Public Enterprises in Peru

Public Enterprises in Peru

Public Sector Growth and Reform

Alfred H. Saulniers

Westview Press
BOULDER & LONDON

Westview Special Studies on Latin America and the Caribbean

Published in 1988 in the United States of America by Westview Press, Inc.; Frederick A. Praeger, Publisher; 5500 Central Avenue, Boulder, Colorado 80301

Library of Congress Cataloging-in-Publication Data
Saulniers, Alfred H., 1945–
  Public enterprises in Peru.
  (Westview special studies on Latin America and the
Caribbean)
  Bibliography: p.
  Includes index.
  1. Government business enterprises—Peru. I. Title.
II. Series.
HD4123.S28 1988   338.7'4'0985   87-34602
ISBN 0-8133-7565-7

Printed and bound in the United States of America

The paper used in this publication meets the requirements of the American National Standard for Permanence of Paper for Printed Library Materials Z39.48-1984.

6   5   4   3   2   1

Contents

Tables

Graphs and Figures

GRAPHS

FIGURES

Preface

This book helps fill the void in teaching materials about the Latin American public sector. It began as two case studies of public enterprises jointly carried out by the Office for Public Sector Studies of the University of Texas at Austin, which I directed, and the Universidad del Pacífico in Lima. Over the years, the cases expanded into a detailed analysis of the overall growth and dynamics of Peru's rapidly changing government portfolio. The resulting book focuses on the external environment for public enterprise action and develops an interlinkage framework to explain the dynamics of company growth, finances, efficiency, and profits in response to changes in that environment.

The manuscript took shape during a year's leave from the Austin campus, during 1983 and 1984, spent in East Africa in association with the Eastern and Southern African Management Institute in Arusha, Tanzania. The strong, positive reactions from government officials and public enterprise managers of Kenya, Tanzania, and Uganda to the lectures I gave about the Peruvian case testified to the broader applicability of the interlinkage framework in explaining company behavior and led to publication in Tanzania of an early version of excerpts of the sixth chapter (Saulniers, 1985f).

After my return to Austin, Richard Webb, then President of Peru's Central Bank, and Carlos Zuzunaga, President of the Peruvian Center for Applied Research, with assistance from the Friedrich Ebert Stiftung, provided me a unique opportunity, namely a forum to test out my ideas about Peru's public enterprises' relationships to the government before a group of Peruvian public enterprise managers and government officials. The debate during the two-day seminar proved lively, the criticisms well founded, and the experience both enlightening and humbling. The published results of the seminar have fueled the debate about the role of public enterprises in Peru from 1968 to 1980

(Saulniers, 1985g).

A six-week stay at the Universidad del Pacífico, under the auspices of the Fulbright Commission, enabled me to update the material in the manuscript and provided countless opportunities for discussions with colleagues there, at other universities, and throughout the government. My seminars to public enterprise executives at Pacífico and at the Graduate School of Business, ESAN, forced me to revise my ideas about the influence on decision making of time constraints and other pressures faced by managers in actual practice. Additionally, my lecture in the Applied Workshop Series sponsored by the Friedrich Ebert Stiftung gave me the chance to pull together several of the more provocative themes, having a broad Latin American impact, for presentation to a highly qualified Peruvian audience (Saulniers, 1985e). The spirited exchange contributed to further revisions and, hopefully, to a more meticulous book.

This book would not have been possible without the encouragement and support of Bill Glade who, as Director of the Institute of Latin American Studies, was instrumental in shaping the debate about the nature of the public enterprise process in Latin America. He urged publication of preliminary findings from chapter six as part of the Technical Papers Series of the Office for Public Sector Studies (Saulniers, 1985h). His keen interest in the evolution of the Peruvian portfolio and its meaning for understanding the *problematique* of public enterprises spurred me to detail the Peruvian evolution in a more thorough fashion than available elsewhere, while remaining conscious of the implications of the evolving paradigm for public enterprise studies in general.

Outside of Peru, several colleagues, eminent pubic enterprise or public administration scholars and practitioners in their own right, have read all or parts of early drafts of the manuscript. They include Gene Bigler in Washington, Edwin Jones in Jamaica, James Katorobo in Tanzania, V.V. Ramanadham and Barbara Grosh in Kenya, Enrique Saravia in Brazil, and Henry Dietz, Bill Glade, and Larry Graham in Austin. Former students, Peruvians and Peruvianists, read the manuscript as well, including Brian Branch, Louis DiSipio, Greg Estep, Luis Fernández, Conrad Herold, and Julio Revilla. While the manuscript draws much of its strength from the detailed and pointed comments of these readers, any remaining deficiencies are mine. Finally, successive generations of students in my graduate seminar in public sector studies at the University of Texas provided a testing ground for ideas and, by sharp questioning, forced me to hone the arguments and better the exposition. Greg Estep proved an excellent graphics consultant and translated some of the numbers into forms with higher visual impact than the original tables.

In Peru, my debts are legion. For reasons that become apparent in the text, many of my sources, both inside and outside of government, cannot be individually acknowledged. My institutional ties, however, since 1970, remain a matter of public record and provide a general way of expressing thanks by using institutional precision to cover individual anonymity. To my colleagues at the Banco Central de Reserva, Escuela Superior de Administración para Graduados, Instituto Nacional de Planificación, Ministerio de Economía, Finanzas y Comercio, Universidad Católica, Universidad de Ingeniería, and Universidad del Pacífico, I owe a debt of thanks. They have all, in some way, contributed to the outcome of this book. Public enterprise officials, some of whom may not be included in the above, willingly provided their time to answer questions and to provide hard information. This book is clearly in their debt.

My wife, Suzanne, and daughter, Catherine, have long suffered time demands caused by various drafts and revisions. Suzanne read several versions of the manuscript, offering up many worthwhile suggestions. Catherine provided drawings to lift my spirits. It is to them that I dedicate this book.

Alfred H. Saulniers

Peruvian Exchange Rates: 1968-1984

Year	Soles per dollar (Year-end)
1968	43.36
1969	43.57
1970	43.41
1971	43.38
1972	43.38
1973	43.38
1974	43.38
1975	45.00
1976	69.37
1977	131.56
1978	196.68
1979	250.75
1980	342.61
1981	506.97
1982	989.67
1983	2,271.17
1984	5,695.98

SOURCE: Central Bank Annual Reports.

1

Introduction and Overview

INTRODUCTION

In 1958, when *Fortune* magazine first included a directory of large industrial corporations outside the United States, its top 100 companies included only five government-owned firms and none came from a developing country.[1] By the mid-1980s, the *Fortune* lists of the top 500 companies regularly contained more than sixty government-owned firms, with more than twenty in the top 100, many of them from the developing countries, especially from Latin America.[2] In 1983, two of the top ten Brazilian firms were government owned as were three in the Dominican Republic, four in Mexico and Venezuela, five in Argentina, and seven in Peru.[3] This book examines public enterprise[4] growth and development in one Latin American country, Peru.

Prior to 1970, public enterprises remained a neglected topic of analysis for Latin Americanists. The recent advent of annual *Fortune*-like country-specific and continent-wide industrial listings, has made their role more apparent. These show that Latin America shares a common characteristic with other areas: the importance of public enterprises in infrastructure and basic industry. However, the standard approach of concentrating on large infrastructure and industrial firms neglects an essential consideration: in Latin America, public enterprises do everything. According to records of the Office for Public Sector Studies of the University of Texas at Austin, Mexico, in 1981, had almost 250 public enterprises in manufacturing; 155 firms in finance, insurance, real estate and business services; 62 in wholesale and retail trade, restaurants and hotels; and lesser numbers in transport storage, and communications, agriculture, hunting, forestry, fishing, mining and quarrying, and in traditional electricity, gas and water utilities. The above figures predate the September 1982 bank nationalization (Saulniers, 1985b).

Public enterprises are stereotyped as losers and "parasitic parastatals," yet, they lose money far less often than is commonly believed. The stereotype arises, in part, from spectacular and repeated losses by a few firms, including such pathological cases as Argentina's petroleum producer, YPF.[5] British and Italian government firms are held up as a paradigm of inefficiency, yet their performance more reflects their inadequate operating conditions than public or private ownership (Saulniers, 1985d:viii). In fact, most public enterprises on the *Fortune* list show profits and compare favorably with private firms. Detailed financial comparison of Latin America's large firms indicates that type of ownership rarely accounts for statistically significant differences in behavior (Saulniers, 1985b). Indeed, public enterprises regularly earn an operating surplus, notwithstanding government price controls that distort company performance and result in low rates of return to capital.[6]

Public enterprises arose for many reasons. Governments often cited ideology, fear of foreign ownership, and national security in creating them, but they also acted to relieve natural and economic disasters, in retribution for past grievances, to rescue failing private firms, to reinforce personal privilege, and out of sheer accident. For Latin America, the traditional historical view that the public portfolio grew according to some unidirectional, additive, inevitable historical logic has been debunked by recent in-depth studies of the nineteenth and early twentieth century state.[7] These studies show governments owned an important share of the means of production earlier than the second quarter of the twentieth century.

Classifying firms according to known motives for public ownership does not capture the essence of portfolio development by failing to properly acknowledge the importance of accidents and unplanned or unexpected circumstances. Rapid portfolio growth and "accidental" shifts in composition have often occurred through nationalizations of banks, financial holding companies, or the family holdings of deposed dictators.[8] For example, Peru's 1970 takeover of the Banco Popular doubled the government's portfolio as more than thirty private companies, formerly in the bank's portfolio, became public without motive, i.e. with no explicit decision ever taken on whether the public interest was best served by public, rather than private, ownership [See Chapter 2]. Similarly, IRI, the Italian industrial development holding company, one of Europe's largest public enterprises, was founded in 1933 to temporarily acquire banks that were threatened with collapse, but, in the process, its objectives changed by accident as it found miscellaneous unrelated firms in the banks' portfolios.[9] Mexico's September 1982 bank takeovers also increased the portfolio at least a third and current privatization efforts have led to the disposal of shares in some of the accidentally nationalized firms.[10]

Most classifications also do injustice to conjunctural nationalization which takes place when the government is forced to acquire firms, sometimes against its overall interests, by unplanned or unexpected circumstances. The standard rescue of a bankrupt firm to safeguard jobs or to recover debts exemplifies conjunctural nationalization. Likewise, many worker-forced takeovers in Chile during the early 1970s resulted from the conjuncture of short-term forces over which the government often had little or no control.[11]

Both accidental and conjunctural nationalizations are concentrated in agriculture, industry, and services. Other sectors of the economy often show broad sectoral similarities. For instance, basic infrastructure, including electricity, gas, water, and wastewater, is overwhelmingly public, often the result of rational nationalization based on explicit intervention motives including externalities, infant industries, and control of the commanding heights.[12] Overall portfolio size and its haphazard growth through incorporating the portfolios of financial firms have been systematically neglected in part because countries use national accounts standards which exclude public financial institutions from definitions of public enterprises.[13] Accidental and conjunctural nationalization should receive more attention to better understand the nature and scope of government action.

Analysis of large infrastructure or industrial firms too often serves as the basis for overgeneralizing about the nature of government ownership and its role in the economy, yet, such firms are only a small minority of public enterprises.[14] Peru's portfolio serves as an example. In 1982, the two largest firms, less than 2 percent of the portfolio, accounted for 40 percent of sales, and the top 10 percent of firms had 76 percent of sales. In marked contrast, 8 percent of firms had annual sales of less than $100,000 and 23 percent less than $1 million.[15] Indeed, in 1982, several Peruvian companies, not considered above, had no sales, but existed either in a pre-development stage for large, natural resource-related projects or in a post-closure, pre-final liquidation limbo. Ranking firms by sales or assets ignores the numerous small and medium firms that constitute the bulk of the portfolio.

Scholars face a major impediment in extending analysis beyond large companies in infrastructure and industry: the lack of readily available and accurate data on the smaller companies. Legal codes in some countries prohibit government authorities from excessive interference in companies organized under the law of mercantile societies or under non-standard legal patterns and interference is often broadly interpreted to preclude data gathering. As a result, government and the media often report data on large sectoral flagship companies while neglecting others. The MINEROPERU system serves as an example. It and its two main subsidiaries in ferrous and nonferrous mining often figure in reports of government monitoring agencies or in informed analyses of Peru's public enterprises; its twenty additional holdings rarely do (Gallegos et al., 1985:43–44).

This book goes beyond the standard approach to public

enterprises by undertaking a detailed analysis of Peru's entire portfolio. It avoids the "big company problem" by including data on all firms, regardless of size. It goes beyond the stereotype of parasitic parastatals to show which Peruvian firms earned profits, which showed losses, and why. It improves on the traditional approach to classifying motives by demonstrating that many public enterprises resulted from accidental or conjunctural factors. It avoids the national accounts definitional problem by comparing both financial and nonfinancial firms. It meets all these objectives by combining an institutional approach to the analysis of events with an economist's perspective on accounting and economic data.

The effects of massive government intervention in a country's productive sector have never been adequately documented. Most country-based studies suffer from two major problems. First, they usually rely on outsider information and inadequately report internal action. Unfortunately, outsider information is often incomplete and deliberately or inadvertently distorted by government authorities. Deducing the basis for and consequences of government action is only slightly more rewarding than the blind man's proverbial search for a black cat in a lightless room. Second, they rarely examine more than a handful of companies, justifying this notable omission of the smaller and medium sized companies on the basis of cost efficiency. Unfortunately, the big company problem leads to extrapolating the behavior of the average firm in the portfolio from a sample limited to the largest companies. Such induction is as invalid as is describing the consumer behavior of the average American pre-World War I family based on an analysis of spending patterns of the Vanderbilts, Goulds, Harrimans, and the other families that frequented Saratoga Springs and Newport. In examining the economic and financial evolution of Peru's public enterprises, this book overcomes the outsider problem by relying heavily on direct, insider information and it overcomes the big company problem by drawing conclusions from more complete portfolio information.

OVERVIEW

With Independence, Peru inherited public enterprises; since then, Peruvian leaders have never agreed on their uses and hence Peruvian governments always changed public enterprise policies. These features of an evolving government presence in the productive sector within an unstable, changing policy environment characterize public enterprises in many countries and Peru is no exception.

Since independence, two long-term trends, on which are superimposed various shorter-term cyclical fluctuations, have determined Peru's portfolio size and composition. Ideologically dominated long trends and cycles only recently surfaced in the theoretical literature on public enterprises (Boneo, 1981b).   Peru's are particularly well marked. The first was a long-term downward trend in portfolio size, which lasted from the mid-1820s to the War of the Pacific. From a numerical high reached in 1824, a long continual decline set in until the 1870s when the Chilean occupiers eliminated most remaining firms. The second long trend lasted from the War of the Pacific until the mid-1970s, during which time the portfolio grew in a discontinuous fashion for more than 80 years. Peru's trends aid in discrediting the traditional view that Latin American public enterprises arose following trade disruptions caused by the great depression and the second world war.

By 1968, according to Latin American standards, Peru had a small, but growing portfolio. Under the military government from 1968 to 1980 and the civilian ones in the 1980s major changes occurred in portfolio size and composition, changes that compressed the evolution of other Latin American countries during the previous three to seven decades. Because the time period was so short, because key government internal documents are still available, and because many the key decision makers are still readily accessible, study of Peru's public enterprise portfolio provides valuable insights not only into the public enterprise growth process in Peru, but insights that are generalizable to other world areas and to other time periods.

Underlying this book is an institutional framework applied to dissect the interplay of governmental institutions and to reveal the excessive frictions that can build up from interorganizational interaction. Other authors have examined how general political and social factors constitute linkages between public enterprises and "polity, society and economy."[16] The main premise of interlinkage systems analysis is that public enterprises do not exist in isolation. Instead, they are unique elements strongly tied to the rest of the government within a wider national and international system. I narrow the focus to the intergovernmental subsystem to demonstrate that just as imperfections within the system can adversely effect public enterprise performance, so too, any improvements in the system can generate positive effects.

Analysts often try to make sense of the haphazard and chaotic process of creating public enterprises by systematically classifying motives for their creation into taxonomies. Classifications are common, indeed almost every public enterprise-related article or book proposes a different one, and they are usually based on some combination of underlying political, ideological, or economic grounds. There is, however, little underlying rigor or consistent application to this approach. I have analyzed conceptual and practical problems with the taxonomic approach elsewhere (1983, 1985c), but some issues bear on the Peruvian experience. Chapter 2 examines the weaknesses of post-hoc categorizations about Peruvian government motives in creating a public enterprise under conditions where: decisional issues are complex and ambiguous; creation motives are many and varied; each potential actor in the creation decision may express individual preferences; and true motives for government intervention may be deliberately concealed from the public behind more politically acceptable ones. These factors combined make classification of the true motives impossible.

Defining operating strategies became difficult when management could not decipher those ambiguous or complex motives, could not establish priorities among multiple motives assigned by different principles, or could not uncover deliberately concealed motives. Other problems arose when government authorities' external evaluations held companies accountable to those ambiguous and often conflicting criteria. Continual and rapid changes in company objectives further muddled the twin issues of goal definition and performance evaluation. To understand Peru's problems, Chapter 2 examines the disoriented method and inconsistent motives that guided its portfolio growth after 1968.

Standard top-down approaches to public enterprises stress the role of central government authorities in defining strategy, periodically reviewing strategy implementation, and continually monitoring company performance. Each of these three tasks delicately balances the government's duties as owner of company equity, trustee of the national interest, and designator of any extra-entrepreneurial functions against the company's entrepreneurial rights to autonomy and flexibility in management decision making. Chapter 3 examines four standard top-down systems: planning, budgeting, committee coordination, and information networks to differentiate among intrastate actors. Continual difficulties resulted from inadequate coordination among the unwieldy bureaucracies of the principal government oversight agencies. Those difficulties, arising from inexperienced staffers, an unproven and weak control system, excessive reporting requirements, and overlapping and contradictory control signals were compounded by persistent interagency power disputes.

A handful of public enterprises, heavily concentrated in natural resource fields, became a potent economic force whose performance determined many of Peru's macroeconomic or sectoral indicators. Chapter 4 examines the evolution of the leading public enterprises' income, profits, subsidies, taxes, employment, investment, debt, and value added. The chapter's rigorous analysis justifies the repudiation of many popular myths and reveals many pitfalls in judging public enterprise evolution and performance.

Domination of macro indicators by a few large public enterprises makes it difficult to generalize about average firm performance. Under certain conditions, standard private-enterprise derived financial indicators may be applied to judge public enterprise behavior. Chapter 5 determines those conditions by examining the conceptual bases for indicators of financial soundness and stability, internal efficiency, and profitability. The indicators are scrutinized for five company groups distinguished by size or sector of activity. The results of the analysis confirm the direct link between government policy and enterprise performance.

Similarities in the evolution of economic and financial variables across firms or sectors lead to the inevitable conclusion that government-imposed external environmental factors invariably constrain public enterprises. Standard policy approaches do not encompass the links that bind public enterprises to the rest of the public administration system. To remedy that failing, Chapter 6 develops a new conceptual policy paradigm around a set of inter-linkages within the public administration system that influence public enterprise performance and applies it to Peru.

Some other issues lie beyond management control because they comprise the decision-making sphere of central government authorities. Among these, macro issues, such as defining the role of public enterprises in the economy and providing an adequate legal framework for action, can have a noticeable impact on individual company performance. Chapter 6 analyzes the macro-level instability and uncertainty that characterized the Peruvian government decision making after 1968.

Asking the correct questions is the first step to finding out the right answers. Chapter 7 reviews the material presented earlier to provide a basis for debunking myths, clarifying misconceptions, and clearing misperceptions about public enterprise growth and development. Five key areas, where incorrect questions are usually asked, come in for detailed criticism including: the purportedly weak and limited Latin American state intervention in the economy; supposed ahistorical public enterprise growth patterns during the 1970s; public enterprises' image as perpetual loser; purported parasitism of government subsidies; and supposedly planned and executed government actions. Based on the application of the interlinkage paradigm, Chapter 7 applies a conflict management perspective to derive policies for initiating, correcting, or maintaining a successful public enterprise system.

EXCLUSIONS

Many potentially interesting areas of public enterprise analysis receive short shrift or are abandoned altogether in this book. The remainder of this chapter serves as a guide to alternative sources of Peru-specific information on some specialized topics that are relegated to a supporting position and are deliberately not given full treatment.

First, the book is not a case compendium. Although a major gap exists in the management literature for cases about public enterprises, Peru counts several cases of varying quality and focus. An early set criticized government meddling through the SOGESA steel mill, the EPF petroleum company, the CPV shipping line, and the CORMAN electric company (CDES, 1965). Case studies of three Arequipa public enterprises founded by the regional development authority are contained in INAP (1976b). They are the Yura cement factory, the DAASA food dryer, and the ESAR water and wastewater installations. Elsewhere, I examined the position of two marketing companies during the late 1970s: SUPEREPSA and ENCI (Saulniers, 1979a and b). The latter case was revised and included in a compendium of cases of Latin American public enterprises (Saulniers, 1980). Under Ministry of Industry auspices, five cases were prepared using the same methodology covering the 1977 to 1979 period: SIDERPERU; the two fertilizer companies, FERTISA and Cachimayo; the Yura cement factory; and the denatured alcohol installations (MITI, 1981a to e). The cases were prepared by a conservative-dominated ministry that opposed public enterprises. The SIDERPERU investment analysis was later expanded into a thesis at Catholic University in Lima and subsequently published (Ponce, 1985a and b). Branch took a detailed look at five companies slated for privatization by the Belaúnde administration in a Masters' thesis done at the University of Texas (1981). They included the ENATA tobacco company, the DAASA food-drying installations, Cementos Lima, MINPECO, and the undeveloped mining concern, EMATINSA. In addition, the public management programs at the Universidad del Pacífico and ESAN in Lima have generated internal case study material.

Second, the book eschews the issues of technical efficiency or internal management. These latter include company organization, delegation of authority, finance, managerial succession, training, promotion, managerial incentives, or other motivational structures. Instead, Chapter 5 examines some financial efficiency indicators. Numerous references to the topic exist in the Multisectoral Commission reports or the related work by INAP (1976a). In addition, slanted or vituperous treatments were a constant feature of the popular Lima press. Finally, two biased sources of information are the case studies of CDES (1965) and MITI (1981a to e).

Third, the book neglects many fascinating labor-related topics, including personnel questions, labor movements, unions, and labor participation in public enterprise management. Instead, it covers employment per se. A good analysis of the Peruvian public enterprise labor situation is that by Bustamante (1981). An earlier treatment done under government auspices is INP-DESCO (1974?c), and public enterprise labor policy is treated in Sorj (1977?:6–12). Legal aspects of labor in public enterprises, including figures on employment by type of labor law for the major companies are found in INAP (1976a), while a later, somewhat shallow treatment of the subject is INP-UNI (1978).

Fourth, the book omits the role of Peruvian public enterprises in foreign trade, including state trading corporations and overall balance-of-payments effects. On this last point, PETROPERU's post-

1978 levels of production provided a major exportable surplus, and thus favored the balance of payments. Three general treatments of the evolution of state trading in imports in Peru are found in Boloña (1977 and 1978) and JAC (1976). An institutional analysis of financial and interlinkage problems affecting the state traders is found in MINCOM (1975). The Peruvian experience in foreign coffee trade is well developed in Lavergne and Caputo (1979). The partners of the state traders come in for special treatment in Nickson (1977). State exporters figure in Campos (1977), while the Latin American treatment of Sánchez and Esteves (1978) relies heavily on Peruvian materials.[17] The legal bases for purchases by all government units including public enterprises are included in a compendium of similar information for all the Latin American countries in Ondarts and Correa (1982:233–244). Sources of bias in the decision by central government authorities to create state traders are examined in the Peruvian context in Saulniers (1981a).

Fifth, benefit incidence of public enterprise policies are mentioned peripherally throughout this book. Particular treatment for early policies is available in INP (1976b), Amat y León (1975), Webb (1977), and Couriel (1979). Sorj examines the effects on another group that he terms "the most important category of beneficiaries of state enterprise expansion, the public enterprise managers" (1983:73). The generally regressive incidence of Peru's public enterprise pricing is examined and contrasted to the Brazilian experience in Baer and Figueroa (1981) and receives passing mention from the IBRD (1981:24). Public and private enterprises were linked through the market as suppliers, customers, and occasionally as competitors. Effects of public enterprise supply and demand on the Peruvian private sector is found in an unpublished report by Branch (1982a). Overall, however, because much of the public enterprise portfolio resulted from nationalization or from compulsory share acquisition by the government, the impact of portfolio growth on some parts of the private sector was negative. Other negative effects stemmed from the largely unmeasurable discouragement of private investment which remained low for most of the military period.

The underlying premise for a growing body of performance improvement literature is that the growth and presence of public enterprises are strongly correlated with increasing and persistent macroeconomic problems, particularly in developing countries.[18] Applying policy options that result from this approach, because they neglect a systems interlinkage framework, often does not meet expectations of decision makers and their policy advisors, and may prompt even more serious and unintended consequences. This book postulates a new policy-relevant theoretical paradigm for public enterprise relations with the rest of government that differs from both the widely accepted top-down *controliste* doctrines and the bottom-up management development framework. Policies grounded in this new paradigm should result in a smoother functioning overall system marked by both greater technical efficiency and higher social efficacy.

NOTES

1. "The Fortune Directory: Part II," *Fortune* 58, no. 2 (August), pp. 115–124.
2. "The International 500: The Fortune Directory of the Largest Industrial Corporations outside the U.S.," *Fortune*, (19 August 1985), pp. 182–211.
3. "Enterprises and Power," *Latin American Newsletters, Special Reports*, No. SR-84-04, (30 October 1984).
4. For purposes of an immediate definition, "public enterprise" means a firm in the economic sense of the term, i.e. that produces or sells goods or services. It has a separate legal personality and its capital is owned in part by the state, whether directly or indirectly. I specifically exclude Peru's social property firms from this definition because their capital was not owned by the state. Böhm summarized definitional controversies that emerged from a conference sponsored by the International Center for Public Enterprises in Developing Countries (1981). See also Jones' formal set-theoretical approach to definitions (1975). I analyze Peruvian definitional issues in Appendix A.
5. Solberg stresses YPF's early mismanagement, financial shortages, and inefficiencies as potentially discrediting the concept of government-owned oil companies (1979). See also Saulniers (1985a).
6. Short (1984) and Shirley (1983:10–17).
7. For traditional views of the temporal evolution of the nature of Latin American public enterprises, see FitzGerald (1974 and 1976b: 119–133); and UNECLA (1971). Revisionist views are found in Bigler (1981); Potash (1959); Revilla (1987); Saulniers and Revilla (1983); Saulniers (1986e); and Topik (1979).
8. The nationalization of Trujillo's property in the Dominican Republic led to the formation of a holding company, CORDE. In Nicaragua, however, the extensive Somoza holdings were split among the sectoral ministries. See Guerrero (1981); Wittich (1983); and Instituto Nicaragüense de Administración Pública (1981).
9. The published literature makes scant reference to accidental public enterprises. On IRI, see Carey Jones, Patankar, and Boodhoo (1974:23) and Holland (1972:57–59).
10. See Fernández Moreno (1983); Murphy (1985:15–19); "Re-estructuración de la indústria paraestatal," *El Mercado de Valores* 45, no. 14 (8 Apr. 1985), pp. 33–37; and idem "Venta de acciones

de empresas no prioritarias con participación estatal," 45, no. 16 (Apr. 22, 1985), pp. 376–377.

11. Peter Winn provides an excellent case study of worker takeovers of the Yarur textile mills in Chile (1986). He notes that only one-quarter of industries socialized under Allende were planned. The rest were uncontrolled seizures by workers, which radicalized the revolutionary process, thereby eroding Allende's relations with the business sector and seriously diminishing his middle-class support [pp. 229–232].

12. Jones and Mason (1982:17–47); Shirley (1983:8); IBRD (1983:48–50); and Ayub and Hegstad, (1986:11). See Saulniers (1985c) for a sectoral analysis of Latin American firms.

13. For a background to international positions on definitional discrepancies, see UN Statistical Commission (1976).

14. Thomas Trebat calls attention to the big company problem (1983:237–238).

15. Figures come from a data base of public enterprises in Peru after 1968 [See Appendix B].

16. Ahmad (1983:49). See also Acosta (1984).

17. The work by Sánchez and Esteves formed part of a larger UNCTAD project to sponsor regional cooperation among state trading organizations in developing countries.

18. See particularly Floyd (1984), Gray (1984), and Short (1984).

2

Growth and Reform

INTRODUCTION

Why are there public enterprises? To answer that question, many analysts develop taxonomies by classifying government motives for creating companies according to underlying political, ideological, or economic grounds. Because virtually every public enterprise analyst favors a different taxonomy, the approach lacks any underlying rigor. Faucher surveyed the literature for representative examples and castigated the approach as "theoretically unsatisfactory or empirically questionable" (1981:9).

I have elsewhere criticized the taxonomic approach and this chapter does not develop a new classification (1985b:2–3). Instead, it summarizes changes in Peru's public enterprise portfolio to demonstrate the shortcomings of an approach that presupposes rationality, continuity in government, stability in goals, and operationality. As shown below, many motives impelled the Peruvian government to create new firms, but they were rarely coherent and hardly consistent. Some creation motives were politico-ideological — wresting sectors from foreign control or severing the national elite from its economic base. Others were economic — to save jobs, rescue failing firms, or stem capital outflow. To them, however, must be added many other, unrecognized and sometimes hidden motives. Moreover, an unknown number of firms were accidentally nationalized and entered the public portfolio without motive. While long-run considerations guided a few government actions, short term gain and rapid response to perceived external changes dominated the bases for action.[1] In general, because Peru's government never followed the standard advice for long-term study and independent review of any proposals to establish new public enterprises, adhocracy has been the only clear public enterprise policy (Sherif, 1973:31).

This chapter's summary description of Peru's portfolio growth fills an important gap in the public enterprise literature, since official or non-official sources rarely thoroughly describe such a process. For Peru, FitzGerald provides the best description, but he skims company creation and restructuring, glossing over the enriching detail (1979). Official documents often confuse reorganization with creation. Uncritically relying on them leads to a historical bias that suggests firms were created more recently than long-term evidence supports.[2] They also underestimate the extent of government intervention by rarely reporting activities of small, often indirectly-held, companies.[3]

Governments created some firms, nationalized others, made some public by accident, and continually reorganized them all. This continual creation/reorganization has resulted in a patchwork portfolio of enterprises in virtually every sector of the economy. These enterprises range in size from the largest Peruvian firm to tiny ones. The government held them under widely different legal statutes so that some were rigidly controlled while others escaped controls entirely.

Analysts of the post-1968 Peruvian economy either assume a functional relationship between government policies and the personality of the head of state that differentiates among the presidencies of General Velasco, General Morales Bermúdez, and President Belaúnde, or they employ intervening variables to delimit sub-periods. Applications of presidential-term analyses to public enterprises include INAP's expansion-contraction model (1979a), Borrani's focus on political variables (1982), Cleaves and Scurrah's six conditions (1980:277–285), Schydlowsky and Wicht's global policy variables (1979 and 1983), and Becker's focus on mining policy (1983). Intervening-variable analyses include Philip's look at intra-military coalitions (1978), FitzGerald's investment analysis (1979), Portocarrero's work on public investment (1982), and Briceño's analysis of changes in mining management.[4] This chapter distinguishes four separate periods from 1968 to 1980, each marked by a dominant public enterprise policy trend, but treats the Belaúnde years as a single unit. The analysis of chapters 2 to 5 demonstrates that this period breakdown proves remarkably robust in explaining growth, the evolution of the control system, changes in macroeconomic indicators, and company-level financial performance.

For three reasons, this chapter untangles some of the interlocked trends in Peru's post-1968 portfolio expansion by stressing "what" happened and "why" it occurred. First, it describes the process as internally defined by Peruvian government officials who formulated policy agendas aimed at attaining specific goals (Tantalean, 1978:202–203). Second, it challenges the standard conclusions about post-1968 portfolio growth that rest on the analysis of the few largest companies, instead of more complete information. Third, it corrects many errors that arise because both official and non-official sources have misread and misinterpreted the historical record.

LONG-TERM HISTORICAL TRENDS

Peru always had public enterprises, having inherited a sizeable portfolio at independence in 1824. The oldest were the revenue-oriented monopolies, called *estancos*, for tobacco, playing cards, coca, hot peppers and tar. Many were later abolished, some reestablished, and others merged repeatedly. Today half still survive, but in vastly different forms. Some firms dating from the 1820s, such as Peru's official newspaper, *El Peruano*, founded by Simón Bolívar in 1825, have changed little. This section examines two long-term trends in the evolution of Peru's portfolio: a numerical decline from the 1820s to the 1870s and a slow, steady increase thereafter.

An important part of the portfolio at independence consisted of lands and properties previously belonging to the Spanish Crown, that formed the public domain.[5] These included farms, the important mercury mine at Huancavelica (Whitaker, 1941), and foundries for precious metals (Camprubí, 1963). Peru's government enlarged the public domain during the War of Independence by confiscating Spaniards' goods and properties and by claiming their abandoned assets. By war's end, the Peruvian government had become the "first and richest property owner" (de Pierola, 1870), owning a substantial part of all important sectors of Peru's economy: urban and rural lands, businesses, houses, mines, mills, smelters, and haciendas. Although no complete inventory of government holdings was ever taken, partial ones indicate a net worth of more than 8 million pesos in 1825, which, if properly managed, could have generated important revenues (Saulniers and Revilla, 1983:22).

The nineteenth century's prevailing liberal philosophy led to a long-term secular decline in the size of the public portfolio through wilful and inadvertent privatization of government property that occurred in several ways. First, during the war with Spain sales from the public domain raised needed revenues. Second, the government sold, auctioned, or rented properties to amortize its war debts.[6] Third, the public domain provided a store of handsome properties to reward major war heroes, while less heroic officers, soldiers, and citizens who had favored Independence were allowed to purchase minor properties at derisory prices. Fourth, the government endowed educational institutions, mutual benefit societies (*beneficencias*), and local governments with revenue producing properties.[7] Fifth, poor accounting and book-keeping systems resulted in systematic looting of the public domain as urban property, farms, and mines were privatized through pilferage.[8]

Yet, during the nineteenth century, Peru's government continually created new companies and participated in joint ventures with private partners.[9] These new firms did not compensate for the shrinkage and resulted in a net portfolio decrease. The new companies deserve more than a passing mention, however, as motives for their creation do not fit our preconceived notions that nineteenth century

Latin American governments intervened largely to underwrite the infrastructure costs needed to support foreign-owned or -dominated exporters of agricultural or extractive products.[10] For example, at times, Peru's governments acted to bolster private initiative in agriculture, mining, and shipping, usually in companies with a local, not export, orientation. It also acted to assure national security, guarantee price stability for basic items, and to make a profit for the government (Echenique, 1952:I:146 and Elguera, 1868). Thus, the explicit domestic orientation of Peru's public enterprises contradicts the accepted view that Latin American government firms were passive complements to foreign companies.

Long-term portfolio decline continued until the War of the Pacific (1879–1882), when most of Peru's remaining public enterprises were liquidated by the Chileans. After the war ended, Peru's new emphasis on public enterprises began a long-term portfolio growth trend that lasted well into the 1970s. For example, immediately after the war, the government reinstated many estancos, including salt and tobacco, in its search for new revenue sources to replace its economic rents from the nitrate deposits lost to Chile and from the long-ended guano boom. In 1887, it monopolized the sale of opium to raise revenue by tapping the product's low price elasticity among Chinese coolies.

As part of a long-term growth strategy, governments relied on joint ventures, many of which still survive, although in altered form. These include the steamship company, Compañía Peruana de Vapores y Dique del Callao, which was reconstituted in 1906;[11] a joint-venture guano monopoly, Compañía Administradora de Guano (CAG), formed in 1909 to rehabilitate the depleted industry and to promote limited conservation;[12] and a company created in 1896 to collect taxes and to administer the opium monopoly.[13] These three ventures merged private with public interests while generating more revenue.

Peru briefly, but unsuccessfully, also experimented with government-owned banks (Camprubí, 1957, 1960). However, it was only during the late 1920s and early 1930s, a politically turbulent period, that the government made an important set of additions to the public portfolio by creating a modern financial infrastructure including the central bank and sectoral development banks for housing, industry, agriculture, and mining.[14]

In 1938, under the Benavides administration, Peru began petroleum exploration. This occurred in response to diplomatic prodding by the Mexican legation, fired by Cárdenas' nationalization of the foreign oil companies (Pinelo, 1973:44). During 1948, the petroleum enterprise underwent its third name change and reorganization to become the Empresa Petrolera Fiscal (EPF).[15] EPF remained lackluster, however, since fifteen years after its creation, it still had not received bylaws (CDES, 1965:39). Later, just as Mexico had done with PEMEX some thirty years beforehand, Peru's government thrust EPF to the fore in 1968, following the takeover of the International Petroleum

Company, as the embodiment of Peruvian nationalism [See below].

New portfolio additions, in the 1940s and 1950s, were linked to industrialization and increasing urbanization. The former created demand for basic industrial goods which the private sector could not supply, while the second expanded demand for modern services. In the early 1940s, the Prado administration provided the legal basis for creating firms to promote industrialization or to ensure the continental defense (Ley 9577).[16] Security motives, linked to World War II, pushed the government to adopt the recommendations of a pre-war study to boost industrial capacity by creating basic infrastructure in iron, steel and coal (Rothrock, 1969:93). It formed multisectoral, multi-objective regional development corporations modeled after the Tennessee Valley Authority (TVA). The Corporación Peruana del Amazonas was set up in 1942 to promote agriculture, mining, and industry on the Eastern slopes of the Andes.[17] The Corporación Peruana del Santa was founded in 1943 to bring industry and new jobs to the Santa River valley by using the available hydroelectric potential to create an iron and steel complex. Modern service firms also date from the 1940s. In 1945, the Ministry of Aviation established a government-owned airline, SATCO, to provide strategic service to provincial cities. The airport authority, CORPAC, was formed to service commercial air transport.

During the 1950s, the portfolio continued to grow. New regional development corporations were formed to decentralize decision-making and public works. Some later spun off industrial activities. Initially, government efforts were limited to reconstructing the earthquake-damaged cities of Cuzco and Arequipa. Later, strong pressures, exerted by members of parliament from areas whose natural resources provided most exports and income taxes, forced the government to create regional agencies throughout the country, increasing the portfolio still more. The result was a hodgepodge of regional programs with little individual autonomy. They were finally unified under the umbrella of the National Fund for Economic Development (FNDE) in 1956 (L. 12676).

Other public enterprises were continually added to the portfolio in the late 1950s and early 1960s. During 1956, the steel mill at Chimbote was spun off from the Santa regional development corporation to become SOGESA. The Mantaro Electrical Energy Corporation (CORMAN), another TVA-copy, dated from 1961 to exploit the Mantaro river's hydroelectric potential and to promote regional industry. A government-owned hotel chain, Compañía Hotelera del Perú, was created in 1964 as a subsidiary of the newly-formed tourist promotion corporation, COTURPERU. Also in 1964 the Banco de la Nación (BN), was created to administer tax collection and manage the estancos.[18] The government formed the Servicios Eléctricos Nacionales (SEN) in 1966 to coordinate its electric sector actions.

By 1968, the portfolio contained remnants of all companies formed in the past. Since government policies were often changed, modified, countermanded, revoked, and later reinstated, public enterprises had been created, dissolved, merged, or allowed to atrophy at different rates and at different times.[19] The self-styled Revolutionary Government of the Armed Forces that took power in October 1968 gave an important role to public enterprises. By the mid-1970s, the Peruvian state had again become the principal agent in the economy and could again lay claim to being the "first and richest property owner." However striking it may have seemed at the time, the public enterprise growth did not represent a major break with past policies. Instead it continued the long-term trend to greater government direct intervention in the economy that dated from the 1890s.[20]

Peru's public enterprise historical evolution corroborates Boneo's hypothesis that long-term underlying trends plus short-term ideological movements determine the portfolio (1981b:7). Both the long-term secular portfolio decline from the 1820s to the 1870s and the long-term gradual rise thereafter depended, in a complex and ever-changing fashion, on the interplay between economics and ideology.

The presence of two long-term trends in Peru suggests that a modification of the Peacock and Wiseman public expenditure growth hypothesis could account for both growth and decline of a public enterprise portfolio (1961). In its general form, the hypothesis states that temporary changes in acceptable spheres of government activity lead to more permanent changes. Thus, following a temporary increase or decrease in the size of the public portfolio, much like a ratchet effect, the tolerable level of state presence in the economy either increases or decreases until the next round of temporary disturbances creates a new tolerance level. From Independence to the 1870s, accepted levels of government intervention in Peru's economy underwent continual retrenchment, leading to a decreasing portfolio. After the 1880s, tolerance levels consistently increased, with the opposite effect.[21] Likewise, contemporary evidence exists, based on the experience of many countries, that upward changes in the acceptable levels of government intervention made the intended privatizations of the 1980s more difficult than expected. The hypothesis that a single, complex underlying phenomenon explains both portfolio growth and decline merits further examination.

PERIOD I: SETTING THE BASES

From October 1968 to early 1970 many of the Velasco administration's public-enterprise actions originated in the strengthening and streamlining of the state apparatus.[22] In the Manifesto and Statutes of the military government reform-minded officers communicated their intent to shake the Peruvian state to its foundations (*El Peruano*, 4 Oct. 1968). To reach their goal, they reorganized institutions ranging from individual agencies to entire ministries in thirteen wide-ranging shakeups during the first three months of military rule, including the National Planning Institute (INP), Ministry of Education offices, the petroleum producer (EPF), the government chorus, and the institute for the blind.[23]

The reorganization shuffled ministerial responsibilities, dismembered some cumbersome organizations, and broke up the unwieldy Independent Public Subsector (SSPI) by rearranging its constituents under different ministries [See Appendix A].[24] The names of some existing companies were changed, some companies merged, new firms were created, and ongoing privatization was halted (D.L. 307-68-HC). Among items on the reforms' hidden agenda appears to have been deliberately reducing any existing public enterprise autonomy (de la Melena, 1973:28).

Table 2.1 lists major public enterprise changes following the 1969 shake-up. Formation of the National Port Authority (ENAPU) illustrates the complicated restructuring process. First, the Port Administration Directorate in the Ministry of Finance and Trade temporarily became the General Directorate of Water Transport under the new Ministry of Transport and Communications. Later, it was merged into ENAPU along with the previously independent port authorities of Callao, Chimbote, and Salaverry (D.L. 17526). Such multi-stage, multi-agency regroupings dragged out the reorganizations for months or even years.

The takeover of International Petroleum Company's (IPC) oilfields and refinery at Talara in October 1968, and their consignment to the small existing public enterprise, EPF, constitute the most dramatic events of Period I.[25] The government took over the remaining IPC operations in early 1969, including the Lima Concessions, a joint venture with the Compañía Petrolera Lobitos. The enlarged EPF later evolved into PETROPERU (Petróleos del Perú) with the objective of undertaking all state entrepreneurial activities in the sector.

The takeover clearly defies simple categorization. Only one or two background items bear repeating. A long-standing dispute between successive Peruvian governments and IPC had aroused such nationalist feelings that it evolved from a producer-regulator conflict to one involving the Peruvian nation, its people, and their honor. A last-minute wrangle over payment terms in a settlement reached by the Belaúnde regime erupted into a major scandal and, in the opinion of most observers, precipitated the coup. Although, at first glance, the IPC case appears to be a standard disciplinary action directed at a foreign, private enterprise, evidence exists that sheer expediency influenced the takeover to legitimate and unify the new regime by maximizing the symbolic political content of asserting national dignity and preserving national security. First, the nationalization was well timed, coming less than a week after the coup. Second, the year before the coup, military strategists already had studied symbolic uses of a potential IPC

TABLE 2.1: PUBLIC ENTERPRISE TRANSFERS OR LIQUIDATIONS: MINISTERIAL REFORMS: 1969

OLD NAME/CONTROL AGENCY	NEW NAME/CONTROL AGENCY
Administración Portuaria de Chimbote	Empresa Nacional de Puertos/MTC
Administración Portuaria de Salaverry	Empresa Nacional de Puertos/MTC
Autoridad Portuaria del Callao/SSPI	Empresa Nacional de Puertos/MTC
Caja Municipal de Crédito Popular/SSPI	Caja de Crédito Popular/MEF
Canal 7 de Televisión/ME	Same/ONI-Presidency
Corporación de Saneamiento de Arequipa/SSPI	Empresa de Saneamiento de Arequipa /MV
Corporación de Saneamiento de Lima /SSPI	Empresa de Saneamiento de Lima/MV
Corporación Financiera de la Reforma Agraria/SSPI	Suppressed/MEF assumed obligations
Corporación Nacional de Comercialización Agraria/SSPI	Not specified/MA assumed functions
Corporación Nacional de Fertilizantes /SSPI	Empresa de Fertilizantes/MIC
Corporación Nacional de Promoción Agraria/SSPI	Suppressed/MA assumed functions
Corporación Nacional de Turismo/SSPI	Empresa Nacional de Turismo/MIC
Corporaciones Departamentales de Desarrollo (N = 10)/SSPI	Status undefined/MEF
Diario Oficial El Peruano/MGP	Same/ONI-Presidency
Dirección de Administración Portuaria /MHC	Empresa Nacional de Puertos/MTC (Intermediate step: Dirección General de Transporte Acuatico)
Estanco de la Sal/Fiscal Monopoly	Empresa de la Sal/MIC
Estanco de Tabaco/Fiscal Monopoly	Empresa Tabacalera/MIC
Fondo Nacional de Desarrollo Económico /SSPI	Status undefined/MEF
Junta Nacional de la Vivienda/SSPI	Empresa de Administración de Inmuebles /MV(Other tasks split within MV)
Juntas with special status (N = 4)/SSPI	Status undefined/MEF
Laboratorios Fiscales de Industrialización de la Coca y Derivados/SSPI	Empresa de la Coca y Derivados/MIC
Radio Congreso/Legislature	Same/ONI-Presidency
Radio Nacional del Perú/MGP	Same/ONI-Presidency
Servicio Especial de Salud/SSPI	Supressed/MS assumed functions
Sociedad Siderúrgica de Chimbote, S.A. /SSPI	Empresa Siderúrgica/MIC

SOURCE: Reforma, 1969.

takeover for maximum propaganda effect in documents prepared at the war college, CAEM (Tantalean, 1978:190). Third, after the expropriation, newspaper accounts showed public opinion dramatically shifted from generalized opposition to yet another military government to reserved support for a nationalist solution to a long-standing dispute, leaving only lingering doubts about a non-democratic regime.[26] Fourth, internal regime politics influenced the takeover, since maintaining a hard line on the IPC question immediately consolidated a viable, nationalist cabinet–level coalition (Philip, 1978:89–92). The internal nature of the motives meant that the IPC takeover did not foreshadow heavy reliance on public enterprise and, indeed, administration spokesmen publicly stated that expropriation would not be a policy linchpin.[27]

More interesting implications can be drawn from the immediate entrusting of IPC's assets to EPF. First, it demonstrated that government could use public enterprises to manage the assets of an entire sector that came under government control. The government later followed this pattern of expediency in marketing minerals and fish products, and in taking over the fisheries.

Second, it showed the public enterprise unpreparedness for assuming newly imposed responsibilities.[28] In March 1968, EPF had proposed to President Belaúnde the immediate takeover of only the *nonproducing* parts of the oilfields.[29] According to this plan, IPC would have continued producing oil under EPF supervision. Pinelo suggests that Carlos Loret de Mola, president of EPF's board of directors, doubted EPF's ability to handle the entire La Brea and Pariñas operations. Loret de Mola, naturally, denied that interpretation.[30] The government later continued to neglect efficiency in thrusting on other companies more than they could reasonably handle (Saulniers, 1981a).

Third, it indicated the immediate nature of government objectives in failing to anticipate consequences of public enterprise-related actions. This stemmed both from the military lack of business experience (Einaudi and Stepan, 1971:13, 42–43) and from a marked distrust of placing managerially- experienced civilians, particularly those with business backgrounds, in power positions (Philip, 1978:102). Poor planning often forced the government to retreat when faced with unexpected results. For example, although EPF initially could decide on wages, salaries, and purchasing under the same conditions as a private firm, within months the government took over wage decisions, imposed tight budgeting and fiscal oversight, and controlled purchases (D.L. 17265; D.L. 17655).

Other developments occurred in addition to the administrative reform and the IPC takeover. The government created EPSAP, a food and fisheries marketing and service company, by merging several barely-related agencies in 1969.[31] Although EPSAP was created to import and export foodstuffs, to control domestic marketing of basic food items, and to support local agriculture, FitzGerald noted that with the Ministry of Agriculture overwhelmingly preoccupied with administering the agrarian reform, EPSAP's main objective became "securing adequate deliveries [of food] to urban areas at politically tolerable prices" (1976a:51). EPSAP was later split into EPSA and EPSEP to respectively market food and fish products.[32]

Other early changes included the national-security motivated forced sale of all ITT shares in the Lima-based telephone company,[33] and the creation of the telecommunications company, ENTEL (D.L. 17526 and 17781). In a move to introduce efficiency, the BN was authorized to hive off non-banking activities, including tobacco, salt, and rice marketing, to other government units.

Period I ended in March 1970 with an attempt to reinforce the ministerial lines of command over public enterprise operations (D.L. 18183).[34] The law contained standard provisions such as determining long-term policy and approving the budget. Other provisions, such as approving all contracts above a specific value, approving annual reports, and deciding the disposition of profits, depreciation funds, pension reserves, and the income from the sale of fixed assets, would have removed important powers from their proper place at company level, dramatically slowing down important company operations. Fortunately, for the companies, the cabinet reversed itself two weeks later, overthrowing this strong attack on managerial autonomy with a new law that replaced the "power of approval" with much weaker "power of recommendation" or "prior knowledge" (D.L. 18191).

From 1968 to 1970, the Peruvian government's public enterprise posture resulted as much from neglect as from deliberate policy. The cabinet, top- and mid-level government management, and the public mostly turned their attentions elsewhere. First, the IPC-related events and their foreign policy consequences demanded attention. Thus, a senior Peruvian government official complained in May 1970, "You should understand that the principal political leaders of the military government for almost 18 months have been almost exclusively preoccupied with whether the United States would apply the Hickenlooper Amendment" (Sharp, 1972:13–14). Second, the long-simmering fisheries dispute with the U.S. also attracted interest.[35] Third, a comprehensive agrarian reform was reshaping the rural property structure.[36] Fourth, the military faced an overriding internal concern, namely how to work out a viable governing coalition between officers with conservative and radical positions.[37]

Conclusions

Close examination of the events during the first eighteen months of the Velasco administration provides no hint of public enterprises' later importance. By early 1970, the government objective of reforming the public administration had been met, at least on paper, but the Velasco administration did not appear to place high value on public enterprises. The firms were analyzed, diagnosed, and reorganized, then occasionally used judiciously as policy tools for mixed motives when politically expedient and with a heightened sense of *coup de théâtre*, as in the splashy IPC nationalization. The administration rarely showed a real understanding of company needs for stability and support, as in the messy EPSAP and port authority reorganizations. This dramatic, politically inspired use of public enterprises that maintained the companies in a state of internal turmoil, as shown below, later tainted central government action.

PERIOD II: A SWEEP OF COMMANDING HEIGHTS

By early 1970, the Velasco government had marshalled its forces. From 1970 to 1973, it eliminated or severely undermined the economic power bases of the oligarchy and major foreign groups, taking over both private companies and private-sector activities and entrusting them to public enterprises. During those four years, the ownership structure of the commanding heights shifted from private holdings to government control of: foreign trade, finance, basic industry, mining, fishing, the media, and public utilities.[38] Some moves were planned, others simply occurred as the public portfolio grew in a haphazard and uncoordinated fashion. The period ended with the Cerro de Pasco Corporation's nationalization in December 1973.[39]

The strategy fit military leaders' perceptions of nationalization as moves against the perceived power structure: "The sad and desperate truth is that in Peru, the real powers are not the Executive, the Legislative, the Judicial or the Electoral, but the latifundists, the exporters, the bankers, and the American [U.S.] investors."[40] Military officers widely assumed that "breaking the monopoly positions of the élite and the foreign firms" would be a sufficient condition for the release of a great reserve of latent dynamics in the Peruvian economy" (Thorp and Bertram, 1978:304). Although some outsiders argue that the Velasco government tried to implement a state capitalist model of production and accumulation, top officials later admitted accumulating companies and sectors without an overall guide.[41] Recognizing that Peruvian military leaders persistently acted without an overall model and without regard to the nature, role, organization, or expectations of the resulting public enterprises is crucial to understanding the intra-governmental dynamics of the period [See Chapters 3 and 6].

The government pursued dual strategies. First, the cabinet promulgated various sectoral laws to reserve major sectors of the economy for the State as personified in embryonic public enterprises. President Velasco announced the new action guidelines in a speech on April 6, 1970 (1970:4). He stated that natural resource exploitation and basic industries would eventually revert to public enterprises under conditions of gradual fadeout of private participation.[42] Second, the government elevated short-lived opportunism and well-orchestrated improvisation to a high art by plucking bits and pieces from the private sector whenever possible and converting them to public enterprises.

Foreign trade dominates the commanding heights of Peru's economy, hence the government took over the two most important export-earners in April 1970. First, marketing of fishmeal and fishoil was nationalized and entrusted to the new state trader, EPCHAP.[43] Later, the government created CERPER in January 1971 to complement fishmeal and fishoil marketing by providing quality control and warehouse facilities, services that previously were privately supplied (D.L. 18745). Second, the government took over all minerals marketing expecting to increase Peru's mining revenue through better contract negotiations and by avoiding concession fees. It created MINEROPERU to coordinate its minerals production and management (D.L. 18225 and 18436).

Mining is also important to Peru's economy.[44] A September 1969 measure gave mining companies strict time limits to come up with a detailed critical-path planning and financial analysis for their undeveloped concessions or lose them without compensation.[45] By September 1970, ASARCO's Michiquillay and the Lampa Mining Company's Berenguela concessions reverted to the state.[46] In October, several Cerro de Pasco Corporation concessions, including Tintaya, Ferrobamba, Chalcobamba, and Antamina followed.[47] Finally, in December two more came under government control, Andes del Perú's Cerro Verde and Southern Peru Copper Corporation's Quellaveco.[48] MINEROPERU was told to develop all concessions that had reverted to the state. Thus, although mining was not nationalized, government action ensured no further expansion of private mining, except for Cuajone.

The General Mining Law, issued in mid-1971, assigned important roles to the state as possible producer, actual controller, and potential partner in joint ventures (D.L. 18880). While it left the existing level of government activity unchanged, the law's stress on partnership with foreign capital contradicted government moves to take over important concessions (Thorp and Bertram, 1978:304). Not surprisingly, therefore, foreign mining firms resisted risking large amounts of new capital. By 1973, only a few large private mines survived. After protracted negotiations, one of these, the Cerro de Pasco Corporation, accounting for more than a third of the value of mining sector output and 30 percent of its employment, was nationalized in December 1973. It became a new public enterprise, CENTROMIN.[49]

Meanwhile, PETROPERU consolidated control by purchasing three of Peru's four remaining private petroleum companies: Standard Oil of California's Refinería Conchán-Chevron, Lobitos Petroleum Company's 50 percent share in the Lima Concessions, and the small Petróleo Ganzo Azul Ltda.[50]

Industrial development also received special attention. The General Industrial Law (LGI) was based on the premise that the state could only obtain strategic control by owning all industries with strong forward linkages. The law's two most important provisions a) reserved all basic industries[51] for the state, and b) potentially reserved other branches subject to later decision (D.L. 18350). While the first provision affected few existing private firms, the vague threat of unlimited future nationalization contained in the second provision effectively deterred any new industrial investment. The LGI expected that existing private firms would gradually be absorbed into the portfolio. Some cement and basic chemical manufacturers bitterly contested nationalization, while the government bought other industrial firms under threat of expropriation.

In late 1971 the government created ENCI to import industrial inputs, a motive downplayedm then finally dropped by successive administrations. The changes in ENCI's objectives were viewed by a ministry official who drafted the original decree as a distortion of the founders' intent.[52] The government also stripped TVA-like SOGESA of railroads, ports, and other ancillary operations, and renamed its steel mill SIDERPERU (D.L. 19034).[53]

In January 1972, the government created an industrial promotion agency (INDUPERU), whose early projects included joint ventures with Perkins Engine and Volvo to make diesel motors (MODASA), and with Massey Ferguson to produce tractors (TASA).[54] Later INDUPERU received a hodgepodge of miscellaneous firms stripped from the regional development corporations including the Cementos Yura, INCA, and the Cachimayo fertilizer plant.[55]

Financial companies also received attention. Officials strengthened the BN by allowing it to compete with private banks; granting it lucrative monopolies on foreign reinsurance and on financing fishmeal and fishoil exports; and designating it the government representative in the purchase of foreign shares in the Banco Internacional and the Banco Continental.[56]

The portfolio also doubled in 1970 through accidental nationalization. An improvised preemptive-strike rescue-mission led to the purchase of 85 percent of the Banco Popular in June 1970 when the government saved the Prado holding from bankruptcy to prevent its distress sale to a Chase Manhattan affiliate, the Banco Continental (D.L. 18307). The purchase also brought the Banco Popular's portfolio into government hands. Because the bank had acted as venture capitalist and because it had foreclosed on many firms, a diversified set of more than 30 companies became public by accident. Businesses included real estate; textile firms; movie theaters; a minor newspaper, La Crónica; and, it was widely rumored, a bordello. While some companies were later closed and their assets sold, many remained in limbo, without the legal status of a public enterprise, yet always subject to criticism as poorly-run government concerns in inappropriate sectors.[57] In late 1981, government officials vehemently denounced the government-owned movie theaters for making money by showing soft-core pornography. They argued that the government had no business in show business, dissembling a strong ideological aversion to public enterprises behind a public appeal to morals (interview, 1981).

COFIDE, the development finance corporation, also dates from early 1971. Modelled after Mexico's Nacional Financiera, COFIDE was to participate in joint ventures with private capital and sell its shares on the Lima stock exchange after the companies became financially independent. Rolling privatization never succeeded, however, because COFIDE was forced to assist other public enterprises, committing, by

1973, 70 percent of loans to public petroleum, electricity, and transport projects (COFIDE, 1974?). The government later admitted COFIDE's de facto role and made it sole financial intermediary for medium- and long-term credit to public enterprises (D. L. 18807). By the end of 1973, the Peruvian government, directly or indirectly controlled banking. The few remaining totally private banks were of minor importance.

Fishing also experienced the traditional rescue operation combined with a preemptive strike. In 1970, private firms controlled fishing and expected to keep it since official spokesmen repeatedly stated that they envisioned no major increase in the government's direct role.[58] Later, circumstances changed as the anchoveta disappeared, after years of overfishing, during a particularly strong sweep south of the warm El Niño current. In May 1973 the government expropriated all private fishmeal and fishoil producers and created PESCAPERU to hold their assets (D.L. 20000 and 20001). Fishing Minister Tantalean justified expropriation as necessary to safeguard the government banks' loan exposure and to safeguard workers' jobs on the 1,500 ships and more than 100 factories.[59] Nonetheless, a hidden motive mattered more than the publicly-admitted ones; namely the fear in some government circles that financially stronger foreign firms would better weather the crisis and take over the industry.[60] Knowledgeable observers noted that fishing expropriations exceeded the military government's initial agenda (Lowenthal, 1983:421) although it fit the pattern of unsystematic and improvisational takeovers seen earlier with the Banco Popular, the security companies, the supermarket chain, and the airline[See below]. After completing the conjunctural nationalization, the government's stake in fishing exceeded 90 percent (Tantalean, 1978:13).

The press was not neglected. In March, 1970, the government expropriated two important daily newspapers, *Expreso* and *Extra* turning them over to worker-run cooperatives (D.L. 18169). In so doing, the government opportunely invoked conjunctural nationalization and took advantage of a 2-week strike to stifle open criticism of its policies and to implicitly threaten to take over other newspapers, a threat it finally carried out in July 1974.[61] In pragmatic terms, the newspapers provided government sympathizers with access to a broader audience than the turgid official newspaper, *El Peruano*. In political terms, expropriation hit directly at Belaúnde's former prime minister, Manuel Ulloa, the papers' principal shareholder.

The broadcast media came under government control in November 1971, when the General Telecommunications Law expanded a previously marginal role into clear domination by mandating minimum state equity in all radio and television stations. The government advanced reasons of national security and promoting basic education to justify the measure.[62] Initial supervision of the government's radio and television interests was thrust on ENTEL, which ran the long-distance telephone, telex and telegraph systems.[63]

The Electric Sector Law created ELECTROPERU, in September 1972, as a holding company to unify the government's activities.[64] A complementary law capitalized the public domain concessions given to private companies, making the state a majority shareholder in some companies, while it acquired others outright.[65]

Railroads in central and southern Peru were intervened, in April 1971, on the grounds that the Peruvian Corporation, owner and operator, had defaulted on foreign obligations guaranteed by the Banco Industrial.[66] The default was long-standing, as the government had paid the company's external debt service for the previous four years. By September 1972, all government railroads were reorganized as a single company, ENAFER.[67]

A private air carrier, APSA, ran into financial troubles in 1973. To show the flag, the Air Force commercial line, SATCO, first received permission to operate internationally. Later it served as the backbone of a new government carrier, AEROPERU.[68]

Many small companies passed into government hands, usually without major planning. As but one example of this type of nationalization, the foreign-owned private security firms were acquired early in 1971.[69] Other small government companies were reorganized, such as the munitions, uniforms, and drugs manufacturers, plus the defense mapping agency that were merged into the military's industrial complex, INDUMIL (D.L. 20231). When INDUMIL's bylaws were issued, however, as a result of internal struggle, the mapping agency remained independent.

Politically motivated opportunism dictated the takeover of a private supermarket chain. When bankruptcy appeared imminent, the government could not afford to have the chain close, since most stores were located in upper and upper-middle class sections of Lima that were rife with suspicion and criticism of the Velasco government. In mid-September, the government supplied the legal basis to continue operating a bankrupt firm for the public interest and applied the law ten days later to the Super Markets. EPSA was named administrator and opportunely reopened the stores for the fourth anniversary of President Velasco's rule.[70]

Conclusions

The Velasco government dramatically increased the public enterprise portfolio from January 1970 to December 1973. The net effect resulted from the convergence of sector-level policies coupled with irregular and unplanned action.

The government swept entire sectors into the portfolio or made enormous breaches in private sector defenses. Thus, public enterprises were principally incidental means to achieve particular ends; they were not ends in themselves.[71] The new ownership structure brought about greater industrial concentration as entire sectors previously organized as oligopolies, such as minerals marketing, or which were competitive, such as the fishing industry, became government-owned and government-created artificial monopolies.

By 1973 the military concern with additions to the public enterprise portfolio had changed. Much of the fervor of the true believer's lightning strikes against the established bastions of private economic power had dissipated as those bastions had fallen progressively into government hands. The military could more easily enforce internal unity and focus when on the offensive against specified objectives such as IPC, Cerro, or the oligarchy, but by 1973, the somewhat duller, less-exciting and definitely sluggish occupation of the commanding heights had begun. As the former chief of the Air Force, General Rolando Gilardi stated, "after 1973 much had happened and it was time to catch our breaths" (Tello, 1983:I:211).

One issue connected with Peru's rapid shift in the scope of government activity needs clarification: did the Velasco government intend that public enterprises become so powerful. Such a question may be interpreted in two ways. If it is interpreted as whether the government intended to take over the commanding heights of the economy and entrust their management to public enterprises — the answer is a definite yes. Two months after the coup, then Prime Minister, Ernesto Montagne, in his first economic policy address to the nation, clearly indicated that the State would play a much stronger productive role (*El Peruano*, 6 Dec. 1968.) The commanding heights formulation was employed by his successor, General Mercado Jarrín, in similar general terms five years later, "statization will be a step that the State undertakes towards those basic, strategic and priority industries, and in some aspects of foreign and domestic trade which serve the country's interest and that of the national majorities" (*El Peruano*, 18 May 1973).

If the question is interpreted as whether the Velasco regime carefully studied implications of a large, legally autonomous, public enterprise portfolio on control and management of both the economy and the administrative system, and carefully planned each move beforehand, the answer is an unqualified no. Not only do former government officials admit they acted without an overall model, the analysis of events until 1974 clearly illustrates the improvisational nature of many reforms. Chapter 3's analysis of contradictory strategy definition, review and monitoring mechanisms and Chapter 6's examination of inadequate institutional coordination mechanisms support these findings. One of President Velasco's chief advisers, General José Graham, later summed up the military position in describing the self-styled revolutionary core as "a group of good faith and with good intentions, with a fixed agenda that signalled the transformation of structures, but whose practical application needed study"

(Tello, 1983:I:235).

The speed and lack of preparation of the takeovers make it painfully clear that, if at all explicit, military aims were to rapidly excise the sources of private economic power, irrespective of the consequences for long-term public enterprise organization.[72] As Stepan claimed after examining the pre-1968 military literature in detail, "At the philosophical level, the goals of greater state direction and greater worker involvement in the enterprise were affirmed, but organizational recommendations about the shape of the economy were vague" (1978:142). Thus, the portfolio grew through fits and starts, with wheezes, lurches, and improvisations.

PERIOD III: MOPPING-UP OPERATIONS

From 1974 to 1977, the government consolidated its presence on the commanding heights.[73] Many factors favored consolidation. First, attention to constantly shifting political alignments through the illness and replacement of President Velasco displaced concern with portfolio growth.[74] Philip convincingly argues that during this period "the state apparatus served more as a battleground over which rival factions competed than as an instrument devoted to a common purpose" (1982:443). Factionalism was not only internally generated, however, it arose, in part, from a gradual erosion of military cohesiveness in the face of external pressures (Amat y León, 1979:46). Second, according to former ministers, President Velasco himself orchestrated a political shift to the right, slowing the pace of nationalizations, to consolidate already gained territory and to avoid excessive leftward drift (Tello, 1983:I:339). Third, a deteriorating economy distracted key civilian and some military leaders who devoted much time and energy to developing strategies of military extrication and regime termination (Stepan, 1978:293). Fourth, by 1974, new pickings were slim and little of substance remained to be wrested from the private sector. Fifth, the new social property movement captured government attention. Social property received a legal basis in May 1974 but it fell from favor in 1977 after rapid growth.[75] Sixth, military attention turned south to the perceived threat of a Chilean invasion, emphasizing military preparedness and arms purchases (Cotler, 1983:27–28). Seventh, the conjunction of so many negative factors seriously undermined the military's confidence in its own capacities[76] which resulted in a government that "did not possess a single coherent set of motives and its actions were not always consistent through time" (Booth, 1983:157).

During the mopping-up period, military authorities learned that nationalization was not a simple command-result procedure, but instead proceeded through multiple levels including: intent to acquire a company, physical takeover, and legal transfer. By 1974, the nature of portfolio growth changed from the early 1970s heavily romanticized and dashing takeovers of private firms based on barely-discussed and newly-printed laws, to routine bureaucratic consolidation and precise attention to legal detail. Although sectoral laws often stated intent to acquire a company, or led to its physical takeover, they often left nationalization legally unfinished. The government also tinkered with companies by changing their responsibilities or by shifting their lines of command in an attempt to better manage the fragmented portfolio. Creation of new companies rarely occurred.

The period started with the signing of the Mercado-Greene Agreement. In February 1974, Peru and the United States finally settled all outstanding claims by U.S. firms against Peru for earlier nationalizations.[77] Mopping up was underway. An early key move was the revelation of the Plan Inca to the public on Independence Day, July 28, 1974. Most of its public enterprise-related elements were already accomplished, which largely reflects the "planning by hindsight" method employed to draw up the plan [See Chapter 3 below].

The government also tinkered with traders. All existing state traders came under the newly-created Ministry of Commerce (D.L. 20488). Thus, MINEROPERU's trading department became MINPECO, which involved splitting minerals marketing from an Army ministry and granting it to an Air Force ministry and led to vigorous protest in the cabinet.[78] Later, ENCI received responsibilities for additional product lines (Saulniers, 1980).

Industry was represented by a set of minor actions. The W.R. Grace paper and chemical plants entered the portfolio as did shares in the FERTISA fertilizer complex on the outskirts of Lima, the Pucallpa paper mill, and the QUIMPAC chemical company.[79] COFIDE rescued a small shipyard, PICSA Astilleros, to recover funds lent by the BIP (D.L. 21189). The Navy shipyard, SIMA, temporarily managed PICSA before it was entrusted first to a committee, and later to the BIP for liquidation. INDAER, a light manufacturer based on the Air Force repair service, was set up in mid-1975, but never had more than a paper existence, since the government refused to capitalize it, and the Air Force preferred retaining its repair service for other, more pressing duties. The company was indefinitely suspended from its nonexistence in 1979 (D.L. 21149; 22605).

In finance, most non-banking activities were spun off. Consequently, two insurance firms, Reaseguradora Peruana and Popular y Porvenir were purchased and received all the BN's insurance activities (D.L. 21087; 21088).

In mining, the protracted dispute with the Marcona company over nationalization of the iron-mining complex was settled in September 1976 (D.L. 21636; 21644). The dispute arose from intra-governmental differences of opinion between mining and administrative experts who saw only a technical problem needing quick settlement and President Velasco who personally insisted on the problem's political nature, involving issues of dignity and national sovereignty (Bejar, 1976:212). Agreement was only reached after Velasco's ouster, resulting in a new public enterprise aptly named HIERROPERU. In 1975, Gulf's petroleum operations in Peru were taken over and merged into PETROPERU, but final legal settlement was delayed (D.L. 21144).

In fishing, the government moved to rationalize companies by reallocating equipment and selling excess assets (D.L. 20523). By 1976, PESCAPERU had sold 420 ships on extremely liberal terms; later that year, it transferred an additional 513 ships to small worker–owned firms; by 1978, it had closed more that 60 of the 99 original processing plants.[80] In an important provision, PESCAPERU kept proceeds from selling assets after a paper transfer of funds to the public treasury and back again as a capital infusion. Post-1980 legislative barons, seeking funds to staunch the central government deficit, sought to seize all revenues arising from the sale of company assets.

The media dispute was resolved when the government abruptly expropriated all major daily newspapers[81] in July 1974 and assigned "sectoral representatives" as managers and editors (D.L. 20680, 20681). The moves temporarily stifled further overt criticism and provided the government's civilian supporters with a powerful propaganda apparatus to mobilize popular support against "minority" [read pre-1968] interests.[82] In December 1974, ENRAD was created as a holding company for radio and television shares, three years after their expropriation, a sign of earlier improvisation (D.S. 007-74-OCI). Three information office dependencies were created: ESI, the government's news service; CINEPERU its film maker; and PUBLIPERU, its publicity agency.[83] Their monopolies made them important [See Chapter 6]. When the Ministry of Economics and Finance Printing House, IMEF, was downgraded from a public enterprise to a mere ministerial dependency, a new Empresa Editora was formed in early 1976 to take over some of its printing duties and to publish the official paper *El Peruano* (D.L. 21139; 21420).

ELECTROPERU brought small electric companies in Piura, Huancayo, Chimbote, Arequipa, and Paita into the national system.[84] Trujillo's water and wastewater facilities were reorganized in late 1976 as ESAT, a public enterprise (D.L. 21688). Central authorities took the Lima Provincial government's transport company, APTL, in June 1976 after years of disastrous losses, reorganized it, and renamed it ENATRU (D.L. 21513). The government created a betting agency, EPAPRODE, hoping to earn huge profits to be channeled to recreational sports, particularly soccer (D.L. 20803).

Conclusions

The public enterprise treatment during the early Morales

Bermúdez' administration bore many similarities to that of the late Velasco years. Although the policy environment had changed, most measures from 1975 to 1977 only extended those begun earlier. In the thrust for consolidation, no major policy changes occurred.

PERIOD IV: SANITIZING

In 1978 a newly-elected constituent assembly began deliberations; in 1980, the electorate returned President Belaúnde to office. Most public enterprise actions of this period were intimately linked to a gradual return to democracy. As part of the smooth transition, finance officials sanitized the portfolio as it came under increasing public scrutiny (Silva, 1981:40). During this period, government austerity measures increasingly constrained public enterprises as the portfolio came under internal scrutiny.

After 1978, the government orientation clearly shifted away from public enterprises. Javier Silva Ruete, the Minister of Economics and Finance, signalled the shift in a speech to business executives by noting that state direct intervention had to be productive, generate wealth or jobs, or regulate the market, and should not exist "simply for the sake of being there." He added that "because of enthusiasm, we have entered too much in the economy and ... in some cases, state intervention acts as a brake on the development process" (1978:252). Under Silva, the government followed three main strategies: privatization through the sale of shares; drastic, and often confusing, portfolio restructuring; and low- or no-cost capital transfers.

The government's first strategy, attempted privatization of shares in companies no longer deemed important, implemented a recommendation of the private sector-dominated Bruce Commission [See Chapter 3]. Privatization was a sensitive issue, however, that had to be handled carefully. Its legal basis was contained in a little-noticed modification to the stock exchange commission by-laws (D.S. 0015-78-EF). Later, an overlooked budget revision enabled Ministers to recommend the "suppression, merger or restricting" of public enterprises, and their "total or partial sale" if company activities were not tax-related or reserved for the state.[85]

Although cabinet members only proposed minor companies for sale, local buyers showed little interest. Depressed economic conditions, the lackluster list of companies up for sale, and the government's inability to come up with a working privatization plan contributed to their reluctance.[86] Although slow to detail sale procedures, the government exhaustively detailed entitlements to the expected income: Treasury would get all revenue, but public enterprises would be compensated for the sale of shares of subsidiaries by 10-year, 10 percent interest bonds with a 2-year grace period (D.S. 022-79-PM and D.L. 22402). The poor investment quality of the proposed bonds dispirited company financial managers, who were already hard pressed to cope with 70 percent inflation. Unenthusiastic executives may have contributed to the program's failure. As privatization attempts waned, the government tried restoring financial solvency to one sale candidate, PEPESCA.[87]

The second strategy consisted of portfolio restructuring. Many shake-ups dated from the short government tenure of Gabriel Lanatta Piaggio, a private businessman, with whose nomination the government tried to restore business confidence. As in earlier reorganizations, public enterprises were shuffled between ministries, but this time, several of them got lost in the shuffle. Government officials justified the moves as promoting more rational resource use, increasing public enterprise profitability, and boosting government efficiency (D.L. 22439). Results fell far short of expectations.

For example, the state traders, which in 1977 accounted for 87 percent of Peru's exports and formed the most coherent trading group in Latin America, came in for virulent attack (Sánchez and Esteves, 1978). They were dismembered and the Ministry of Commerce abolished.[88] Under the new structure which merged Commerce to Lanatta's Industry ministry, EPCHAP, the fishmeal and fishoil trading corporation was split;[89] MINPECO went to the Ministry of Energy and Mines; and ENCI, stripped of its industrial input role and merged with the insolvent EPSA, went to the newly reunited Ministry of Agriculture and Foodstuffs.[90]

Industrial changes in 1978 also greatly affected Paramonga: it was merged with other paper factories; it was transferred ENCI's newsprint import business; and it was saddled with an unfinished, unwanted, and technically inefficient paper mill built by INDUPERU.[91] The paper mill proved so disastrous, particularly after a drought literally dried up supplies of the main input, bagasse, that MEF assumed all remaining obligations ($12.4 million U.S.) with the Finnish suppliers in early 1980 (D.L. 22865).

MINEROPERU, too, received long-overdue transfers. In June 1980, MEM surrendered all shares in the profitable Minera Condestable.[92] At the same time, the Banco Minero transferred the San Juan de Lucanas silver mine to MINEROPERU (D.L. 23205).

The third strategy involved building up company equity at minimum cost to the government via creative equity financing and taking overdue decisions. As an example, the government increased its equity in ENCI by 6-fold in early 1980, but more than 70 percent of the increase came from ratifying asset transfers for mergers dating back to 1974. The rest came from approving profits reinvestments, which had been pending for up to six years (León Flores, 1981:13). The government also assumed company debt, as with Paramonga and SENAMA, the agricultural machinery arm of the defunct EPSA (D.L. 22935). It cancelled and capitalized inter-enterprise debt as with S/. 1.1 billion owed by AEROPERU to the airport authority, CORPAC.[93]

The government also financed firms by clearing up its own arrears. In June 1979, it promised PESCAPERU payment of 5-years' subsidy arrears, then amounting to $11.5 million U.S., but the settlement did not cover interest charges on BN loans that excessive treasury delays forced on PESCAPERU to maintain operations (D.L. 22440). Later, the government agreed to pay an additional $8.4 million in interest (D.L. 23005).

Arrears to PETROPERU were partly paid with funds the government borrowed from a Chase Manhattan-headed consortium of foreign banks in early 1979. Even this $388.6 million loan was insufficient to repay all its debts (D.L. 22477) [See Chapter 4]. Finally, only two weeks before leaving power, the government agreed to pay subsidy arrears going back several years (D.L. 23110).

The government funded large companies by allowing them to capitalize back taxes, future taxes, and future profits.[94] Most taxes and forced profit remittances were recent, a result of increased revenue needs of the mid-1970s. Managers of cash-starved firms had resented the measures and often placed tax and profits payments in escrow accounts pending resolution of company claims against government (Saulniers, 1981a). Capitalizing the frozen assets acceded to company demands and, because it involved funds not directly under government control, was low-cost. A similar option allowed firms to capitalize future income taxes or import duties, measures that involved no current outlays and that reduced government revenues during the early years of the Belaúnde administration.

Creation of two new firms stands well apart from the dominant trends. Moraveco, the light equipment manufacturer, was intervened in October 1979 after years of persistent losses had forced it into insolvency. Under a new government-named board of directors, the company capitalized its debts to public enterprises as the first step to financial recovery (D.L. 22733; 22734). ECASA was spun off from ENCI in January 1980 to market rice.[95] Its early results augured badly. By 1981, ECASA showed enormous deficits since it was forced to subsidize three distinct groups by purchasing rice from local farmers at higher than world market prices; by selling rice to urban consumers at far lower that world market prices; and by saving local millers the need to borrow working capital.

Conclusions

From 1978 to 1980, the portfolio underwent politically and financially motivated sanitizing. The government followed three main strategies: privatization through the sale of shares; drastic, and often confusing, portfolio restructuring; and low- or no-cost capital transfers. The result, by mid-1980, was a portfolio that presented the appearance of financial health while concealing deep-rooted problems.

PERIOD V: DISORGANIZED DIVESTITURE

In July 1980, the second Belaúnde administration came to power with unbridled zeal and the goal of undoing the excessive statism of the previous twelve years. Pledging to return to a modified market economy, the president's party, Acción Popular, promised dramatic restructuring of the state's entrepreneurial activities by greatly reducing the number of totally owned firms and by opening most of the portfolio to majority private investment.[96] Belaúnde's partners in the ruling coalition, the Popular Christian Party, espoused an even more limited, Chicago-style economic role for the government, namely guaranteeing the workings of a free and competitive market (CIUP, 1980:275). Both groups coincided in the need to reduce the role of public enterprises from being principal agents of national development to last-resort suppliers of social or economic infrastructure to support private development. Clearly, the portfolio was slated for reassessment.

The new administration vested early reassessment in yet another Multisectoral Commission appointed to overview the problems of Peru's public enterprises. Tulio de Andrea, president of COFIDE, and a noted economist in his own right, headed the Commission, but resigned amid the furor that greeted its final report that took a more objective stance on public enterprises than the strong privatization slant expected by top government officials (Comisión, 1981). [See Chapter 3].

Reorganization could not wait for reassessment, however, and government officials forged ahead without clear overall directions and without studying the impact of their policies either on the companies or on the economy. The executive issued a new law on the Entrepreneurial Activity of the State in mid-1981, while the Multisectoral Commission prepared its report and without the Commission's collaboration or advice (D.Leg. 216, interview, 1982). The Decree, intended to systematize all norms applicable to public enterprises, restated the vaguely-worded provisions of the new constitution on areas of government intervention: promoting the economy, providing public services, undertaking national development, and assuring the nation's security. The decree provided a laudable, although inconsistent and unhonored, framework for action: minimize costs while providing "reasonable" quality services; use "technical" criteria to set prices; employ "sound" financial administration; and base investments on worthwhile returns.[97] Public enterprise activities had to be carried out within stringent austerity guidelines and under constantly revamped management systems.

Prime Minister Ulloa asked the World Bank to assess the portfolio and lend an international cachet to Peru's divestiture efforts. The Bank's report reflected objectivity in its treatment of company economic and financial data and provided an excellent base-line study of the portfolio (1982). It also mirrored the confusion in Peru where: conflicting lists of privatizable firms circulated at top government levels; officials had yet not assessed market or political constraints; and they had not planned selling strategies nor studied the mechanics of transfer (interviews, 1981).

Three interlocked, often contradictory, trends marked the Belaúnde years: creation of privileged public enterprises; privatization of marginal firms; and perpetual reorganization. Peru's government created few new public enterprises after 1980. When it did, privileged reasons overcame ideological reluctance. Housing, it may be expected under an architect President whose first administration had heavily emphasized housing projects for Lima's middle class, most benefited. Only two months after taking office, President Belaúnde created yet another housing bank, the Banco de Materiales (BM) (D.L. 23220). It joined two other public banks in the sector, BANVIPE and BCHP, raising inevitable questions about inefficient duplication of effort. The BM, however, was told to support building, expansion, and improvement of basic housing.

The Ministry of Housing also received a newly-created holding company for the water and waste-water companies, SENAPA (D.Leg 150). Although SENAPA was expected to centralize policy-making for the sector, its creation contrasts sharply with the breakup of holdings in other sectors, such as industry, where INDUPERU's shareholding activities had been transferred to CONADE. SENAPA also founded five new subsidiaries, becoming the largest single creator of public enterprises during the Belaúnde administration.[98] Housing clearly had a privileged position.

The armed forces ranked highly in privileged public enterprise development. Both the army and navy had important firms. The air force did not because its company, INDAER, had been deactivated in 1979. Under Belaúnde, however, INDAER was reactivated in order to chase the Peruvian dream of developing a national aircraft industry (D.Leg. 134). Later, INDAER held discussions with the private Italian manufacturer, Aero Macchi.[99]

Involuntary and accidental nationalization played a lesser role during the Belaúnde years. Three banks closed as a result of dubious banking practices. Two of them were liquidated, but the third, SURMEBAN, was reorganized as an INTERBANK subsidiary. This move, designed to bolster private sector confidence in an already-shaken banking system, added three SURMEBAN subsidiaries to the portfolio via accidental nationalization. Customs clearing houses and warehouses in Callao ranked with low priorities in public enterprise creation, nonetheless, they, too, entered the portfolio.[100]

Divestiture was a main focus of the administration. Piecemeal, special-interest privatization, consisting of the sale of government assets to benefit groups or individuals in or close to the administration, formed the divestiture counterpart to the privileged creation of public enterprises.[101] Greatest urgency was shown for the media. Under the special legislative powers delegated to the executive in 1980, an early decree called for the immediate return of newspapers and radio and television stations to their former owners, who later received indemnities for the capital losses their companies suffered while under government ownership (D.Leg. 3, 76). Additionally, special exemptions from the labor stability laws allowed owners to restructure the existing management (D.Leg. 39). Prime Minister Ulloa's two newspapers were among the first returned under the provisions.

Radio and television firms followed the newspapers. Ten radio stations were returned to their former owners who received compensation similar to that paid the press barons (D.Leg. 79).[102] Still later, the apparent conflicts of interest in the sale of some assets from the suppressed SUPEREPSA to a consortium of legislators and current and former officials of the Ministry of Economics and Finance and Central Bank were so glaring that they even provoked stories in the conservative newspaper, *El Comercio*.[103]

Where special interests could not be called into play, general privatization criteria were missing. After legislative attempts at passing a divestiture law failed, CONADE proposed a major draft that would have applied general principles to the transfer process, identified both areas of government action and current companies subject to sale, and stated precise conditions and mechanisms for conducting the sales.[104] After repeated delays occasioned by Acción Popular supporters, the senate approved the draft law, but it was tabled in the house.

With general principles missing, privatization was left up to individual ministries. INDUPERU, the sectoral holding, came in for sharp action in a conservative, PPC-headed ministry. It was liquidated and the companies in its portfolio transferred to CONADE. INDUPERU's important feasibility studies were sold "by the kilo" with no efforts made to recover costs.[105] In other actions, MITI pushed strongly for lower tariffs. Those on imported steel acted to the detriment of SIDERPERU, a company plagued for years by stagnant production levels, increasing short-term debts, underutilized capacity, deteriorating capital stock, and local competition (Gutiérrez, 1983). Labor-union generated political pressures forced the administration to further invest in the company.[106] Lowered rates on PVC cost Paramonga half the market; lowered rates on tractors forced TASA's eventual closing (interview, 1985).

MITI cancelled the 100 percent nationalization of Cementos Lima to achieve an out-of-court settlement of three pending legal suits by former owners (D.S. 038-80-MITI/DM). The government ultimately paid the disputed shares at 1974 prices with no additional compensation.[107] The conservative team at MITI also cancelled the tobacco monopoly held by ENATA, which although it may have outlived its usefulness, had roots in colonial times (D.Leg. 20).

The MEM took less dramatic action. Its companies remained

public mainly because Minister Kuczynski believed that local businessmen lacked the resources to buy and run them (1982:19). However, acting on the premise that public enterprises were inefficient, bureaucratic, subject to non-commercial goals, and forced to follow ill-advised procedures, MEM limited their future expansion and reduced their current activities. Thus, MINPECO's marketing monopoly was withdrawn, leaving private producers free to choose their own marketing channels (D.Leg. 109). Similarly, private companies, not PETROPERU, were targeted for major expansion of petroleum production.[108]

In mid-1981, the government attempted privatizing the public enterprises' legal environment when a flurry of legislative decrees issued by the executive reorganized most firms under the law of mercantile societies.[109] The move was expected to remove constrictions on management, leading to greater flexibility and initiative. The new legal bases gave companies greater freedom in hiring, firing, and salary decisions. However, control agencies employed the cover of legal changes to greatly extend their influence over public enterprises. The INP increased control over planning efforts by 60 percent, from less than 50 firms to more than 80 (INP, 1982). The CGR quadrupled its staff in expectations of monitoring the operations of all directly and indirectly held companies.[110] Thus, privatization of the legal environment, instead of freeing managers from central government restrictions, increased the already stultifying controls.

Privatization by surrender also occurred. For example, as the joint-venture tractor assembler, TASA, lost its 63 percent market share to increasingly competitive imports allowed in under the more liberal customs schedule, it repeatedly dropped production. Finally, it ceased operations altogether and paid off workers, leaving the field to foreign tractors (interviews, 1981, 1985).

During 1982 and 1983, the CONADE subsidiaries tried to set the more general policy that the central administration was unable to do. Distressed privatization occurs when a set of economic, financial, or administrative problems impel a company's divestiture (Glade, 1983:91). Some members of the Acción Popular party had long called for privatizing any public enterprises that could not cover current costs. ICSA applied this and other criteria to begin closing down minor firms in its portfolio.[111]

Privatization took still another aspect as many public enterprise monopolies were withdrawn, paving the way for new, private entrants. The state traders felt the brunt of this privatizing assault. MINPECO's minerals marketing monopoly was withdrawn and ENCI's marketing monopolies were dropped for coffee, corn, and cotton.[112]

Portfolio reorganization and restructuring also reigned during the Belaúnde years. In addition to the more than twenty large companies reorganized under mercantile society law, other firms were merged, carved up, or suppressed. Most underwent changes of name, management style, and control structure. Reorganizations were complicated, multistage affairs, similar to those carried out in 1969. Thus, the three largest urban water and wastewater suppliers, those in Lima, Arequipa, and Trujillo, were merged with the Dirección General de Obras Sanitarias of the Ministry of Housing and emerged as four new companies: SENAPA to orient national water and wastewater policy, and three regionally decentralized companies to implement policy: SEDAPAL, SEDAPAR, and SEDAPAT (D.Leg. 150). One benefit of the reorganizations was the disappearance of PUBLIPERU, the military's ideological watchdog for public enterprise advertising. It was merged with the old information service, ESI, to form a new news and advertising agency, ANDINA.

The public enterprise holding system was reorganized, as COFIDE was divided into three parts: the Corporación Nacional de Desarrollo (CONADE) would set policy; Inversiones Cofide (ICSA) would perform as a holding company; and COFIDE S.A. would monitor the outcomes (D.Leg. 157). CONADE languished as intra-bureaucratic struggles soon stripped it of any real power. In 1982, less than 18 months after CONADE's creation, the executive included a proposal to liquidate it in the budget, a move beaten back by its supporters in Congress. Outmaneuvered, but not defeated, CONADE opponents tried repeatedly to strip the holding of supervisory power. They finally succeeded in 1984 as key responsibilities were transferred to the MEF (Ortíz de Zevallos, 1985:126–127).

CONCLUSIONS

Chapter 2 examined the institutional evolution of Peru's public enterprises from 1968 to 1983 to demonstrate the analytical weaknesses of simple approaches that merely classify companies according to known motives for creation. The chapter clearly shows the difficulty in discerning true motives and the complex fabric of motives, both hidden and apparent, that marked the portfolio's evolution. In the descriptive analysis, five distinct periods are identified.

Each period exemplifies a different public enterprise policy mix. The notions that a single guiding strategy called "state capitalism," underlay the military government actions or that three policies prevailed, one for each president, are not sustained. Although a dominant policy marked each period, many other motives led to company creation, resulting in a partially coherent process of portfolio growth and change that provides an unsound basis for constructing and operationalizing a taxonomy.

Some firms entered or left the portfolio for ideological reasons; others were wrested from foreign control; in other cases the Peruvian government wanted to capture the rents from natural resource exploitation; still other firms were nationalized for "security" reasons; some became public to take advantage of economies of scale; many entered the portfolio as a result of natural or economic disasters; and some bankrupt private firms were rescued through nationalization. Thus, while the government took some actions with conscious long-run economic, ideological, political, or strategic considerations in mind, most were undertaken to fulfill constantly changing short-run personal, economic, political, and social objectives, and others were simply accidental. For some companies creation motives were manifest; in most other cases, they were undisclosed. The net result was a perpetually disarticulated portfolio without sound conceptual foundation that consisted of a vast number of companies, each with specific objectives that may, at times, been laudable, necessary, and occasionally openly discussed prior to creation, but, as admitted by government officials, lacked any overall coordination (Silva, 1981:86).

Clearly, as time passed, the government's public enterprise posture evolved considerably. There is only slight exaggeration in saying that it evolved from a naive belief that creating public enterprises would solve all Peru's problems, which marked the early 1970s;[113] to a manipulative belief that public enterprises could be bled almost indefinitely to benefit producers, consumers, and the government without regard to their financial health, which marked the mid-1970s; to the Machiavellian belief that produced symptoms of financial health without regard to long-range effects on the companies, which marked the late-1970s. The early-1980s were marked by government policies that simultaneously blamed public enterprises for most of Peru's economic ills while employing them for private benefit.

Because public enterprises were invariably viewed as particular means to a specific, sectoral, and short-term end — and not an end in themselves — the government rarely considered the impact on public enterprise of meeting goals that were often unclear, hidden, or changing. Aníbal Meza Cuadra, former minister of Transport and Communications touched on the problem when he denounced past perceived injustices by the Peruvian Corporation and claimed that the only solution "necessary was decision and dignity" (Tello, 1983:I:371). There was clearly no thought for the future.

NOTES

1. Long-run economic considerations in the public enterprise creation decision have been amply surveyed by Jones (1975:146–152), Pryor (1976:8–20), Sheahan (1976:205–222), Shepherd (1976a:33–40), and Trebat (1983:31–34). For Peru, even official sources stressed portfolio growth by rapid accretion (INP, 1980a:I:82–86).
2. INP (1976a) and INAP (1984) equate the date of current legal base with creation.
3. INP (1976a). See Chapter 3 for legal impediments to coverage of many firms by government monitoring agencies.
4. Interview with Luis Briceño Arata quoted in Becker (1983:211).
5. For an examination of the nature, size, growth, and management of Peru's public domain during the nineteenth century see Saulniers and Revilla (1983) and Revilla (1987).
6. Estenós (1825). Irregularities in privatization of a pitch mine in Northern Peru led to lingering litigation which, almost 150 years later, after a contested settlement with the International Petroleum Company, precipitated General Velasco's 1968 military coup (Pinelo, 1973:3–30). Likewise, property in the Cerro de Pasco area confiscated from 25 Spaniards during the Independence struggle and subsequently privatized reentered the public portfolio at the end of 1973 (*Gaceta*, 10 July 1825).
7. The *beneficencias* were a holdover from colonial times. They carried out good works, and ran cemeteries, hospitals, and almshouses. FitzGerald erroneously attributed them to the twentieth-century (1979:190).
8. Saulniers and Revilla (1983:26).
9. Saulniers and Revilla (1983), Saulniers (1985e:16–21), and Revilla (1987:86–117) survey Peru's nineteenth century public enterprises.
10. See ECLA (1971), FitzGerald (1974 and 1976c), INAP (1979a:8–13), and Bronstein (1981:1–19) for synopses of the conventional wisdom about the historical roots for public enterprise formation in Latin America. INP-DESCO (1974?a:3–7) uncritically applies that framework to Peru using erroneous dates for public enterprise formation, dissolutions, and mergers.
11. Controversy exists about the company's origins. The government formed the Compañía Peruana de Navegación in 1860 as a wholly-owned firm (Saulniers and Revilla, 1983). Kuczynski placed the foundation of the modern CPV in the 1930s (1977:14), while FitzGerald placed it in the 1940s (1979:190). Although the private partners agreed to sell out to the government in 1939, asset transfer remained incomplete until a reorganization from 1944 to 1946, when the company name was shortened (Rothrock, 1969:96).

12. Lanatta summarizes CAG legislation (1944). After a bewildering succession of changes during the 1960s and 1970s, the CAG eventually became part of ENCI (Saulniers, 1980).
13. By 1912, after undergoing several name changes and reorganizations, as the Compañía Recaudadora de Impuestos it received a monopoly on all tax collection except customs and guano. (Ley 1566 in *Anuario de la Legislación Peruana*, vol 6, pp. 103–105.) After its 1963 expropriation, it became the nucleus of the Banco de la Nación.
14. When created, although the government did not own all the Central Bank's shares, it exercised control by naming board members and by claiming most of the profits for the Treasury (CDES, 1965:87).
15. Previous incarnations were the Petroleum Department of the Corps of Mining Engineers and the Establecimientos Petroleros Fiscales (CDES, 1965:39). Finding an adequate institutional form for Latin American governments' petroleum ventures often took time (Saulniers, 1985a:253).
16. Appendix C details the levels of Peruvian laws.
17. The source for more complete information on previous names and creation dates is Saulniers (1986).
18. For background to BN predecessors from 1896 to 1912, including the Sociedad Anónima Recaudadora de Impuestos, the Compañía Nacional de Recaudación, and the Compañía Recaudadora de Impuestos, see Saulniers and Revilla (1983:15–16). Rothrock (1969:86) and CDES (1965:105) examine the immediate predecessor, the Caja de Depósitos y Consignaciones.
19. Appendix A compares conflicting estimates of the numbers of public enterprises in 1968.
20. Among Peru's leading social scientists, Julio Cotler has tried to stress the abrupt nature of the change in the economic role of the state (1975:44–45; 1983:19–27).
21. In addition to the Peruvian case, scattered evidence exists to justify the extension of the hypothesis to explain the growth of public enterprises. The Nora Report noted that the French nationalizations came in "successive waves" (France, Groupe, 1967:15). Similarly, Sherif noted that public enterprise portfolios often grew "as a discrete series of climactic efforts or as a succession of bunches of new entrants" (1973:12).
22. Wils noted the preparations for later reforms (1979:199–200). An unpublished MEF report called the early years an "adequating stage" (*etapa de adequación*) of government agencies to their new roles (DGAF, 1978:5).
23. *El Peruano*, various issues.
24. This transformation occurred after open press discussion, and commentators widely hailed it as long overdue. *El Peruano*, 5, 7,

and 9 Nov. 1968. See also Sociedad Nacional de Indústrias, 1969:40. Notwithstanding the extensive press play prior to the reform, Cleaves and Scurrah include the 1968 administrative law as an example of closed decision making carried out in relative secrecy (1980:88). Others have thoroughly examined the public administration reform noting both the emphasis on military-style decisionmaking and military control of key positions Jaquette (1975:418–420); Cleaves and Scurrah (1980:68–72); Becker (1983:29); and *Reforma* (1969).

25. I omit a bibliography about the takeover. Interested readers may consult Ocampo (1970) for local reactions. Pinelo (1973) and Philip (1978:53–74, 1982:243–255) provide longer-term perspectives in English.

26. Luttwak's coup handbook stressed that "conveying the reality and strength of the coup" and "manipulating national symbols" should mark the immediate post-coup information campaign (1968:175–176).

27. Goodwin reported that top Peruvian officials even offered to sign a treaty renouncing the use of expropriation (1969:89).

28. Pinelo states that most Peruvian technical petroleum talent worked for IPC, not for EPF (1973:156), while Loret de Mola noted only that EPF had personnel of widely varying competence (1978:249). The military clearly neglected internal efficiency in deciding on creation, a sad foretaste of things to come, since military intelligence estimates in Plan Inca castigated the EPF as bureaucratized and inefficient (*Plan Inca* in Tello, II:290).

29. Pinelo (1973:137–138). [Emphasis in original]. Loret de Mola reproduces the documents and the proposed decree law (1978:114–120).

30. Pinelo (1973:138), Loret de Mola (1978:248).

31. These included the National Fertilizer Service, the National Slaughterhouse and Meat Packing Service, the National Market Administration Service, the National Agricultural Marketing Service, and the National Agricultural Machinery Service (D.L. 17533 and 17734).

32. Cleaves and Scurrah treat EPSAP's early problems (1980:202–213).

33. D.L. 17860. See Shane Hunt (1975:313–316) and the interview with Aníbal Meza Cuadra, former minister of Transport and Communications (Tello, 1983:I:365–368) for background and analysis of the ITT sale.

34. Philip and Wils place the major turning point a few months later with the proclamation of the General Industrial Law (LGI). However, Philip analyzed sectoral laws and the encouragement of worker participation (1978:3) while Wils focussed on the entire industrial sector, not only on public enterprises (1979:199–200). Quijano placed the break in April 1970, when President Velasco

announced a more coherent view of the military agenda (1971:66). Other early analyses qualified the unity of the 1968–1969 period as one of "prudent appropinquations" between the government and private industrialists (Fernández, 1977) or one of legitimation of the entire process (Guerra, 1983:82). Rose's analysis of internal military dynamics also pinpoints early 1970 as a crucial period (1981:61).

35. On the fisheries dispute, see Loring (1972) and Llosa (1972).
36. See Strasma (1972:187–201) for an early treatment of land reform issues. The following provide a longer-term perspective: Bourque and Palmer (1975:179–219); Harding (1975:220–253); Havens, Lastarria-Cornheil, and Otero (1983); Cleaves and Scurrah (1980:103–130); and Caballero (1977, 1980).
37. The clear early choice for radicalism was later reversed. Pease (1977:55–70), Philip (1978).
38. Hunt was among the first to popularize the "commanding heights" notion in English-language analyses of the post-1968 Peruvian process (1975:343). His usage of the term, as denoting a substitute for the private sector, contrasts sharply to other opinions that public enterprises take over the commanding heights to "either accelerate other economic activities or regulate private sector operations along proper lines" (Ramanadham, 1974:10).
39. Philip placed the break at the beginning of 1973 based on his finding that widespread opposition by the non-oligarchic bourgeoisie had led to a drop in private sector investment (1978:133–134). The drop, however, merely continued the long-term trend which dated from the mid-1950s. Cleaves and Scurrah note the conjuncture of four forces in 1973: loss of the momentum of state growth, deteriorating control by the Velasco group over the military and civilian apparatus, declining foreign reserve levels, and a deepening internal debt largely fueled by public enterprise subsidies (1980:213). FitzGerald views the 1969–1973 period as a whole, marked by new accumulation under state control following a restructuring of ownership (1979:147). Sorj considers a unified 1968–1973 period of relative public enterprise autonomy (1983:83). Wils places the break later, between April and July 1974 (1979:200). Guerra emphasizes President Velasco's ill health in explaining the end of expansive takeover in mid-1973 (1983:82–83). Notwithstanding these alternatives, changes in portfolio growth and shifts in company operations [See Chapter 5] support a division in December 1973.
40. CAEM, Centro de Altos Estudios Militares, (1963) *El estado y la política general*, quoted in Stepan (1978:254).
41. FitzGerald, 1983:67–71. See also remarks by Dammert:28, Moncloa:63 and Portocarrero:84 in Lauer (1978). Unresolved cabinet disputes between those who favored a state capitalist

solution and their opponents gave a lurching character to government action. Former COAP head, José Graham Hurtado incisively depicts competing positions in Tello (1983, I:251–252).

42. Hunt analyzes the repercussion of this position for foreign investment (1975:312–313).

43. D.L. 18212. Former Minister of Fisheries Javier Tantalean details government takeover motives and provides a biased view of EPCHAP's early history (1978:269–302).

44. Becker provides an excellent and comprehensive review of post-1968 mining policy and policymaking in Peru (1983:49–71).

45. D.L. 17792. According to Becker, insiders interpreted the law as applying strong political pressure to speed up Southern Peru's negotiations on the Cuajone mine (1983:106). The tactic repeated a mid-1968 Belaúnde government threat to withdraw the Southern Peru, Cerro, and Anaconda concessions unless plans to get projects underway were speeded up (Kuczynski, 1977:246).

46. R.D. 0401-70-EM-DGM; R.D. 0402-70-EM-DGM; and *El Peruano*, 6 Oct. 1970.

47. *El Peruano*, 30 Oct. 1970. Although Cerro's critical path analyses were ready on time, ministry officials pressed for additional details and for hard financing arrangements, which the company could not provide.

48. D.S. 023-EM-DGM and R.M. 1165-70-EM-DGM. Andes del Perú was an Anaconda subsidiary. Quellaveco came into the public domain when ministry officials reduced the maximum permissible radius for grouping nonferrous mining operations from 10 to 5 kilometers so that "the state could get a foothold at Southern" Fernández Maldonado (1983:28) and Tello (1983:I:177).

49. D.L. 20492. Ballantyne (1976) provides the background to the takeover. Becker (1983:132–165) and Sánchez (1981) reproduce key documents and analyze the negotiations.

50. DGCoP (1975?:399). Although PETROPERU took over the petroleum companies during 1973, the Standard Oil disputed payment remained unsettled until 1974's Mercado-Greene Agreement. Hunt (1975:319–320) and Arnold and Hamilton (1978:267–268).

51. Basic industries included steel, nonferrous metallurgy, heavy chemicals, fertilizers, cement, and paper.

52. D.L. 19023. and interview (1980).

53. See MITI (1981a), Gutiérrez (1983), and Ponce (1985a and b) for details on SIDERPERU. The World Bank, one of the steel mill's major backers, later alleged that "[s]erious mistakes in design turned the plant [SIDERPERU] into an economic disaster" (IBRD, 1979:405).

54. D.L. 19272. Also *El Peruano*, 21 Dec. 1972. Stepan discusses the contract specifications (1978:280–281).

55. D.L. 19985 and 19986. The social mobilization agency, SINAMOS,

briefly controlled the ex-regional development authority firms before INDUPERU.

56. D.L. 18118; D.L. 18370; Comunicado Oficial 003-70-MEF; and D.L. 18425. Banco Internacional and Banco Continental purchases resulted from a law that restricted foreign ownership to a maximum of 25 percent of a bank's shares (D.L. 17330). The Banco Continental takeover led to a bitter public battle over the generous price paid by the BN as abstruse accounting methodologies received full press coverage. Hunt reported a price of 5.7 times market value and 3.1 times book value (1975:316). de la Melena thoroughly treats changes in BN attributes from 1968 to 1973 (1973:57–60).

57. Eleven ex-Banco Popular firms in the Santa Catalina Textile group were to be sold to their workers in 1973 (D.L. 19948). Gallegos et al. trace 32 companies in the group 12 years after government acquisition (1985:15–23).

58. Tantalean (1970:204–208; 1971:75–76).

59. Government bank exposure amounted to $123 million U. S., or 58 percent of the outstanding loans to fishing.

60. Tantalean later admitted the hidden motives in his polemic book (1978:307).

61. D.L. 20680, 20681, 20682. General José Graham indicated that top officials maintained constant contact with the striking workers and that a strong anti-government editorial precipitated the takeovers (Tello, 1983:I:248).

62. D.L. 19020. The following 11 radio stations had 25 percent of their shares expropriated: Empresa Radiodifusora Victoria, S.A.; Radiodifusora Radio Reloj, S.A.; Empresa Difusora RadioTele, S.A.; Radio Disco, S.A.; Empresa Radiodifusora Excelsior, S.A.; Radio Atalaya, S.A.; Empresa Radiodifusora Once Sesenta, S.A.; Promotora Siglo XX, S.A. Radio el Sol; Cadena Nacional, S.A.; Emisoras Populares, S.A.; and Emisoras Nacionales, S.A. In addition, 5 television stations had 51 percent of their shares expropriated: Teledos, S.A.; Panamericana Televisión, S.A.; Compañia Peruana de Radiodifusión, S.A.; Bego Televisión, S.A.; and Radio Continental, S.A. in Arequipa (D.S. 026-71-TC).

63. D.L. 19373. The Peruvian government already owned the standard public stations and its Radio Difusora Amauta, S.A. had been listed for sale since 1967 (R.S. 1330-68-HC-BN).

64. D.L. 19522. Previously, CORMAN supplied power to Lima and Ica; CORSANTA supplied it to the Chimbote-Trujillo region; SEN owned about 250 small and medium plants in isolated areas; and SINAMOS had small scattered plants. Enrique Saravia observed that Peru's large holdings dating from the early 1970s followed Brazilian models and were widely expected to import Brazilian efficiency (personal communication, April 1985).

65. D.L. 19521. CORSERELEC in Ica and SEAL in Arequipa became

mixed enterprises (Wolfenson, 1981:79–82). Trujillo's was bought (R.S. 001-71-EM-DGE).
66. Comunicado Oficial 004-71-MTC. The Ex-Im and World Bank loans dated from the early 1960s to modernize rolling stock and locomotives. Aníbal Meza Cuadra, who oversaw the nationalization, provides an indignant view of the background to the takeover (Tello, 1983:I:369–371).
67. D.L. 19431. The Peruvian Corporation's embargoed property was formally auctioned in November 1972. Under rigid bidding qualification only one bid was presented — ENAFER's. (*Andean Air Mail and Peruvian Times*, October 6, 1972, "Banco Industrial del Perú: AUCTION," p. 4.). See also Hunt (1975:317–318).
68. R.S. 0115-73-TC-AE and D.L. 20030.
69. D.S. 016-71-IN. These included: Vigilancia, S.A.; Protección de Plantas, S.A.; Seguridad Industrial, S.A.; and Protección Industrial.
70. Saulniers, 1979a; D.L. 19525; R.S. 1009-72-AC. *Andean Air Mail and Peruvian Times*, 6 Oct. 1972, and *idem*. "Supermarkets Re-Open Under State Management," p. 4.
71. See also FitzGerald. (1976a:32).
72. Bangladesh provides a similar example of poor military-enterprise relations (Sobhan and Ahmad, 1980:549–550).
73. Timing reflects stylistic differences in portfolio growth and change. President Velasco's death in December 1977 coincides with a shift in government behavior patterns.
74. Stepan notes exceptionally sharp intra-military conflict during the 1975–1977 period (1978:293).
75. By mid-1979, 57 social property firms existed, compared to 3 in 1976, the result of a much faster growth rate than that of the public enterprise portfolio from 1968 to 1973. *Autogestión*, (1979:18) and Palacios (1983:127).
76. North (1983:268). While North refers to military confidence at all levels, General Mercado Jarrín indicated widespread overconfidence in military aptitude for company management in claiming in 1964 that the Army had long possessed "manpower equipped and trained to act successfully in industry" (1964:6).
77. See Arnold and Hamilton for details on the background, the negotiations, and the settlement (1978). The views of Generals Edgardo Mercado who negotiated the settlement and Miguel Angel de la Flor who signed it are found in Tello (1983:I:305–306) and (I:78–87) respectively.
78. D.L. 20784. Much later, ex-energy and mining minister, Jorge Fernández Maldonado called the breakup a "major error in the Revolution" (1983:31).
79. D.S. 005-74-IT-DS; R.M. 1101-74-IT-DS; R.M. 1100-74-IT-DS; and D.S. 220-75-EF.
80. PESCAPERU, 1981. An advertising supplement in *El Peruano* (4 Sep. 1978) reproduced a 371 page computer listing of surplus

equipment valued at approximately $7.5 million U.S.

81. *Prensa, Comercio, Correo, Expreso, Ojo*, and *Ultima Hora*.
82. Thorndike gives an insider's view of the takeover (1976:29–30), while Booth (1983) provides historical perspective. McClintock indicates that the abrupt press expropriation suggests improvisation (1983:284).
83. D.L. 21173; 21245; 21099.
84. R.M. 018-74-EM-DGE, R.S. 235-75-EM-DGE, and D.L. 21256. Bassino and Cruz provide background on the 1975 acquisitions of ELECTROLIMA and Hidrandina (1975:ix).
85. D.L. 22264, Article 26. The budget revision was overlooked because the cabinet immediately thereafter passed a notorious personnel reduction law that attracted all the attention. The budget revision, with its important privatization provision, was even omitted from an official, supposedly comprehensive list of public enterprise-related statutes (INAP, 1979a, Anexo 3). Privatization, however, figured strongly in Minister Silva Ruete's presentation to business executives, who reacted by interrupting his speech with applause (Silva, 1978:252).
86. The firms proposed for sale included PEPESCA, DAASA, FETSA, ENATA, FUNAPER, Sociedad Agrícola "Orrantia," Espectáculos, S.A., Norsac, S.A., Empresa de Teátros y Cinemas, S.A., and Desmotadora Nacional, S.A. (D.S. 131-78-PE and D.L. 22402). Many were so minor that they had never appeared on the exhaustive company lists prepared by the Multisectoral Commissions.
87. The government repaid PEPESCA's debt to other public firms and gave it EPSEP-owned wharves and other construction at Paita plus some of PESCAPERU's surplus equipment. PEPESCA capitalized all transfers as new government equity (D.S. 165-78-PE).
88. Hints of these policies appeared in the foreign trade subcommission reports of the Bruce Commission (Comisión, 1977g).
89. In the EPCHAP split, PESCAPERU was to market fish products, while foodstuffs went to ENCI.
90. D.L. 22151, R.M. 366-78-ICTI-CO-CE, R.S. 089-78-ICTI-DM, D.L. 22232, D.L. 22439.
91. D.S. 0108-78-EF; D.S. 026-78-ICTI-CO-IND-SE; and D.L. 22333. INDUPERU profited from the transfer. It received S/. 200 million to cover its "services" in developing the paper mill. BCRP (1979a:117–122)
92. Minera Condestable shares had been donated by the Nippon Mining Company and a private individual (D.S. 022-80-EM-DGM).
93. The method by which the government repaid AEROPERU's debt to CORPAC merits mention — a 6.5 year, 0 percent interest, 1-year grace period loan. Under the assumption of continued 70 percent inflation, these terms wiped out three-fourths of the loan's present value while promising to repay the entirety (D.L. 22874).

94. From February to mid-July 1980, the following companies were financially restructured: MINPECO - D.L. 23041 of May 14; HIERROPERU-D.L. 22906 of Feb. 26 and D.S. 111-80-EF of May, 29; MINEROPERU-D.L. 23122 of July 9; SIDERPERU - D.L. 23196 of July 19; ELECTROPERU - D.L. 23115 and 23126 of July 9, and D.L. 23200 of July 19; ENTEL - D.S. 138-80-EF of June 18; and Moraveco-D.L. 23098 of the same date.

95. ENCI Board of Directors Acuerdo 01-80.

96. The Acción Popular party platform planned equal-share or majority private-national joint-ventures for AEROPERU, ELECTROPERU, ENCI, ENTEL, EPPA, HIERROPERU, INDUPERU, MINEROPERU, MINPECO, Paramonga, and PESCAPERU. See CIUP, 1980:80–82. Cogent observers noted that the proposed joint ventures would absorb at least $500 million US from the Peruvian capital market, and doubted the absorptive capacity of local investors. *Perú Económico*, "Un círculo que aun no cierra," Vol. 3, No.6(June, 1980).

97. D.Leg. 216 is reprinted as a Belaúnde administration failure to rationalize the portfolio in Saulniers et al, (1985:271–284). Chapter 6 analyzes inconsistencies in the legal apparatus.

98. New SENAPA subsidiaries included: SEDACUZCO, SEDALAM-BAYEQUE, SEDALORETO, SEDAPIURA, and SEDATUMBES.

99. *Latin America Regional Reports*, p.3.

100. *Andean Report Peru Banking Portfolio 1983*, p.36. Subsidiaries were PROCASA, SERPESA, and ALMACENA.

101. Glade employs the more neutral "claimant-induced privatiza-tion" in describing the same phenomenon (1983:90–19). Branch provides detailed evaluations of early Belaúnde administration privatization efforts (1981, 1982b).

102. Compensation for all media firms took the form of subsidized-interest loans and tax credits.

103. "Aclaran venta de inmueble de Super Markets," 27 Aug. 1985. Officials implicated in the potential conflict of interest included the Minister of Economics and Finance, the former General Manager of the Central Bank, and a leading congressman from the president's party.

104. Ortíz de Zevallos (1985:108). See also the version passed by the Peruvian Senate (Senado:1983).

105. Grisolle, writing from an insider's perspective, called the sales a "curious mechanism for promoting [industrial] development" (1983:5).

106. Excise taxes imposed on SIDERPERU's production and earmarked to support the new University of Chimbote, accomplished what direct measures had been unable to do. SIDERPERU's prices in the Lima market were forced higher than those of the competi-tion. *El Comercio*, "Aporte de Síder-Perú a U. del Santa casi llega a mil mlls. mensuales," 18 Aug. 1985 and interview, 1985).

107. Branch analyzes the background and solution to the Cementos Lima conflict in detail (1982b:162–195).
108. Companies with which contracts were signed under Kuczynski include: Superior Oil, Royal Dutch Shell, a Hamilton Petroleum-Petroinca consortium, and Belco. Two other contracts were deferred at the last minute by falling world market prices: Elf Aquitaine (a French public enterprise) and the Union Texas-Mapco consortium (Kuczynski, 1982:61).
109. The following companies were reorganized as corporations: Alcohol Industrial S.A., CORPAC S.A., CPV S.A., ELECTROPERU S.A., EMSAL S.A., ENACO S.A., ENAFER S.A., ENAPU S.A., ENATA S.A., ENATRU S.A., ENTEL S.A., ENTURPERU S.A., EPSEP S.A., HIERROPERU S.A., INCA S.A., INDAER S.A., MINPECO S.A., PESCAPERU S.A., PETROPERU S.A., SIDERPERU S.A., SIMA S.A.
110. "Contraloría en 1981 amplía acción a 200 empresas estatales," *El Peruano*, 4 Jan., 1981.
111. Firms that were bankrupt or being liquidated by mid-1984 included ALAMBRESA, Avícola Cencerro, DAASA, FUNAPER, HELITUBCA, Iquitos Plywood, MHASA, Mina Aguila, and TASA. See ICSA (1984).
112. D.Leg. 109; D.S. 161-81-AG; R.S. 126-81-AG; and D.S. 56-82-EFC.
113. Sherif described this widespread naiveté as "public enterprise as *deus ex machina* that could sufficiently ensure accelerated development" (1973:5).

3

Strategic Failures

INTRODUCTION

The standard problem in public enterprise control and account-ability focuses on the contradictions between the company's need for autonomy and the government's use of the company to serve the public interest.[1] The problem is posed as follows: Because public enterprises produce and sell goods and services, government author-ities must grant them sufficient autonomy to carry out entrepreneurial tasks; but, because governments use public enterprises as policy tools, authorities must limit managerial discretion to ensure meeting social goals. Contradictions arise between the microeconomic role of inde-pendent company and the macrosocial role of government agent. The standard solution to this problem is to design mechanisms that simul-taneously define and rank the company's objectives and strategies to provide a coherent basis for effective management action. Such mechanisms also provide criteria for management and government to use in evaluating company effectiveness and efficiency.

Peru spread strategic responsibility for its public enterprises over several agencies, including, but not limited to, the overseeing ministry, the INP, MEF, inter- and intra-ministerial committees, special commis-sions, the comptroller general, and the development corporations.[2] This splintered state apparatus, with its strong potential for division and dissension, led to internal coordination problems that resulted in the systems' inability to provide a coherent basis for effective manage-ment action.[3]

The resulting confusion is an excellent case of failure in defining, setting, reviewing, and monitoring public enterprise strategies. As shown in Chapter 2, Peru's public enterprise portfolio grew through agglomeration via the conjunction of different issues. Disorganized portfolio growth was matched by inconsistent and contradictory oversight systems based on vaguely-stated objectives that were often impossible to attain, used ad hoc evaluation criteria, led to strong negative externalities, and took no heed of tradeoffs among objectives.

This chapter reviews Peru's control failure by examining four separate subsystems: planning, budgeting, commission or committee coordination, and information monitoring.[4] Planning merits special attention because it provides medium-term perspectives to guide company actions and against which they may be judged. Budgeting systems provide similar short-term orientations and guidelines. Commissions or committees may effectively reduce systemic operating frictions. Information gathering and analysis systems should provide useful data for both company management and external controllers. In Peru, each subsystem shows flaws in conception and execution.

DEFINING STRATEGY–THE ABDICATION OF PLANNING

In a modified market economy, such as Peru's, planning's most important role is to define basic strategies. This involves formulating policies for providing goods and services through public enterprises and determining the organizational structures necessary to achieve those policies.[5] National plans detail basic strategies, whether to serve as a model for company plans or because they are aggregated from documents prepared at the company level. Planning systems usually remain powerless to implement basic strategies because they have limited coercive ability, but they have a role in review and monitoring.

After taking power in 1968, the Velasco administration upgraded the National Planning Institute (INP) by raising its budget substantially in real terms and by letting it hire a larger and more highly qualified staff. The national plans prepared by INP are examined below.[6]

Planning Strategies 1971-1975

Drafts of the medium-term, 1971–1975 plan, the first prepared by the revamped INP, circulated during 1970 and the cabinet approved the final version in May 1971.[7] Many important public enterprise changes during 1970 should have been present in the plan. They weren't. The plan consistently stressed that a vague and indefinite "state" would have new roles as a development promotor and leader, intervening directly and indirectly in the economy, but it barely touched on the practical matter of implementation[8] Indeed, when the plan mentioned public enterprises, it repeatedly assigned them a support position to a private sector-oriented development. The uncertainty and confusion was initially revealed when, of the ten Horizontal Commissions that brought together public sector policy makers during late 1970 to prepare the draft plan, none dealt specifically with public enterprise issues (R.S. 013-70-PM-AL).

Following the major portfolio changes after 1968 one would expect the plan to clearly state that public enterprises would be instrumental to Peru's development. However, there was no general statement of their planned importance and only three vague, partial strategy references: expansion, profits, and efficiency. The expansion strategy deemphasized them, as it stressed transforming the entire public sector to become "a stimulus to private sector participation in activities... not reserved to the state" (*Plan 1971–1975*:15). They were assured only a direct role in future natural resource exploitation. The profits strategy indicated that public enterprises would account for most of the planned increase in savings on government account by shifting to "activities capable of generating surpluses" and by boosting efficiency (:26–27).[9] The efficiency strategy, part of total public administration reform, included reorganizing the development banks and creating an agency to coordinate public enterprise management training, technology, and profits (:70).

To varying degrees, the sectoral plans mentioned public enterprises. The strongest references concerned basic industry, and mining (*Plan 1971–1975*:26). In industry, the state was expected to "practically assum[e] the leading role" in directing industrial expansion to attain permanent and self-sustained development, yet public enterprises were marginal to planned reforms that stressed de-bureaucratizing the government, instilling industrial promotion attitudes, and bypassing bureaucrats who resisted change (:41). Another sign of low priority is that public enterprises figured in only 2 of the plan's 36 industrial policies: creation of an industrial holding company, and ensuring them adequate means to meet plan targets (:121–123). Because the plan assigned public enterprises such a marginal role, Walter Piazza, a leading private businessman, concluded that their major role would be to support private firms by providing cheap inputs (1971:219).

The Plan stated that LGI provisions reserving basic industries for the state would be gradually implemented by acquiring a minimum of 50 percent equity in paper mills and cement plants according to a "well-developed" program (:117). It presented a wish list of industrial projects that included building steel complexes at Nazca and Talara, and plants for nonferrous metals, chemicals, petrochemicals, phosphoric rock, and salt (:115–116). A stress on gradualism contradicted the proposed leading industrial role.

In mining, the plan proposed a similar gradual approach to take over foreign decision-making capacity, but took no note of changes that had already taken place (*Plan 1971–1975*:41). The plan stated that private mining concessions without feasible short-term development plans would revert to MINEROPERU (:42), but all the major concessions had already been taken over by the time of the plan's second draft in December 1970. The plan also failed to mention the most important development in mining, MINEROPERU's new minerals marketing monopoly.

In fishing, public enterprises would continue to provide traditional support for private firms, except in marketing where a planned government monopoly would increase Peru's share of the surplus (*Plan 1971–1975*:42). Again, actions far outstripped expectations. EPCHAP had received a monopoly in April 1970, before preliminary drafts of the plan were written.[10]

Although the Velasco government viewed state-directed development through public enterprise as possible, planning policies were poorly defined, poorly articulated, and inconsistent. Anomalies in the 1971–1975 plan lead to two important conclusions. First, planners placed such a low priority on public enterprises that they were unable to incorporate changes that occurred prior to and during the plan exercise. Second, because plans stressed growth through an amorphous "state," public enterprise strategies were usually vague and unclear or, where detailed, stressed a gradualist approach that contradicted both previous actions and later portfolio growth. A self-serving INP document published in 1980, attributed the inconsistent strategy definition to "asynchrony between the worthwhile plans and studies carried out by the National Planning Institute and their implementation" (1980b:79–80).

Conspiracy theorists such as Zimmerman (1975) and Sánchez (1983:13) argue that published plans deliberately concealed government aims in an attempt to gull the private sector and to prevent countermeasures from being taken. They surmise that a handful of radical officers hid their true intentions, even from the rest of the cabinet, to use public enterprises to negate the economic and political power of foreign companies and the national elite.[11] While conspiracy theories may explain pre-coup behavior, they hardly explain the planners' inability to follow and incorporate current events, neither do they justify the repeated corrections of errors in control and monitoring systems, nor the growth via agglomeration that occurred after 1968. A more likely scenario was confusion in INP about the role of public enterprises, a confusion that was compounded by the INP's marginal role in overall policymaking. Internal evidence indicates that the growth of Peru's public enterprise portfolio resulted from the attempt to meet a few vaguely-identified, imprecise objectives in an uncertain time horizon and within an unknown constraint field.[12] Neither conspiracies nor plans really mattered.

Planning Strategies 1975–1978

The second medium-term plan, from 1975 to 1978 overlapped the mopping-up operations. Consolidation, its key strategy, was the reason the plan paid more attention to public enterprises. It stressed the need to consolidate the state's economic position in all major sectors (*Plan 1975–1978*:38–39) and to integrate company plans into the overall planning framework (:30). Public enterprises had been partly integrated into regional plans (:35); sectoral plans gave their production and supply goals (:95–107); and the investment plan detailed their major projects (:121–152).

The plan also proposed to increase regulation of firms and to reorganize the portfolio as a belated response to earlier rapid growth. However, the proposed reorganizations, regulations, and consolidations were not implemented because the plan was scrapped.

Planning Strategies 1977–1980

Events quickly left the earlier plan behind. The mid-1975 change in regime removed some ideological underpinnings of the 1975–1978 plan, while rising inflation and exchange rates made many of its economic assumptions obsolete. As a result, INP drew up a new medium-term plan, midway through the planning period, called Plan Tupac Amaru after the mythical figure of the revolution. It featured a major shift in government thinking: a planned transition to civilian rule, a new constitution, and general presidential elections.

In other ways, Plan Tupac Amaru was consistent with earlier plans: there was no special public enterprise section, no general strategies for them, and they were marginal to sectoral objectives or policy guidelines. However, concern about their organization resulted in a statement of intent to enact norms for state entrepreneurial activity and to establish worker participation mechanisms (*Plan 1977–1980*:26). Actions fell short of expectations, as normative law drafts circulated at top government levels and would remain unpassed under the military [See below]. Increased worker participation tried to merge two administration concerns, but it too stagnated. In other areas, public sector planning was made compulsory so that the government could better tap any public enterprise surplus; companies were increasingly subjected to the national control system; and the subsidy policy was slated for reexamination (*Plan 1977–1980*:18; 20; 35). The sectoral plans contained little new for public enterprises.

Planning Strategies 1979–1982

The 1979–1982 plan incorporated a major innovation: a special public enterprise section (*Plan 1979–1982*:30–34). It detailed, erroneously at times, the portfolio growth from 1950 through the late 1970s and stressed that the government had acted on two basic motives in creating public enterprises: correcting distortions in the market economy and converting the state into a dynamic development agent. The narrative constituted gross oversimplification of the facts [See

Chapter 2].

The plan candidly admitted that no explicit management strategy existed because the government's public enterprise actions were mutually inconsistent (:33). For example, firms could not fulfill their investment targets because government price controls made it impossible for them to generate the needed savings. The plan also admitted that the subsidy policy used in setting prices, did not redistribute income to the poor (:33) The plan reiterated two explicit public enterprise policies: to pass a normative law of state entrepreneurial activity and to boost efficiency (:145).

Planning Strategies 1982–1985

The 1982–1985 plan updated the historical section of the previous plan with recent changes (*Plan 1982–1985*:61–68). It championed the finally-passed Normative Law of the State's Entrepreneurial Activity as resolving organizational problems and it noted a drop in the number of firms due to closures or mergers (:64).

The proposed tactics were repeated from earlier documents: to implement complete legal consistency; to increase efficiency; to make firms self-financing; and to transfer funds from public enterprises to the central government (:177). The plan added two new objectives that reflected the regime's private sector bias: to invite national and foreign participation in joint ventures and to privatize companies in sectors no longer deemed strategic or socially necessary (:177).

Conclusions

Peru's planning system failed to adequately set or to reconcile medium-term public enterprise strategies because it never formulated policies for providing goods and services through them and nor did it determine the organizational structures necessary to achieve those policies. At best plans provided companies with "mere indicative guides of desirable behavior" (Moncloa, 1978:128). The earliest plans neglected the portfolio's growth in size and importance. The exclusion resulted in plans that remained at a high level of abstraction. Although public enterprises were later included into the plans, they were not part of the planning process. A measure of INP's ineffectiveness is that Azi Wolfenson, a former executive president of ELECTROPERU, in enumerating central government hindrances of public enterprise operations, stressed problems with the sectoral ministry and the MEF, but omitted mention of the INP altogether (1981:310).

The planning system not only failed at setting strategies, it never specified evaluation criteria against which the public enterprise actions could later be measured. Ideally, criteria would carefully balance economic against social or political objectives but, Peru did not. According to former economics and finance minister Javier Silva Ruete, the government never clearly defined its exact social goals.[13]

Plan Inca — Hidden Agenda or Planning by Hindsight?

On Independence day, 1974, General Velasco claimed that a "secret plan" had guided the government's major actions since taking power in 1968. Thereafter the subject of much speculation and examination, the plan was trumpeted in a book by Velasco's press secretary, Augusto Zimmerman (1975).

Plan Inca was divided into 31 sections, each section contained a skeletal outline of the situation, an objective, and a list of concrete actions to be taken.[14] The plan sections were not well integrated, indeed, Evelyne Stevens referred to it as a hybrid of "high-level abstract values and low-level concrete objectives and strategies for action" (1980:86).

Internal evidence, widely examined at the time, suggested that the version that existed in 1968 was vastly different from the one eventually released.[15] Later, members of the Velasco team admitted tampering with the document after 1968. General Arturo Valdés professed membership in the COAP team that later expanded the original 1968 document into its published form (Tello, 1983:II:277). Former foreign minister de la Flor claimed that the list of concrete actions was completed and brought up to date as authorities became aware of new problems or as steps were taken to solve those already listed (Tello, 1983:I:62). Former energy and mining minister Fernández Maldonado concurred, "there was a clear consciousness of what we must do without saying that we had total and complete understanding. As we advanced in the revolution, we began to see our horizons more clearly, making our ideology more precise, and perfecting our program" (Tello, 1983:I:124).

Given Plan Inca's 1974-hindsight perceptions of pre-1968 reality, its references to public enterprises are revealing, especially in the light of the Velasco administration's early actions. For example, the plan characterized EPF as "bureaucratized and inefficient" (*Plan Inca* in Tello, II:290), but among its first acts, the military government entrusted EPF with managing one of the nation's largest companies. In fishing the plan indicated that state would absorb large-scale fishing and marketing and rationalize the sector, but excess capacity only became crucial after the disappearance of the anchoveta in the early 1970s (Roemer, 1970:88). In mining, the plan stressed using a solvent public enterprise to take over production, refining, and marketing (:295–296), but MINEROPERU showed accounting losses in all years but one after 1974. Other public enterprise actions were planned for electricity, foreign trade, and communications, but in two of these three sectors, the Velasco government's actions were at odds with Plan Inca, while in the third, the actions responded to external factors that became important after 1968. These discrepancies do more than provide internal evidence of plan tampering, they reveal that by 1974 the highest policy levels still had not faced the possibility of contradictions between the microeconomic role of a public enterprise and its macrosocial role as government agent. Public enterprises were simply the means to implement policies set elsewhere.

Plan Inca shows other important policy insights. It did not authorize the planning system to set, review, and monitor public enterprise strategies, but the INP constantly sought more power to do so. It did not include public enterprises in the section on company reforms, corroborating the hypothesis of lack of understanding of their role as microeconomic agency. Further, it did not mention them in the section on administrative reform, indicating a lack of understanding of the communication channels necessary to carry out the role of macrosocial agent.

In summary, the hindsight-derived agenda failed to provide any mechanisms for setting public enterprise strategies, for periodically reviewing them, or for monitoring their implementation. At best, it provided a de facto summary of the major portfolio changes prior to 1974 and hard evidence that top policy makers did not yet understand problems of achieving long-term institutionalization of their reforms through public enterprises.

REVIEWING STRATEGY–THE HINDRANCE OF BUDGETING

The budgetary process is a structural link between public enterprises and central government. It provides government authorities with recurrent opportunities for strategic review of expenditures, programs, and objectives. Budgets normally do not set strategy because their analytical context is usually limited to results of the last budget cycle. Well designed and implemented budgets can, however, aid in monitoring strategy attainment. This section analyzes Peru's budgeting system.[16]

Finance ministries invariably monitor public enterprises through the budget's control of investment funds and subsidy allotments or its request for dividends. In Peru, these concerns were reinforced by the planning system's abdication of setting anything more than vague guidelines. General Morales Bermúdez, then Minister of Economics and Finance, tried to use the budget to fill the policy vacuum.[17] Within three months of his ministry's creation (D.L. 17521), its functions were broadened from standard tax, budget, and financial matters to include broad quasi-planning powers "to harmonize national economic policy in the short run, in accordance with the general government policies and the plans for economic and social development, coordinating and executing the Annual Economic Plan *with the participation of the National Planning Institute.*"(D.L. 17703, June 1969) [Emphasis added].

Budgets could not provide the strategy definition abdicated by the INP because most public enterprises were legally exempt from budget requirements. Only the small minority of firms organized under public enterprise law was required to submit to the government budgetary process. Differential treatment of public firms made overall strategy definition or review impossible.

Peru's budget system grew as the portfolio did. Ad hoc portfolio growth resulting from short-term considerations was matched by ad hoc heaping of budgetary controls that responded both to real short-term financial requirements and to the alleged inadequacy of earlier controls. One consistent feature marked the system: it neglected broad goal attainment issues to focus, instead, on forms and finance.

In 1968 and 1969, public enterprises not only formulated their own budgets for inclusion in the national budget, they operated under fewer constraints than did other agencies (D.L. 17556). They could fill staffing vacancies, create new management positions, and vary their budgets, actions forbidden other agencies. They were even exempt from post-hoc control by the Comptroller General (CGR).

Beginning in 1970, government authorities used the budgetary process to impose tighter financial control and reporting requirements on the companies (D.L. 18088). They had to send monthly reports on cash-flow and quarterly reports on current income and expenditures to the annual economic planning group and to the economic affairs directorate of MEF (DGAE). Although reporting is basic to the exercise of control, it only becomes useful under certain conditions that Peru's system failed to meet. For example, the budget set no time limits for sending in reports nor did it mandate their analysis. As a result, reports were sent late, if at all, and simply filed by the recipients (interview, 1978). In a move with broad implications, the 1970 budget made the CGR responsible for verifying adherence to budget norms [See below].

As the portfolio grew, the twin problems of coordinating its overall policy and of controlling individual companies became more acute. In an effort to solve the problems, budgets placed more controls and reporting requirements on public enterprises and introduced toothless review and monitoring mechanisms. The 1971-1972 budget obliged public enterprises to transmit monthly reports on budget execution to the MEF, INP, and CGR via the supervising ministry (D.L. 18700). The monthly reports still were not subject to analysis, however, and continued to expand the files. Although the INP had to be notified of some budget changes, it had no formal review mechanism to analyze them. The budget also set maximum limits on central government transfers to public enterprises, which led to a substantial buildup of arrears [See Chapter 5].

The 1973–1974 budget law further increased reporting requirements and, for the first time, required INP and MEF monitoring.[18] It also imposed stringent financial programming, subjecting public enterprises to a strict budgetary calendar that required them to forecast annual sales, production, purchases, market position, investment, and personnel, as well as annual and monthly income statements and cash flow (DGCP, 1972:800). If well thought-out and properly implemented, the forecasts would have greatly strengthened the quality of information available to top management. However, the government could not agree on programming techniques, reporting forms, or forecasting mechanisms. During the budget exercise, paperwork and procedures were continually changed, while companies were tightly held to the original schedule, so that the process became one of repeatedly submitting new and usually overdue forms, instead of forging a useful management tool. In bureaucratic power terms, central government confusion was the outcome of a struggle between the INP, MEF, and COFIDE who sought to impose strict centralized controls over company production and investment decisions, and the sectoral ministers, backed by the President's Advisory Committee (COAP), who pushed for decentralization. The proponents of decentralization won, although MEF did impose a condition for prior consent for some budget changes that resulted in serious delays, forcing many companies to begin the 1975 fiscal year without approved budgets (INP, 1978a:6).

By 1974 portfolio growth had slowed, but the number of agencies involved in the budgetary process continued growing. Once a company's controlling ministry initially approved a draft budget, seven other clearances were needed before the Minister's final approval could be given.[19] Monitoring increased as INP and MEF now prepared biannual budget execution reports; sectoral planning offices provided quarterly financial management reports; and Sectoral Management Committees[20] periodically evaluated company financial statements and recommended corrective measures to the Cabinet [See below].

By the 1975–1976 period, public enterprise managers had acquired sufficient experience and political clout to begin reversing the trend to greater reporting requirements (D.L. 21057). Reduced paperwork benefited both company executives who no longer had to prepare the forms and ministry officials who lacked enough trained evaluators. However, specific conditions still burdened companies. For example CENTROMIN had to draw up an annual imports calendar for approximately 30,000 items not locally available (Comisión, 1977d:9). One provision of the budget law went counter to the trend, namely, an open-ended data-gathering authorization for two groups, the DGPP and DGCP, which led to an "alarming increase in requests" that company officials viewed as unwarranted (Comisión, 1977e:11). The process of budget modification was also eased, requiring only the minister's approval, with notification of the appropriate central government authorities, provisions that, while reducing the number of steps needed for approval, assigned to the minister decisions that formerly were the prerogative of boards of directors.[21]

The 1977 budget law reduced the number of required company reports and limited semi-annual reviews to the INP and MEF (D.L. 21765). Although it returned power over most operating budget changes to the boards of directors, because of deteriorating economic conditions, the investment budget could only be altered via a Supreme Resolution jointly signed by the sectoral minister and his colleague in MEF. By 1978, power of approval was also returned to the sectoral minister, but it could only be exercised after the DGPP and the INP had analyzed the proposed changes (D.L. 22049).

The continuing financial crisis led to a Priority List for Public Sector Investment, which was the first serious attempt to centrally rank projects according to how well they fulfilled medium- and short-term planning strategies. The system was justified as putting a lid on subsidies, given the BN's inability to keep covering company deficits and the worsening treasury situation. However, because the INP and MEF could not deal with investment project documents fast enough, new delays, compounded by high inflation and continual devaluations, led to outdated investment budgets even before completion of the review process.[22]

The Silva Ruete budgets for 1979 and 1980 tried to centralize control over company finances and to tie them more closely to the country's austerity guidelines (D.L. 22399, D.L. 22749). Most notably, the budgets shifted control over profits disposition to the Silva-controlled Interministerial Economic and Financial Commission (CIAEF). They also made changes in company investment conditional on prearranged financing; required companies to budget for incurred but unpaid expenses, including government obligations;[23] and forbade imports of capital equipment without available funds to pay customs duties. In recognition of high inflation, boards of directors received power to increase investment budgets to cover higher local costs or more expensive imports. They could not, however, reschedule projects without prior INP approval. The budget process was also simplified so that final approval rested with the sectoral Minister before transmittal to the INP, CGR and MEF.

The Belaúnde budgets tried dual tactics. First, they freed public enterprises from most reporting requirements.[24] Companies only had to prepare bi-annual reports on budget execution. Indeed, the 1981 budget removed so many reporting requirements that it even omitted to mention who would get the reports, an oversight later remedied. Second, they imposed the same austerity measures on companies as on the rest of government. At first, hiring and contracting were frozen and purchases of many goods were blocked. Later budgets placed stringent restrictions on management practices. Thus, BN's monopoly on company banking was reinstated, companies had to spend at least one third of their advertising budgets through public enterprises, and the CGR's grip on the companies was tightened. By 1982, any local or foreign operation that incurred debt needed prior CGR approval.

Conclusions

Peru's budgeting system failed to define a public enterprise strategy because most government-owned companies were excluded from budget requirements. It also failed to monitor public enterprises because budgets focussed on filling out forms and imposed increasingly complicated reporting systems on the firms. The budgets posed other problems because they focussed on finance, which led to superimposed and increasingly complicated clearance levels for approving new projects and changing budget items. To even further complicate the issue, in lieu of pre-budget guidance about levels of resource availability, managers were repeatedly told how to fill out forms and reports correctly (DGCP, 1972).

The controliste approach stemmed, in part, from Peru's inexperience in bringing public enterprises into budgeting. Short-term considerations led to the ad hoc heaping of controls and reporting requirements based on financial needs or perceived problems in the system while the government could not even analyze the resulting reports. Consequently, control was not exercised at all in the early years when most reports remained unread. Later, the increasingly complex approval structure caused bottlenecks that lowered government efficiency. Slow approval procedures, in turn, had negative consequences for public enterprises. Company managers viewed the budget process as impeding entrepreneurial dynamics (Wolfenson, 1981:310). Although the government received repeated recommendations to boost government and company efficiency by removing its centralized budgetary requirements, it steadfastly refused the advice.

Inter-agency disputes weakened the budget system. As the INP incorporated public enterprises more fully into planning documents, its limited institutional role in setting strategy was eroded by MEF control over the budgetary process. By early 1975 INP's power of approval had been almost entirely withdrawn, replaced by the much weaker requirement of prior notice; INP pre-fiscal year budget approval also disappeared by 1978. The Minister of Economics and finance then held sole power of approval and the INP was left with after-the-fact notification. MEF thus eclipsed the INP.

OVERSEEING STRATEGY–DISREGARDED COMMITTEES

In Peru, committees oversee both strategic and every-day affairs of public enterprises. According to Ramanadham, committees are handicapped by having limited executive power over enterprises, by being subordinate to the controlling ministries and, if they lack proper structure, by merely serving as a forum for discussing conflicting opinions, without resolving any problems (1974:85). Peru's experience with committees clearly corroborates his findings.

Strategic Review

From 1975 to 1981, three Multisectoral Commissions conducted strategic reviews of Peru's public enterprises, examining their most pressing problems and proposing solutions. The first commission, authorized by the cabinet in October 1975, brought together representatives of the INP, the MEF, and INAP with top company executives. Its thorough final report examined key public enterprise issues. First, it noted that different statutory forms led to variations in effective government control. It suggested alternatives including reducing the number of permissible forms and creating a single holding company for all parastatals (Comisión, 1976:20-21).

Second, it looked at labor problems that arose because workers in the same company could fall under different statutes. The resultant parallel legal and administrative structures to cover wages, salaries, and bonus structures led to higher costs. Labor organization depended on statutory form, so that some firms had unions while in others labor could not organize. This led to unequal treatment. Because the government regulated hiring, firing, wages, and promotions, company management was restricted, which led to inefficiency. The report proposed new laws to remedy the three problems (Comisión, 1976:10-12).

Third, the report criticized the budgetary process for "creating rigidities and delays" (Comisión, 1976:12). It proposed giving boards the power to modify line items providing post hoc notices were sent to the relevant authorities (Comisión, 1976:27). It recommended sharply decreasing reporting requirements.

Fourth, it criticized government policy on taxes and profits remittances, particularly the 1974 profits disposition law that forced companies to pay out half of *anticipated* profits before approval of yearly financial statements (D.L. 20810). Because the law confused anticipated profits with cash flow, companies were sometimes forced to borrow to meet treasury payment deadlines.[25] The report noted that the law promoted inconsistent profits tax treatment: firms legally considered public enterprises lost control of at least 50 percent of their profits, while firms organized under mercantile society law could reinvest up to 99 percent of theirs, irrespective of the government's share of equity. It proposed simplifying the laws, eliminating institutional rigidities, and treating all government-owned companies consistently (Comisión, 1976:28).

Fifth, it censured the poorly designed control and auditing system later characterized as used to "asphyxiate, immobilize and crush the public enterprises" (Comisión, 1977c:3). The system was based on hierarchical supervision by four agencies under the direction of the CGR.[26] The commission proposed vast revisions of the system to correct two bad practices: Companies could only hire CGR-approved external auditors and internal auditors were jointly responsible to top management and the CGR.[27]

Sixth, it recommended creating a set of committees to define basic policies, to coordinate policy achievement, and to resolve disputes among public enterprises that lacked a practical arbitration system.[28]

There is little indication that Commission recommendations were ever adopted. Recommendations to solve public enterprise problems were lost, perhaps deliberately, among similar calls for action by other Commissions concerned with different problems.[29]

The government's response was to form yet another Multisectoral Commission, named the Bruce Commission after its president, Alberto Bruce Caceres, the General Manager of PETROPERU, in November 1976. The new commission was mandated to propose means of increasing public enterprise efficiency and to draft a public enterprise normative law.[30] It included prominent private sector representatives on almost all 18 subcommissions. Its basic premises were that Peru's portfolio had: no overall orientation, inadequate coordination and control systems, an inadequate legal framework, and inadequate compensation for controlled prices.

The Bruce Commission returned four startling recommendations. First, it proposed that public enterprises operating in sectors not reserved for the state should be transferred to social property firms, cooperatives, or private firms. This proposal originally figured prominently in the report of the international trade subcommission, two of whose four members, including the president, Dionisio Romero, were from the private sector.[31]

The second recommendation, concerning monopoly public utilities and industries reserved to the state, divided the commission. A minority favored maintaining the status quo while the majority supported opening the sectors to private initiatives.[32]

Third, the Commission stressed the cost to the treasury of subsidies to compensate firms for inadequately priced goods. It blamed the government for inarticulated subsidy and pricing policies and proposed that the government define both global subsidy and company pricing objectives. It also blasted price setting procedures as so slow that newly approved prices were often unable to cover newly risen costs and so politically motivated that authorized prices almost invariably fell short of company requests. It proposed speedups and simplifications. It noted that subsidies were often late, or never paid, with the build-up in arrears forcing companies to borrow, thereby increasing costs [See Chapter 4].[33] It observed that subsidies were never readjusted to cover rising prices of imported inputs stemming from repeated devaluations. It proposed punctual public treasury payments and simplified administrative mechanisms for adjusting subsidy levels.

Fourth, it criticized the control system and strongly recommended an end to political intervention by leaving management decisions to the *técnicos*. It proposed longer terms for the government's nominees as board members, with a stop to politically motivated turnover. It urged a simplified control system, simplified procedures for internal and external accountants, and greater management options in meeting goals (Comisión 1977b:12–13).

The third Multisectoral Commission, appointed in March 1981, balanced private with public sector delegates. It was charged by the Belaúnde administration to recommend a new entrepreneurial role for the Peruvian state, to evaluate public enterprises, and to recommend needed changes. It was the least heeded of the three commissions, beset by a combination of factors that undermined its efforts. First, the zeal of the Belaúnde reformers for reorganizing or dismantling the state apparatus could not be contained while waiting for commission results. Ministers reformed their ministries' portfolios while the commission met. From its formation on March 13 to its last meeting on 21 August 1981, 27 companies were reorganized at ministerial level, one was dissolved, the entire holding system changed, and the four key ministries restructured. The commission's final report listed changes over which it had no jurisdiction.

Second, some agencies viewed the commission as trespassing on their territory. Branch reports little cooperation by BN, INP, and INAP with the commission's information requests (1981:256). INAP dealt the most severe blow by drawing up a new law of entrepreneurial activity, unbeknownst to the commission, that stripped the commission of most of its functions.

Third, because the commission's members and technical staff were largely unfamiliar with either Peruvian state entrepreneurial activity or its control systems, they devoted more time than expected to self-education rather than to carrying out the commission's assigned activities (Branch, 1981:255).

Fourth, the Commission failed to take into account that central government officials really did not want a true evaluation of the current situation of the portfolio. Ghai indicates that, in other countries, government authorities widely use public enterprises for "patronage, as a device to channel resources to the ruling political party, [and] to build the economic base of the political leaders. The plundering of the state resources...clearly discourages the objective analysis of the operation and performance of public enterprises" (1982:163). Indeed, Belaúnde administration insiders expected the Commission to provide either an exposé of the supposedly corrupt practices of the previous regime or an indictment of the financial state of companies in the current portfolio that would justify their intended privatization. Instead, they got a non-ideological, albeit shallow, report on the current state of the portfolio and, consequently, shelved it (Comisión, 1981). Three months later, the commission's president, Tulio de Andrea resigned from CONADE in a lurid ideological split with the administration.

Everyday Affairs

Many countries use inter- and intra-ministerial committees to oversee and guide public enterprise policies. Peru is no exception, but it employed a complex and overlapping committee structure that led to functional duplication and inefficiency, that blurred lines of authority, that fostered jurisdictional conflict, and that made excessively high demands on a limited pool of top executives.

The financial sector demonstrates the overlapping committee functions and composition. The Consejo Superior de la Banca Estatal, composed of the presidents of government-owned banks, was formed to advise the Minister of Economics and Finance on financial policy issues (D.L. 17521, 17868 and 19577). Two other committees, formed in 1972, one to supervise development banks and COFIDE the other to supervise state-owned banks, had almost identical membership.[34] By the next year, the economics and finance minister had eight similar advisory committees.[35] They even remained after the ministerial reorganization of 1973 created the Dirección General de Asuntos Financieros (DGAF) whose duties superseded them all. The Comité de Coordinación de la Banca Estatal de Fomento y COFIDE, however, was only dissolved in 1978 when Minister Silva Ruete set up a new group, the Consejo de Coordinación de la Banca Estatal de Fomento with virtually the same membership (D.L. 22261.)

Another type of committee structure received mixed evaluations. CONSEPEM was set up in the Ministry of Energy and Mines in late 1970 and included the presidents of the sectoral public enterprises, the ministry's directors general, and the heads of the ministry's planning and technical offices.[36] According to civilian ministry employees, the committee succeeded as a coordination agency due to a stable ministerial structure having sectoral firms of similar size and nature. CONSEPEM's success was qualified, however, because many company-level problems could not be resolved in committee (Comisión, 1977d:3). According to other sources, it never coordinated policy because the companies were so large and their projects considered so important that many devices were used to short-circuit bureaucratic dependence.[37] Even relative military rank could be invoked to replace a governmental hierarchy by a military chain of command.[38] Whatever the differences of opinion about the overall effectiveness, persistent problems among Ministry firms were beyond the competence of any committee to resolve [See Chapter 6].

Committees consisting of the minister, the head of the ministry's sectoral planning office, and the presidents and general managers of the public enterprises were mandated by the 1973–1974 budget (D.L. 19864). They met to periodically review company financial management, but there is little evidence that they functioned effectively.

Issue-oriented committees were also tried. Their purpose was to reconcile needs of functional ministries, such as Economics and

Finance, with those of sectoral ministries such as Agriculture, Industry, and Energy and Mines. These included a multisectoral commission to determine foreign investment funding needs, and a foreign-debt monitoring committee.[39] There is little evidence of their impact.

Peru's most important committee, COAP, the President's Advisory Council, did not figure prominently in public enterprise issues. With no definite legal status, but with the power to coordinate pre-cabinet discussion and to propose measures to the executive, COAP should have provided the key to a coherent and consistent overall public enterprise policy. It did not.

The one notable exception to a dismal committee record occurred under Minister Silva Ruete, who built up the Interministerial Economic and Financial Affairs Committee (CIAEF), as his first step in becoming a "Super Minister" (1981:62). He persuaded the Cabinet to grant CIAEF extensive powers, including the right to review all proposed economic legislation before Cabinet submission and the power to present draft laws to Cabinet, bypassing review by COAP (D.L. 22189). Later, CIAEF coordinated foreign trade after taking over MICTI's Trade Secretariat (D.L. 22569). With a powerful CIAEF, Silva could, and did, design and carry out economic policy needing only Presidential acquiescence. Even disposing of such power, he never succeeded in getting approval of a public enterprise law, drafts of which had circulated since 1971 and whose passage was assigned top priority in the 1977–1980 plan.[40] Under Silva, the purported fifteenth draft of such a law reached COAP, but was stymied there.[41] Since, CIAEF could bring drafts of laws to cabinet without COAP's approval, Silva's claim that the public enterprise law was never approved because time expired on the regime, appears doubtful (Silva, 1981:298).

Conclusions

Coordination by both strategic and everyday-affairs committees was flawed. First, committee executive powers were constrained. Except for CIAEF briefly during the late 1970s, committees were limited to examining problems or to proposing solutions, while the ministries executed policy. Second, committees often were relegated to being a forum for discussing conflicting opinions. This occurred even during meetings of the promising Bruce Commission which provided a chance to air policy divergences and to reconcile them into a coherent proposal for solution, but solving the problems went beyond committee ability or mandate.

The three strategy-oriented Multisectoral Commissions received the same mission: to evaluate the policy matrix for public enterprises and to recommend improvements. They focused on the same problems which were apparent to even the most casual observer. Their recommendations were mostly shelved and the system continued much as before. Their proposals contrasted sharply with medium-term planning and budgeting strategies. While the plan proposed imposing greater government control to align company actions with national objectives, the Commissions pushed more freedom for public enterprises. While the budgets imposed more stringent reporting and clearance requirements, the Commissions recommended reducing central government interference in internal management decisions. The central government clearly rejected commission advice.

MONITORING STRATEGY–GENERALIZED FAILURES

Efficient control of a public enterprise portfolio means defining control strategies, employing adequate control instruments, and setting up effective monitoring systems. Monitoring means that central government authorities continually watch over company actions to ensure that strategies are being followed and to provide corrective actions, if necessary, during the process of policy execution (Fernandes, 1986:164–170). The above sections have shown that, in Peru, strategies were missing and control instruments were defective. This section examines monitoring of public enterprises by key institutions: INP, MEF, CGR, CONADE, and ICSA.

National Planning Institute

The INP first analyzed the public enterprises' economic and financial situation for the 1973 fiscal year, as mandated in the 1973–1974 budget (INP, 1975?). The INP merely gathered company-level information, made it compatible, and assembled a final document.[42] Later, the INP improved its analysis, preparing more comprehensive reports on public sector management (INP, 1975, 1978b, 1978c, 1979a). These examined company prices, wages and salaries, employment, and compared budget figures to year-end results.

While INP analyses provided valuable data on part of the portfolio, they failed as a monitoring system for several reasons. First, their coverage was poor. Legally, INP could only get data from about a third of the portfolio, those firms incorporated under public enterprise law. Often these firms set up subsidiaries under mercantile society law to skirt controls. Although the INP recognized its data limitations, it never overcame them.

Second, the INP could not always get the data to which it was entitled. Often, ministries forwarded incomplete data or sent unaudited, internally prepared financial statements instead of year-end, externally audited ones. Financial firms, including development banks, only reluctantly provided information and often neglected to send balance sheets or income statements. When INP received all the data requested, the questionnaires came late, delaying final reports for up to two years, far beyond the time needed for competent monitoring. Third, the INP had no way of analyzing either the entire portfolio or a separate sector because its evaluation procedures treated each firm separately. This micro-financial focus could not reveal needed policy changes for the government's entrepreneurial system.

Fourth, INP analyses stressed financial indicators revealed in income statements, balance sheets, and flow-of-funds statements. They rarely judged the attainment of economic or social objectives. Moreover, they could not monitor investment progress, as mandated in budgets, since financial data bore slight relation to the physical progress of works or construction.

Fifth, inadequate distribution systems meant that INP recommendations were unknown and remained unimplemented. Institutional mechanisms did not exist for coordinating INP recommendations with those of other agencies, so the analyses mainly stayed within the INP, with few copies sent elsewhere. Most importantly, companies received inadequate or nonexistent feedback from INP.

Sixth, INP-company relations were often strained because INP staffers lacked the clout needed to get data and to follow up on evaluations. INP fit Choksi's observation of "[p]olitical and bureaucratic interference by novices with powers totally out of proportion to their ability" (1979:69). Company managers, who often possessed better analytical and planning capacity, resented being evaluated by personnel who lacked the flexibility and moderation that age and experience could have provided (Comisión, 1977g:15). FitzGerald's positive characterization of them, "there is some lack of experience and first-hand knowledge of the economy, partly counterbalanced by an eagerness to learn and experiment," was not shared by company officials concerned with completing specific projects or getting routine approvals (1976a:81). INP staffers thus differed from sectoral ministry officials who often had considerable experience elsewhere before joining government service.[43]

Seventh, disciplinary incompatibility also strained INP-company relations because the INP drew largely from academia, predominantly from the social sciences or planning, while company officials were often trained as engineers or accountants. Different disciplinary training often reflected different ideologies, with engineers and accountants more conservative than social scientists or planners.[44] Their incompatible backgrounds, called the "psychological factor" by Garner (1983:7), meant that both groups viewed problems differently, they assigned problems different priorities, they applied different analytical tools to problem solving, and they communicated with different professional vocabularies. Although backgrounds of INP technicians may have been closer to those of company officials before 1968, thereafter the INP changed in ideological orientation, to emphasize structural change instead of economic efficiency, and hired a different type of staff which led to a major communications gap (FitzGerald, 1976a:81). Eighth, from 1968 to 1980, the INP was a "civilian institution in a military government." The few military officials detached to it were insufficient to enforce directives throughout the administration.[45] After the return to civilian power, the Belaúnde administration compounded the problem by relegating the INP to a subservient position to the ruling party's civic action program, Popular Cooperation.

The INP clearly did not provide effective public enterprise monitoring. Its staffers lacked the necessary background and experience while the system they constructed was flawed by responding neither to its own data requirements nor to the resolution of public enterprise problems.

Ministry of Economics and Finance

The Ministry of Economics and Finance monitored public enterprises through several directorates, led by that of economic affairs, DGAE (R.M. 1117-71-EF.11). DGAE's first report, for the 1970–1971 period, was based on data from the ministry's government accounts unit (DGCoP) and included some accounting ratios based on summary income statements and balance sheets (DGAE, 1972, DGCoP, 1972?). It made only minor recommendations that were not heeded.

In 1973, DGAE's public enterprise monitoring section was spun off as the financial affairs directorate, DGAF,[46] whose lackluster reports merely tabulated data originating in the sectoral ministries or elsewhere in MEF. It began serious analyses in the late 1970s, but the results were strictly classified for internal ministry use, resulting in minimal impact on correcting public enterprise problems.[47]

Budget laws detailed two other directorates, the DGPP and DGCP to monitor the budget and credit operations, respectively. Both relied on information obtained from other ministries, but they could also request data directly from the companies (D.S. 272-70-EF and 009-70-EF). Neither directorate did more than compile periodic summary reports.

The public accounting directorate (DGCoP) prepared a manual for the economic and financial evaluation of public enterprises (1974). It claimed to design a detailed monitoring system to fulfill the government's information needs. Other than in the title, preface and introduction, however, public enterprises were not mentioned. The manual was oriented to private firms and never questioned whether standard financial ratios could be employed. Moreover, it was aimed at firms producing goods, not to Peru's numerous service firms (MTC, 1974:i). Indeed, the sample income statement omitted government subsidies as a possible income item. The system never was implemented.

MEF's most promising attempt at monitoring was a joint effort with INP to undertake a thorough legal, economic, and financial study of Peru's portfolio from 1969 to 1977 (INP, 1978d). It came to an untimely end, having produced a short, initial report, after falling victim to severe budget cuts in mid-1978 (INP, 1978a). A similar fate befell a DGAF Task Force on public enterprises in 1978. After preparing an overview of portfolio growth from 1968 to 1978 to present a methodological framework, the group was disbanded (DGAF, AFS, 1978).

MEF suffered from most of the problems that beset the INP. Its staffers were young, inexperienced social scientists; its data access was constrained by law; it used late or incomplete data; it looked at companies individually; and it zealously guarded its reports. An additional problem was one of approach. MEF's short-run concerns were closely linked to current economic issues, a standard characteristic of any finance ministry. As a result, MEF looked at public enterprises from the operational basis of a tactical agency not as a systematic and strategically oriented observer of events.

Comptroller General

From 1968 to 1983, budgets gave the Comptroller General's office increasing control over public enterprises. In March 1972, it received an overambitious legal mandate to monitor virtually all aspects of public enterprise operations including a company's: personnel; provisioning systems from purchases of inputs to distribution of final product; budgeting from formulation to execution; treasury operations; accounting; "institutional efficiency" from planning, organization, control, and management to their coordination to most efficiently achieve company goals; planning; implementation of public administration reform guidelines; and administration and control systems.[48]

As the portfolio grew, tensions arose between the CGR which sought to solidify its control and managers concerned with the erosion of company autonomy. The CGR abdicated any pretence at strategic control because it lacked both a public enterprise orientation and qualified staff. Instead, it expanded the control system to cover operational and technical questions, an approach incompatible with executive autonomy (Stefani, 1980). The CGR imposed precisely the wrong type of review system, so that the 1977 Multisectoral Commission castigated its interventions as "more about form than about substance, causing unnecessary discomfort" to management (Comisión, 1977f:12). Company executives almost unanimously decried the CGR's actions as leading to "fear of taking decisions;" "fear of action;" or removing the "right to make a mistake" (interviews, 1981). CGR was further accused of applying controls with a counterproductive excess of zeal that constituted as "abuse of authority, absolutist and omnimodal power, [causing] a rupture of autonomy, of management, and of institutional authority" (Comisión, 1977e:1). The CGR tried to refute the charges, laying the blame entirely on company managers who were said to lack "a positive attitude towards the supervising agencies" (CGR, 1977b:45).

Under the Belaúnde administration, the CGR extended its dominion over all firms in which the government had equity.[49] From 1981 to 1985, its personnel grew at a compound annual rate of almost 30 percent, a record for an austerity administration. It also increased its authority to include prior approval for public enterprise borrowing (L. 23249).

By 1982, CGR began a multi-volume annual report on public enterprises (1982). It compiled company legal bases, and auditors' notes to the summarized financial statements. The report was thorough because the CGR could solicit information from all nonfinancial firms irrespective of legal basis and because internal auditors were jointly responsible to the CGR and to company management. Laws forbade the CGR from examining the financial firms. The documents provided valuable data obtainable elsewhere only with difficulty, however, they failed to monitor strategy because they concentrated exclusively on financial indicators; they did not evaluate the attainment of social objectives and they did not differentiate between public enterprises pursuing predominantly social goals and those pursuing predominantly economic ones.

Nevertheless, the reports could have provided valuable feedback for managers and information for ministerial decision making, but the CGR's fetish for secrecy resulted in classified documents mainly for internal use, with few copies circulated to other monitoring agencies. Ministers only received partial reports of information on selected companies in their sectors with no basis to compare their companies to the rest of the portfolio (interview, 1985). They, in turn, could decide whether to pass the information on to company management.

The CGR's findings were not coordinated with those of other agencies, in part because of the power fight between CGR and CONADE [See Chapter 6]. Both institutions had the mandate to monitor the portfolio; they gathered similar information and treated it similarly, then similarly restricted access to it. As a result, both the companies and the portfolio suffered.

Development Corporations

COFIDE's original objective of boosting the private sector was replaced through government-mandated financing of other public enterprises [See Chapter 2]. Consequently, COFIDE was split, in mid-1981, into three corporations, CONADE, COFIDE, S.A. and ICSA, to oversee different aspects of the government portfolio (D.Leg. 206). At the same time, the monitoring authority of its holding subsidiary, ICSA, over its portfolio was increased. The new public enterprise law and its bylaw gave CONADE a major role in setting company policy and in verifying its execution, including an ex-post control of company management (D.Leg. 216, D.S. 375-82-EFC). CONADE never fulfilled that role. Under attack from MEF and CGR officials who viewed power-sharing as a dangerous precedent, CONADE's monitoring role was suspended one month after becoming law.[50] Because its line authority was held in abeyance, most companies reported that CONADE did not even evaluate their operations in 1983 (INAP, 1983:83–84).

CONADE and ICSA, nevertheless, continued to monitor economic and financial indicators for internal use. The resulting documents provide the best coverage of economic indicators at the company level (Eg. ICSA, 1984). Nevertheless, the reports failed to have much impact either on other monitoring agencies or on the companies, since their circulation was limited.

CONADE existed as a politically neutral, technocratic agency in a highly-charged political atmosphere. Its inability to maneuver among the internecine struggles for power and resources had lasting effects on the agency. The forced resignation of its first president, Tulio de Andrea, led to hostile restrictions placed on its second president, Felipe Ortíz de Zevallos, who lasted approximately a year in the new post. CONADE never adequately monitored the portfolio because other government actors resisted, claiming that the task was too important to be left to CONADE's economists.

CONCLUSIONS

Central government strategy definition, review and monitoring are needed for any public enterprise system, but setting public enterprise strategies, controlling their implementation, and periodically monitoring performance are all delicate tasks. They must be performed so that they do not impinge strongly on the autonomy and flexibility of company management, yet they must ensure that any extra-entrepreneurial objectives are also being achieved (Boneo, 1983). Although specifying systems through statutes and translating statutory authority into practice are always difficult, Peru's system stands out as a model failure.

At first, the planning system ignored the increasing entrepreneurial role of the state. Later, the planners belatedly realized their omissions and attempted to rectify them, however, they failed to incorporate public enterprises into the planning system, failed to adequately define public enterprise strategies, and badly implemented review and monitoring systems. Indeed, central government authorities often bypassed the elaborate screening mechanisms whenever a project was assigned a national priority.

Central government planners handicapped company management. Instead of defining clear, attainable, and adequately stated objectives, planners saddled the public enterprises with politically motivated objectives that were vague, mutually contradictory, and contrary to management wishes. Rarely were technical or economic considerations examined when setting goals. Excessive control systems are often justified as keeping public enterprises from becoming irresponsible power centers (Sherif, 1973:3). Peruvian government authorities progressively made the operating environment for many companies intolerable. Decisions on wages and salaries, employment, imports, exports, price-setting, investments, purchases and sales were often made outside the company and communicated to company executives at the last moment. Thus, the controls hindered, rather than helped, efficient resource use.

In Peru, risk aversion, usually an identifying mark of public enterprises, did not result mainly from inherently poor quality management. Instead, it resulted from poor quality control which led to a malaise called *epsitis*, the local name for public enterprise executives' aversion to being subject to the whim of central government bureaucrats. The name refers to the widespread demoralization following the politically-inspired crackdown on executives in EPSA and its subsidiaries.[51]

An adequate strategy definition, review and monitoring system could have been possible under certain conditions. For a start, the Peruvian government should have acknowledged the institutional needs of public enterprises. Instead, it viewed them as tools for executing a particular, often transient, sectoral policy, as ways of tapping badly-needed revenue, or as berths for placing ministerial clients. With policies often changing, ministers never stable, and revenue needs always increasing, public enterprises were continually squeezed to provide more revenue, more jobs, and to do more tasks.

The government also could have sought a political consensus on the role of public enterprises in the economy, to restrain the excesses of ministers and policy makers and bring about a balance of power between central government and the public enterprises. This was never done, leaving each incoming cabinet, minister or board of directors free to assert power to impose a new company structure, new company procedures, and new company managers.

Ramanadham's incisive diagnoses of the ties that normally bind public firms to government agencies are worth recalling (1972:3). He noted that with few exceptions: 1) neither government authorities nor public enterprises are clear about the desired results from supervision; 2) ministries are unable to design good supervisory systems; 3) formal channels between public enterprises and government are haphazard, ineffective and inconsistent; and 4) efforts to improve supervisory systems have rarely been thorough, comprehensive or effective. Peru's record clearly substantiates his pessimistic conclusions.

NOTES

1. The control problem is widely addressed in the literature. Ramanadham provides broad coverage of the issue (1974:79–126) while Fernandes addresses problems faced by administrators and managers (1986).
2. The general organic-statist model fit to Peru by Stepan (1978) makes little functional distinction between intra-state actors. Rose better disaggregates the concept of the state (1983).
3. I do not examine external penetration into different components of governing groups as did Cleaves and Pease (1983:209–210) nor study bi-directional cooptation mechanisms mentioned by Ferner (1983:55–56).
4. The chapter omits company- or ministry-specific systems. Becker examines company-specific control systems for MINEROPERU (1983:20). Although the literature indicts ministerial control systems (Ramanadham, 1974:83–83; Trebat, 1983:70), Peruvian ministries progressively increased their supervisory duties that often led to outright interference with companies. Former fisheries minister Javier Tantalean (1978) provided an off-handed, and perhaps inadvertent, account of his repeated interference in management, purchasing, personnel, recruitment, and commercial activities of fishing sector firms.
5. Thornhill provides a more general view of central government's role in public enterprise administration (1983). Ghai (1982:166) and Fernandes (1986:34–35) examine the relations between central planning and public enterprises.
6. Kilty (1967) and Roel (1968) give a background to Peru's planning. FitzGerald examines planning under the military (1976a:78–92 and 1979:216–259). Klitgaard summarizes the 1971–1975 plan (1971). I omit regional plans since, although public enterprises loomed large in a region's economy, for example, PETROPERU's Talara complex in the north or CENTROMIN's mining operations in central Peru, regional planning offices played no role in setting, reviewing or monitoring strategy.
7. Presidencia, *Plan 1971–1975* hereafter referred to as *Plan 1971–1975*.
8. *Plan 1971–1975*:76–77. For a preview of the role for an indefinite state prepared prior to the 1968 coup, but published afterwards with the approval of the coup leaders, see INP (1968:4–9).
9. Sorj only places the profitability emphasis after 1976, although it was repeated in all plans after 1970 (1983:84).
10. Although EPCHAP's monopoly was expected to take effect on 1 January 1971, COAP, in a meeting chaired by President Velasco in March 1970, decided to move up the effective date by four months to September 1. Later, top ministry officials ordered an

immediate takeover after learning that, contrary to their expectations a fishmeal futures market still operated (Tantalean, 1978:276 and D.L. 18212).

11. Fernández Maldonado supports these allegations in saying that the goals omitted from the plans were known only to a select group who kept them a state secret (Tello, 1983:I:151).

12. Schydlowsky and Wicht similarly claimed that the planning system displayed a lack of understanding of Peru's development problems, showed no clear and consistent vision of the economic goals of the military government, and was based on serious blunders and miscalculations (1983:105).

13. Silva, 1981:38. FitzGerald (1976a:54) recounts problems of integrating public enterprises into the planning system. Schydlowsky and Wicht discuss why managers resisted such integration (1983:106).

14. *Plan Inca* is reproduced in Tello (1983:II:289–310), while its nucleus is found in Zimmerman (1975:105–123).

15. See Lowenthal (1975:32) for early speculation on this point.

16. Premchand (1983) summarizes overall budget links that tie public enterprises to the government.

17. Much later, when Morales Bermúdez had become President, a Multisectoral Commission recommended centralizing all public enterprise decision-making in the MEF (Comisión, 1977c:3).

18. D.L. 19864, Figueroa and Saberbein (1978). INP (1978a:4). For the detailed budgetary requirements to secure final project approval, see FitzGerald (1976a:85–89; 1979:252–253).

19. D.L. 19864. Clearances had to be obtained from the INP, COFIDE, DGPP, DGCP, DGTP, BCRP, and BN.

20. Members included the presidents and general managers of the sector's public enterprises and the head of the sectoral planning office.

21. Easier modifications to the investment budget were not matched by changes in drafting them which still involved the sectoral ministry, the INP, COFIDE, and in some cases, prior consent of the CGR. A report noted that all these groups could and did question reports, even those done by specialized foreign consultants. The resultant delays in project approval not only raised costs, they frustrated and demoralized company officials (Comisión, 1977d:4).

22. The complicated procedures for a foreign-funded project after completion of the feasibility study included: assignment of a sector-level priority by the sectoral planning office; assignment of an inter-sectoral priority by the INP; technical review by COFIDE; review by the Permanent Commission on Foreign Debt (it also approved at all previous steps); review by the DGCP in MEF; analysis by the Committee on Foreign Debt; scrutiny of the loan agreement by the CGR, and finally, approval by the Council of

Ministers (Comisión, 1977d:9). Formal procedures took no account of other commissions and committees.

23. These included fines and surcharges on unpaid, but still-contested, tax bills. However, as shown in Chapter 2, most were later capitalized.

24. L. 23233, L. 23350, L. 23556.

25. Companies were at times forced to borrow from the BN to make quarterly payments *to* the treasury before subsidy payments *from* the treasury were deblocked to BN accounts (interview, 1978).

26. Other controllers included the Sectoral Inspector General's Office, external auditors and the company's own auditors.

27. R. 520-021-72-CGR-AT. Joint responsibility meant that reports, even those covering internal problems, simultaneously went to the CGR and to the board of directors. Managers fumed that all problems were scrutinized externally prior to company action. Additionally, internal auditors could not be dismissed without prior CGR approval (D.S. 001-72-CG).

28. Saulniers (1980) and Chapter 6 examine some long-standing inter-enterprise problems that plagued ENCI.

29. In the four days following the creation of the Multisectoral Commission on Public Enterprises, the following were formed: a Multisectoral Commission to examine development problems in the Department of Piura; one to examine problems of agricultural professionals; one to propose changes in the legal treatment of minors; and one to coordinate all government activities related to industrial zones and industrial parks.

30. R.M. 0190-76-PM-ONAJ. The 1976 commission, declaring that a study of efficiency was beyond its power, had focused on problematic intra-governmental relations (1976: 9) and had drafted laws aimed at solving specific problems (1976: Annex 1–6).

31. The subcommission's January report to Alberto Bruce noted insufficient time between 23 Dec. 1976 and 18 Jan. 1977 [sic] to convene a meeting of all Subcommission members. Therefore, the subcommission president, Dionisio Romero, and an alternate for the other private sector member proposed "personal" suggestions. Notably, they moved privatization, previously sixth in a list of seven recommendations prepared by the full Subcommission, to first place and provided a strong justification. See Comisión (1977f:20 and 1977g).

32. Comisión (1977b:Annex 3). The majority was upheld by the President of the Commission, Alberto Bruce Caceres, while the minority was supported by Remegio Morales Bermúdez, of COFIDE.

33. Although the government authorized payment of overdue subsidies and the interest on the resultant loans and overdrafts, it did not specifically require the treasury to make payment, leaving

arrears for: EPSA's operations from 1975 to 1977; PETROPERU's and EPSEP's for 1975 and 1976; and ENCI's and EPCHAP's for 1977 (D.L. 22050).

34. The Comité de Coordinación de la Banca Estatal de Fomento y COFIDE, formed in 1972, had almost identical membership to the Consejo Superior de la Banca Estatal (D.S. 242-72-EF).

35. Committees included: the Comité de Coordinación de la Banca Estatal de Fomento y COFIDE, the Consejo Superior de la Banca Estatal, the Junta de Política Crediticia Estatal, the Consejo de Política Monetaria, the Consejo de Coordinación de la Banca Estatal de Fomento y COFIDE, the Comité de Asuntos Bancarios y Financieros, the Comité de Seguros, and the Comité Sectorial de Fomento Financiero Regional (de la Melena, 1973: 135–139).

36. Consejo de Empresas Públicas de Energía y Minas D.L. 18433.

37. Thus General Fernández Baca, the first head of PETROPERU, outranked Colonel Fernández Maldonado, Minister of Energy and Mines, until the latter was promoted in January 1969. Similarly, retired General Bossio, the first head of MINEROPERU had been superior to Fernández Maldonado at the Army intelligence school, and at one time, had been President Velasco's commanding officer. Fernández Maldonado later, in a telling *mea culpa*, said that the traditional military respect for hierarchy and seniority was a grave limitation on the dynamics of the Peruvian process (Tello, 1983: 1: 137).

38. Cleaves and Scurrah (1980: 214–215). For a similar reading of the role of military rank in Chile, see Boeninger and Palma, 1978.

39. D.S. 019-71-PM; D.S. 275-72-EF. See Sherif for an overview of issues related to second-tier supervisory agencies (1973: 8–10). Sherif warns that committees can have strong negative effects on public enterprise operating management by making firms more open to political pressures.

40. For years, Silva had publicly promised managers to pass a law removing government interference from their public enterprises (Silva, 1978: 253). He never did and his neglect remained a sore point with them (Wolfenson, 1981: 149).

41. Interview (1980). Exact numbering of the draft is difficult to ascertain. However, in 1971 the INP drew up an early draft (1971). Later, external consultants prepared a 54-page draft, accompanied by a series of justifying documents in 1973 (INP-DESCO, 1974?b). In 1976, the INP circulated another version (INP, 1980b:88). Chapter 6 analyzes discrepancies among draft normative laws and relates them to internal power conflict.

42. Analytical capacity, due to staffing problems, became acute during the late 1970s as poor pay led to an exodus of INP officials holding the public enterprise dossier.

43. Becker appraised the backgrounds of MEM officials (1983:211).

44. See Stevens for the political dimension to disciplinary incompati-

bility (1980:223–224). Becker (1983:210) reports on MINERO-PERU manager-engineers; Hopkins (1967:48) details academic backgrounds of SSPI executives.

45. Cleaves and Scurrah (1980:74). Becker notes that the INP had low status because its "director was a colonel, outranked by the senior generals and admirals on the Council of Ministers" (1983:57). This is only partly correct. Only the first three INP heads, *Jefe del INP*, were colonels when named. The first was removed after a short term, while the other two were promoted to Brigadier General in the next scheduled promotions, generally a few months after taking office. As Brigadier Generals, they were sometimes, though not always, outranked by their cabinet colleagues. All other INP Jefes were generals when named. A more telling indicator of power than military rank, however, is that although INP's head held a Cabinet seat after 1962, INP was *never* elevated to a ministry.

46. D.L. 20134, R.D. 012-75-EF.73.01. DGAF and DGAE were reunited in 1978. (D.S. 127-78-EF).

47. MEF usually classified public enterprise information to avoid giving wider play to potentially embarrassing information. Indeed, most financial information was available elsewhere (interview, 1978 and DGAF, 1978).

48. D.S. 001-72-CG — the bylaws to the National Control System.

49. "Contraloría en 1981 amplía acción a 200 Empresas Estatales," *El Peruano*, Jan. 4, 1981.

50. D.S. 019-83-EFC. Ortíz de Zevallos provides an inside perspective on the attacks and consequences (1985:123–127).

51. Interviews (1978, 1979); Cleaves and Scurrah (1980:213).

4

Measures of Growth

INTRODUCTION

Peru's public portfolio grew after 1968 with a few large companies, mostly in energy and mining, weighing most heavily in a portfolio that exceeded 150 firms. Their weight has important implications concerning the design of monitoring systems. Since governments must closely observe key macroeconomic indicators, such as the impact of subsidies on the government budget or of company foreign borrowing on the balance of payments, it is most efficient to monitor those companies with the greatest indicator impact and it is inappropriate and not cost-effective to subject all public enterprises to the same degree of central government scrutiny. Government resources available to oversee public enterprises are limited, hence they must be deployed for maximal impact by concentrating on a few companies. The argument for streamlining monitoring activities does not invalidate the need to implement a global monitoring system. On the contrary, routine monitoring is necessary to assess performance and to prepare periodic reports. Non-routine, precise monitoring, which covers short-term government concerns, however, is best applied only to those companies with highest performance impact.

This chapter examines the weight of a few large firms in explaining Peru's principal macroeconomic indicators within a broader context of public enterprise theory. Data on income, profits, subsidies, taxes, employment, investment, debt, and value added are analyzed for the portfolio and its largest companies from 1970 to 1984.[1] Conclusions drawn from a wealth of detail rarely accessible to outsiders challenge several assumptions about public enterprises that underlie standard policy prescriptions. A strong case is made that the standard linchpins of policy analysis including nonprofitability, continual need

for subsidies, and perpetual drain on the government budget definitely
need serious reappraisal.

INCOME

Public enterprise income, measured in constant 1973 soles,
increased almost eight-fold from S/. 22 billion in 1970 to S/. 174 billion
in 1982. Graph 4.1 shows most of that increase came from flagship
firms,[2] the largest companies that often served as holdings, and the
state traders in Peru's traditionally strong mining and natural resource
sectors. Banks expanded rapidly only after 1979.

Portfolio growth was discontinuous. The high, sustained,
takeover-fueled growth of the early 1970s gave way to fluctuating, but
still positive growth during mid-decade.[3] Later, growth slowed notably
and, during the early 1980s, stabilized under the Belaúnde administration. Steady portfolio growth until mid-decade has been misinterpreted
to mean steady growth at the company level. However, company
incomes varied as their attributions changed independently of portfolio
growth trends (Saulniers, 1980, 1981a).

Graph 4.1 also shows that utilities, considered traditional public
enterprises, generated little income, only 5 percent or less of the
portfolio total. Similarly, the transporters' share, including railways,

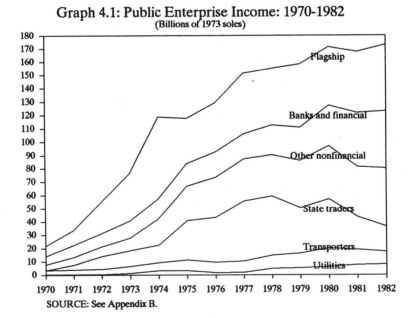

Graph 4.1: Public Enterprise Income: 1970-1982
(Billions of 1973 soles)

SOURCE: See Appendix B.

shipping, and airlines, typically was less than 8 percent. After 1970, the state traders took over marketing of traditional exports accounting, in 1977, for 85 percent of Peru's exports and 30 percent of portfolio income. Their importance fell thereafter. Banks and other financial firms expanded to 24 percent of income in 1982. The six flagship firms, rarely dropped below 30 percent.

Only six public enterprises accounted for half of the portfolio's income. In 1970, PETROPERU was most important, with more than 30 percent. Thereafter, as the portfolio grew, its share declined. Reflecting the increased state presence in mining after 1974, MINPECO, the minerals marketer and CENTROMIN, the major producer, together contributed between 25 and 40 percent of public enterprise income. PESCAPERU's income share dropped from over 10 percent in 1974 to under 5 percent in 1982. Until its dissolution and merger in 1978, EPSA, the populist-oriented foodstuffs importer and marketer, showed rising real income. The BN quadrupled its real income to reach a 7 percent share in 1982.

PROFITS

Pryke summed up the common wisdom about public enterprise profitability: "It is widely believed that their profits resemble snakes in Ireland: there are none" (1971:178). Peruvian firms are interesting to compare to the common wisdom for two reasons. First, they rarely received explicit profit objectives [See Chapter 6]. Indeed, except for the largely disregarded planning documents, government directives during the early 1970s remained suspicious of anything related to private enterprise, especially market-imposed financial discipline and an emphasis on profits (CGR, 1978:2). Second, government spokesmen, including Gen. José Graham Hurtado of the powerful advisory group, COAP, stressed that earning profits was not a major goal for Peru's public enterprises (Graham, 1974:51). This section analyses how companies performed in an environment hostile to profits. It concludes that the portfolio usually earned profits which were hidden by enforced reporting practices and partly channelled to the treasury.

Operating profits measure the surplus which a firm receives from the sale of the goods and services it produces, over the current costs of production.[4] Accounting profits, commonly called the bottom line, add income from all other sources to operating profit and subtract other expenses, including items on capital account and extraordinary items. Peruvian accounting practice defines accounting profits as net of income taxes and of mandatory legal deductions including: workers' share of profits; sectoral community share of profits; research and development funds; and a compensatory nutritional fund. Mandatory deductions easily account for 25 percent of post-tax profits, so that reported accounting profits understate the power of a public firm

TABLE 4.1
Profitability Measures of Major Public Enterprises: 1970-1982
(Millions of constant 1973 soles)

	1970	1971	1972	1973	1974	1975	1976	1977	1978	1979	1980	1981	1982
Operating Profit													
Portfolio	705	774	380	1,764	3,852	592	4,198	8,336	11,419	15,129	10,511	6,127	9,994
PETROPERU	994	295	447	(55)	(3,217)	(2,207)	(898)	(747)	(2,072)	(2,378)	(309)	(32)	679
EPSA	61	(1)	(345)	(1,521)	(2,250)	(1,122)	(579)	(144)	797	436	--	--	--
PESCAPERU	--	--	--	1,214	2,569	1,143	223	1,535	2,106	1,760	108	149	295
CENTROMIN	--	--	--	--	3,151	1,045	1,421	2,576	2,739	5,629	5,116	3,410	1,567
MINPECO	--	--	--	--	105	277	182	291	513	736	320	279	32
Accounting Profit													
Portfolio	971	1,756	1,368	1,215	2,756	1,686	940	2,935	5,414	3,664	3,876	(410)	(11,391)
PETROPERU	529	233	416	329	375	128	244	0	60	67	168	10	40
EPSA	(110)	(166)	(554)	(458)	(1,921)	328	179	2	24	(3,081)	--	--	--
PESCAPERU	--	--	--	2	400	(1,833)	(1,433)	343	1,076	1,514	(727)	(1,342)	(2,524)
SIDERPERU	(615)	(295)	12	138	138	(52)	(379)	(231)	168	38	(97)	(1,101)	(1,703)
CENTROMIN	--	--	--	--	1,125	521	445	863	1,423	2,412	1,755	57	(4,544)
MINPECO	--	--	--	--	60	57	60	126	195	(1,297)	649	37	(306)
BN	653	472	354	657	676	657	562	387	608	523	676	963	1,489
Financial Expenditures of Major Nonfinancial Firms													
All nonfinancial	722	472	425	2,045	2,714	5,011	6,838	20,010	12,948	9,810	8,235	13,287	22,979
PETROPERU	38	49	40	47	206	822	1,766	6,496	3,103	715	312	436	1,098
MINEROPERU	0	18	0	65	0	15	136	193	536	638	912	1,286	4,725
EPSA	170	n.a.	n.a.	473	257	1,017	88,888	6,935	1,855	2,785	--	--	--
PESCAPERU	--	--	--	559	792	825	2,017	2,081	1,974	1,427	1,188	2,111	3,746
SIDERPERU	158	67	47	38	20	155	288	594	848	323	253	1,102	1,999
CENTROMIN	--	--	--	--	164	351	836	1,404	751	664	1,955	3,728	4,840

-- Not applicable
n.a. Not available
SOURCE: See Appendix B

to generate revenue over and above expenses.

Neither operating nor accounting profits measure efficiency, however, since many factors exogenous to company-level decisions also determine profit levels. For example, many companies could exercise market power by operating in monopolistic or oligopolistic markets, while the government exercised its power in rigidly controlling prices of both inputs and final production.

From 1970 to 1982, measured in constant 1973 soles, Peru's portfolio always earned an operating profit, a finding consistent with most countries through different time periods (Short, 1984:151–158). Moreover, profits were period related. As shown in table 4.1, until 1974, they remained low while rising slowly from S/. 0.7 billion in 1970 to S/. 1.8 billion in 1973. Following a sharp decline, profits recovered to peak at S/. 15 billion in 1979. During the Belaúnde years, operating profits fluctuated widely.

A few companies determined much of the variation in the portfolio's operating profits. Before 1973, PETROPERU weighed heavily, but thereafter, it showed consistent operating losses until 1982. Its losses, at times exceeding S/. 3 billion, arose when the government forced it to import high-priced crude oil to supply rising domestic demand at controlled prices. Government policies also forced food marketers to show losses. Their objectives of guaranteeing cheap, subsidized food to urban consumers led to losses for EPSA, the food lines of ENCI, and, later, ECASA. PESCAPERU showed strong operating profits at first but, as it was dismembered, they later fell sharply both in absolute and relative terms. Profits from the mining- related CENTROMIN and MINPECO covered losses elsewhere.[5] After 1979, profits earned by many, small nonfinancial corporations became important and, by 1982, they accounted for almost half the portfolio operating profits.

Public enterprise accounting profits behaved differently [Table 4.1]. Before 1980, Peru's portfolio always showed an accounting profit; after 1980, it had major losses. Profits dropped from S/. 1.8 billion in 1971 to S/. 1.2 billion in 1973; during mid-decade they fluctuated sharply, reaching S/ 5.4 billion in 1978; thereafter, they fell to a S/. 11.4 billion loss in 1982.[6]

Portfolio accounting profits depended on a few large companies. For example, in 1982, PETROPERU's profits were less than 10 percent of their levels a decade earlier. PESCAPERU's deficits usually overshadowed those of all other firms.[7] In 1982, CENTROMIN chalked up almost a S/. 4.5 billion deficit. EPSA also contributed to the problem as its losses rose from S/. 110 million in 1970 to S/. 3 billion in 1979. By 1982, all large nonfinancial firms showed substantial losses, while the BN had a banner year. The financial firms stood out from the rest of the portfolio by earning consistent profits and, except for the agricultural bank during the mid-1970s and the mining bank in 1973 and 1975, finished every year in the black.

The hypothesis that the Peruvian financial system contains mechanisms that caused profits to be consistently transferred from the government's producers and marketers to its financial middlemen merits some investigation. As shown in table 4.1, there was a strong upswing in financial expenditures of the public enterprises until 1977, a trend associated with the buildup in financial institution profit levels.[8] Official statistics do not report profits of financial firms, leading to a vastly distorted image of portfolio profitability.[9] In providing separate treatment, Peruvian authorities follow recognized guidelines laid down in the *IMF Draft Manual on Finance Statistics* (UN, Statistical Commission, 1976:1–6). Normally when examining public enterprise macroeconomic indicators, such as capital formation, omitting the financial sector does not pose a problem (Short, 1984:114). However, because of significant profit differences among Peruvian firms, separate treatment hides the true picture of portfolio performance.[10]

Control over profits opposed company managers to government bureaucrats, as the planners continually expected to use public enterprise surplus for financing overall public sector expansion. During the early 1970s, actual transfers were limited because companies received no targets for profits disposition. By 1974, concern over companies' retaining profits, instead of channelling them to the treasury, led to a law mandating automatic transfer of half of a company's post-tax profits. The other half remained at the company's disposition provided managers could convince skeptical, cash-starved authorities of the merits of specific investment projects (D.L. 20810). Although the law set precise targets for profits distribution, its implementation was badly flawed.

The law placed both a high premium on forecasting accuracy and strong monetary penalties on inaccuracy. Half of all *anticipated* profits were due to the treasury. Whenever actual profits exceeded anticipated profits, the treasury took the excess; in case of a shortfall, readjustment was possible but cumbersome. Consequently, the law hindered productivity growth by slowing the adoption of cost-cutting measures since any resulting boost in profits to exceed forecast levels was, in effect, taxed at a rate of 100 percent. The law also took no account of accumulated losses, so that profits could not be offset against earlier losses, a standard business practice (INAP, 1979a:31). The law also promoted bad cash management. By assuming that income and expenditures held steady through the year, it required equal quarterly payments of anticipated profits, regardless of seasonal cash-flow patterns. Treasury often blocked subsidy payments to firms until they had paid quarterly profits due, at times with short-term loans that could only be repaid with the deblocked subsidy payments. Such rigid procedures increased company financial costs. Moreover, since funds were borrowed from the state banks, the measure forced transfers from nonfinancial to financial public enterprises. The law was abolished in 1979.

Expecting high public enterprise profits and windfall gains from privatization, in 1981, Congress created the Investment and Counterpart Fund of the National Public Sector to provide counterpart resources for foreign-financed investment projects (L. 23337). Its funds would come from: 100 percent of the distributable profits of financial firms, 80 percent of the profits of the nonfinancial ones, and 100 percent of the receipts from the sale of government assets.[11] This law did not confuse anticipated profits, annual profits, and cash flow, but it too fostered inefficiency as managers, faced with an effective 100 or 80 percent tax on profits, became less concerned with cutting costs. Companies resisted the measure by delaying payment on 1982 profits for an average of eighteen months past the legal deadline.

Table 4.2 provides information on profit transfers. From 1974 to 1977, the Treasury received only S/. 900 million from 17 of the more than 150 broadly defined public firms and 50 narrowly-defined public enterprises. The 17 were among Peru's smallest public enterprises and included no flagship firm nor any top profit earner. During mid-1978, MEF officials calculated profits transfers arrears at more than S/. 6.5 billion, or more than 7 times the amount actually paid. D.L. 20810 proved ineffective as a way of channelling more surplus to government. From 1981 to 1983, the Fund proved slightly more efficient in transferring profits, bringing in more than S/. 1.7 billion, because its provisions covered more firms. Thus, even when the portfolio showed a loss, the firms were forced to transfer profits to the treasury.

TABLE 4.2
Profits Paid to Government and Arrears: 1974–1983
(millions of constant 1973 soles)

	1974	1975	1976	1977	1978	1981	1982	1983
Total paid	324	117	347	137	0	399	378	971
Nonfinancial	324	117	347	137	0	241	355	836
Financial firms	--	--	--	--	--	158	23	135
Arrears	2382	1421	914	1783	n.a.	n.a.	n.a.	n.a.

-- Not applicable
n.a. Not available
SOURCE: MEF, unpublished statistics.

SUBSIDIES

When public enterprises show losses, governments may use several mechanisms to cover the deficit including: subsidization from the national budget, giving loans at low or no interest, waiving service charges on existing loans, declaring a moratorium on loan repayments, or eroding the firms' own reserves or depreciation funds. While Peru's government has used all these mechanisms to some extent, this section

TABLE 4.3
Subsidies by Product Line: 1974-1984
(millions of current soles)

	1974	1975	1976	1977	1978	1979	1980	1981	1982	1983	1984[a]
Basic foodstuffs	2,546	4,207	7,145	20,592	4,695	41,790	59,489	66,112	158,897	229,825	154,925
Wheat	2,256	1,806	3,366	11,969	1,751	21,014	26,202	8,499	54,111	42,136	-
Vegetable Oil	-	929	373	4,099	2,250	7,189	4,764	(288)	436	10,955	-
Milk products	-	-	280	973	-	2,366	4,470	2,087	16,345	21,470	74,563
Maize	3	-	1,961	1,980	-	1,076	5,397	(3,344)	1,841	5,439	2,313
Rice	-	1,282	394	-	-	8,957	15,641	59,183	84,686	149,992	78,039
Others	287	190	771	1,571	694	1,188	3,015	(25)	1,478	(167)	10
Sugar	-	-	-	-	-	3,574	15,627	9,500	-	-	-
Fishoil	-	-	-	-	-	-	6,097	-	-	-	-
Subtotal-Foods	2,546	4,207	7,145	20,592	4,695	45,364	81,213	75,612	158,897	229,825	154,925
Petroleum products	3,083	5,717	10,489	36,748	32,226	98,331	-	-	-	-	-
TOTAL	5,629	9,924	17,634	57,340	36,921	143,695	81,213	75,612	158,897	229,825	154,925

[a] Preliminary
- Zero or nil
SOURCE: BCRP, 1985b:3.22.

examines its most common practice, subsidization from the national budget. Other mechanisms, particularly hidden subsidies through inter-enterprise transfer pricing, are examined in Chapter 6.[12]

The income and the accounting profits reported above include subsidies from central government. Economic theory justifies subsidies for companies with economies of scale that price output at long-run marginal cost or to compensate companies forced to meet social objectives. Peru justified its subsidies for social or political reasons, rarely for economic ones.[13]   Table 4.3 provides information on subsidies by product line. Basic grains, such as wheat, rice, and maize, account for most food subsidies, while milk products, edible oils, and sugar make up most of the rest. Petroleum products remained an important item only until 1980.[14]

According to the Central Bank, Peruvian firms needed subsidies to cover rises in the costs of production based on external factors, such as increased prices for imported raw materials, the exchange rate differential, and rises in foreign interest rates (BCRP, 1979:38). INAP estimated that for 1978, more than two-thirds of the portfolio's deficit resulted from recent devaluations (1978a, Anexo 2). However, when government authorities were reluctant to allow prices to rise enough to cover increased costs, subsidies took up the slack, jumping from almost S/. 600 million in 1970 to more than S/. 229 billion in 1983 [Table 4.3]. Successive governments were caught in a dilemma. They lamented the need for subsidies, pledging to reduce the budget drag, while flaunting subsidies as clear proof of a commitment to populism as embodied in the twin pillars of cheap foodstuffs and cheap petroleum products.

Unfortunately, for the companies concerned, the open subsidization policy was largely a sham. The government pledged subsidies through the budgets or through budget amendments, but it repeatedly delayed payments, sometimes for five years or more. Indeed, illusory subsidies were the polite fiction whose myth closely bound the public enterprises to the central government. Such an arrangement, while privately deplored by both parties to the fiction, sufficiently served the purposes of each partner that the arrangement was never changed until *force majeure* — the incoming civilian administration in 1980 — imposed a general settling of accounts. The government benefited by trumpeting its populist face and enforced public enterprise silence by keeping companies on the defensive for their supposed inefficiencies that generated needs for continually larger subsidies. Companies reported the fictitious numbers in their published accounting data to indicate a solvent financial situation. The promise of future payment of subsidy arrears ensured companies' current silence. The cost of the subsidy was met in the medium term by reduced profits and reserves for the public enterprises and by recourse to credit through government-owned banks, with the accrued interest, often after long rancorous exchanges, usually charged to government. By 1980, the system was changed to enable companies to act as agents for the

TABLE 4.4
Nonfinancial Public Enterprise Current Account Subsidies 1970-1979
(Millions of current soles and percentages)

	1970	1971	1972	1973	1974	1975	1976	1977	1978	1979
Total subsidies payable	576	602	786	914	5,629	9,924	17,634	57,340	36,921	143,695
Total subsidies received	0	0	158	792	386	4,735	4,801	2,248	4,982	801
Received/Payable (%)	0.0	0.0	20.1	86.7	6.9	47.7	27.2	3.9	13.5	0.6
PETROPERU										
Payable	0	0	0	0	3,083	5,717	10,489	36,748	56,617	98,330
Received	0	0	0	0	0	0	0	0	0	0
Received/Payable (%)	--	--	--	--	0.0	0.0	0.0	0.0	0.0	0.0
EPSA										
Payable	268	450	670	594	2,546	4,207	7,145	20,592	4,695	--
Received	0	0	158	540	30	3,531	2,541	1,377	1,042	--
Received/Payable (%)	0.0	0.0	23.6	90.9	1.2	83.9	35.6	6.7	22.2	--
ENCI										
Payable	--	--	0	n.a.	783	419	1,078	1,455	2,760	41,790
Received	--	--	0	n.a.	0	787	1,213	510	3,706	469
Received/Payable (%)	--	--	0.0	n.a.	0.0	188.0	112.5	35.0	134.3	1.1

-- Not applicable
n.a. Not available
SOURCE: BCRP, unpublished statistics; BCRP, 1985b:3.05-3.22; and MEF, unpublished statistics.

government by depositing all proceeds from sales into special, product-specific accounts in the BN.

Table 4.4 illustrates the subsidy deceptions by comparing the current subsidies payable by the government with the subsidies actually paid by Treasury to the major recipients. Government payments always fell far short of entitlements, with companies receiving far less in current subsidies than the amount they were due. The government's best performance was in 1973, when it paid slightly more than 85 percent of its subsidy obligations; in 1979, Treasury only paid 0.6 percent. At an early date, the IMF called the government's attention to the triple danger that unpaid 1974 subsidies posed for public enterprises, for inflation, and for the exchange rate, but the message went unheeded (IMF, 1976:22). Indeed, government subsidy arrears were widespread and not limited only to the largest companies.[15]

Economists accept that periodic partial payments of agreed annual transfers serve to keep public enterprises operating more efficiently than do large ex-post transfers (Green, 1976:9). Peru, however, chose the most inefficient subsidy payments of all. It made no regular or semi-automatic ex-post subsidy transfers; instead, it regularly made promises to pay subsidies ex-post, which served to increase uncertainty, inefficiency, and costs. By deferring subsidy payments, the government shifted the burden of its populist policies to the companies themselves and to the economy as a whole. As a consequence, the companies were forced to borrow from government-owned banks, which increased their financial costs and lowered their profits.   The ensuing rapid and forced public enterprise credit expansion also generated demand pressures which were linked to the acceleration of the inflation rate after 1975 and to Peru's subsequent massive devaluations.

Table 4.5 shows government arrears on foodstuffs subsidies by product line and antiquity of debt. By January 1979, EPSA had been merged, but the government still owed it more than S/. 25 billion (almost $200 million dollars) on accounts that dated back a decade. Although the government had twice renegotiated payment of subsidy arrears, the debts remained unpaid (D.L. 21052, 22050). EPSA's imports accounted for more than 95 percent of total arrears, principally wheat, maize, and vegetable oil, all mainstays of an urban diet. Although well-intentioned, Peru's foodstuff subsidies were notoriously ineffective in meeting the government's redistribution objectives. First, they clearly discriminated against Peru's lowest income groups, the rural poor, in favor of higher income urban consumers. Second, in urban areas they did not discriminate among income groups, thereby subsidizing the higher income groups who could afford to pay the entire cost of foodstuffs as well as the poor who couldn't. Successive governments refused advice to better target subsidies to the needy (Saulniers, 1979a).

Government arrears weakened PETROPERU. From 1974 to 1979,

TABLE 4.5
EPSA'S Subsidy Arrears by Product and Antiquity of Debt:
January 1979
(millions of current soles)

	1969	1970	1971	1972	1973	1974	1975	1976	1977
Imports									
Wheat	1	49	20	109	1,117	731	615	2,307	11,499
Milk	-	(2)	(3)	16	(6)	-	-	-	661
Soybeans	-	25	50	1	11	4	-	543	360
Sorghum	-	-	(2)	(12)	16	2	-	-	560
Potatoes	-	-	-	20	10	6	-	17	16
Maize	-	-	-	-	32	298	-	85	1,802
Vegetable oil	-	-	-	-	-	-	-	-	3,569
Local Production									
Potatoes	-	1	1	1	16	37	-	3	-
Seed wheat	-	-	-	-	-	3	5	8	12
Palm oil	-	-	-	-	-	-	-	-	35
Soybeans	-	-	-	-	-	-	-	-	6
Marketing									
Rice	72	107	241	372	(697)	-	-	-	-
Food packets[a]	(3)	5	6	5	1	2	-	-	-
Food support[b]	-	-	-	1	1	-	-	-	-
Abbatoirs, cold storage	-	-	-	-	-	143	-	-	136
Mills, silos, warehouses	-	-	-	-	-	7	-	-	-
Edible oils	-	-	-	-	-	-	-	230	-
TOTAL	70	185	313	513	501	1,233	620	3,193	18,656

a   Bolsas Económicos
b   Apoyo Alimentario
-   Zero or nil
SOURCE: BCRP, 1979a:67.

TABLE 4.6
PETROPERU Subsidy Treatment: 1974-1980
(Billions of soles)

	Subsidies Payable			Subsidies Paid		Arrears	
	Legal Basis	Current S/.	1973 S/.	Legal Basis	Current S/.	Current S/.	1973 S/.
1974	RM 774-78-EM	3.1	2.7	DS 031-76-EF	2.6	0.5	0.4
1975	RM 774-78-EM	5.7	3.1			6.2	3.5
1976	RM 774-78-EM	10.5	3.1			16.7	6.6
1977	RM 774-78-EM	36.4	7.1			53.1	13.6
1978	RM 375-79-EF	32.2	2.8			85.3	16.4
1979				DL 22477	61.0[a]	24.3	14.7
1980	DS 153-80-EF	122.7	3.0	DS 153-80-EF	147.0[b]	0.0	14.1
TOTAL		210.7	21.7			0.0	14.1

a   Corresponds to a $388.6 million debt refinancing whose payment was assumed by Treasury against unpaid subsidies.
b   S/. 12 billion were a capitalization of the government's share in post-1978 profits; S/. 135 billion were charged against unpaid taxes. No cash transfers were made. Subsidies were paid on capital account to cover current account arrears.
SOURCE: MEFC, DGAF, Unpublished statistics.

it was the single largest intended recipient of direct government current account subsidies, yet it received nothing from the treasury. Forced to sell petroleum products domestically at low prices, PETROPERU's only recourse was continual borrowing to cover its cash requirements. The long-term negative effects on the company are shown in table 4.6. Although the government granted ever-increasing subsidies following the 1973 oil shock, until early 1979, the Treasury arrears continually grew. The government then refinanced and assumed PETROPERU's debts and, in early 1980, paid its remaining subsidy arrears as a capital transfer.[16]

A negative effect of settling the arrears was payment with strongly devalued currency, that had reduced purchasing power. For example, when measured in constant soles, figures in Table 4.6 show that PETROPERU only received S/. 7 billion of the S/. 21.7 billion granted in subsidies from 1974 to 1980. Thus, Treasury delays meant that inflation had eroded two-thirds of the subsidy.[17]

Differentials between domestic and international prices had other subsidy implications. After 1978, when PETROPERU's exports spurted, every barrel of oil sold domestically bore the opportunity cost of not having been sold abroad. By 1981, the implicit economic subsidy to consumers from this differential alone amounted to more than $ 1 billion, which exceeded the entire projected public sector deficit (IBRD, 1981:40).[18]

Other analysts of Peruvian public enterprises have calculated implicit subsidy levels on the basis of full-cost pricing, including a normal return on capital. According to this perspective, subsidies have two components: a direct treasury payment, which was often postponed, and income foregone by the companies. The World Bank estimated that, for 1980, the indirect subsidies through income foregone by the companies were more than triple the direct ones (IBRD, 1981:24.). Similarly, Wolfenson showed that treasury subsidies to the electric companies only covered 55 percent of the full-cost subsidy of producing electricity, forcing ELECTROPERU to bear the rest (1981:336).

Subsidies on capital account often helped finance company investment projects. During the late 1970s, the government used capital transfers not only to restructure a company's finances, but often to correct, usually too late, an initial undercapitalization or to compensate for the previously unrecognized long-term cash-flow problems. Subsidies on capital account were much less important than the current subsidies examined above.

Close analysis of subsidies reveals a damaging picture of company-government relations and confirms the official finding that the government never had a global subsidy policy (INP, 1980b:86). Moreover, subsidies were not payments to uneconomic firms, but to cover costs of meeting the government's social and political objectives. They were implemented through mechanisms that crippled the companies' flexibility to respond to external changes and that caused permanent addiction to subsidies. Trebat noted precisely the opposite occurred in Brazil:

> "For the most part, the central government has not meddled excessively in public enterprise operations to the point of demoralizing management and debilitating the firm's financial structure. The public enterprise sector has responded by remaining relatively independent of government subsidy, and the individual firms have not been characterized by waste and corruption (1983:237)."

To hook its companies on subsidies, Peru's government rarely paid on time and, when it made the eventual payment, did so in a manner that levied high monetary and efficiency costs on the companies.

TAXES

Public enterprises may pay taxes on their own income, imports, sales, or other operations and they may also act as government revenue agents in collecting excises on their production or on that of their private competitors. Tax issues are neglected in theoretical and empirical work on public enterprises. Indeed, Robert Floyd, a leading specialist on the topic (1978, 1979), omitted taxation from an otherwise complete survey of topical issues (1984). This section shows that through taxes, Peru's public enterprises transferred large sums of money directly to the government.[19]

Peru's public firms were not always heavily taxed. From 1968 until 1976, their income was exempt from corporate income tax (D.S. 287-68-HC, D.L. 21382), however, the burden of other specific taxes fell almost entirely on public enterprises. For example, in July 1976, a 15 percent tax was levied on traditional exports (D.L. 21528). Because the fisheries and minerals producers had overwhelmingly come into the portfolio during the early 1970s, the incidence fell on the producing firms while collection fell on the state traders (BCRP, 1977:31). Other public enterprises were taxed to finance regional development, for example, PETROPERU's ten-year, 10 percent ad valorem tax on all petroleum production in the Department of Loreto to benefit the Department (D.L. 21678). A similar tax to finance the new university in Chimbote fell on SIDERPERU.

Data in table 4.7 show tax contributions by Peru's public enterprises. Measured in current soles, they rose from S/. 2 billion in 1970 to S/. 696 billion in 1982. They became increasingly important after the tax reform measures in 1976 and contributed more than 60 percent of total government revenue in 1979, falling thereafter. Since

TABLE 4.7
Taxes of Portfolio and Selected Public Enterprises: 1970-1982
(Millions of current soles and percentages)

	1970	1971	1972	1973	1974	1975	1976	1977	1978	1979	1980	1981	1982
PORTFOLIO													
Taxes (S/.)	2,051	2,250	2,383	3,094	6,849	8,547	16,928	35,224	89,708	341,124	283,280	430,777	696,093
as percent of government income	5.3	5.4	5.2	5.8	10.0	9.7	15.2	22.9	34.0	61.8	27.8	28.3	27.9
Subsidies (S/.)	1,884	3,110	3,260	4,852	9,695	19,226	31,559	68,642	74,919	159,906	103,815	24,723	4,000
Taxes - subsidies	167	(860)	(877)	(1,758)	(2,846)	(10,679)	(14,631)	(33,418)	14,789	181,218	179,465	406,054	692,093
as percent of government income	0.4	-2.1	-1.9	-3.3	-4.2	-12.1	-13.1	-21.7	5.6	32.8	17.6	26.7	27.7
PETROPERU(S/.)	1,917	1,959	2,033	2,285	3,561	7,289	14,967	23,285	63,326	278,237	205,935	301,800	575,426
% of total taxes	93.5	87.1	85.3	73.9	52.0	85.3	88.4	66.1	70.6	81.6	72.7	70.1	82.7
PESCAPERU(S/.)	--	--	--	0	621	0	1,041	2,575	6,730	13,113	9,156	12,570	13,579
% of total taxes	--	--	--	0.0	9.1	0.0	6.1	7.3	7.5	3.8	3.2	2.9	2.0
CENTROMIN(S/.)	--	--	--	--	1,460	190	329	4,158	8,194	30,243	33,330	23,588	16,182
% of total taxes	--	--	--	--	21.3	2.2	1.9	11.8	9.1	8.9	11.8	5.5	2.3
BN (S/.)	n.a.	23	33	33	125	151	n.a.	115	192	1,474	6,947	26,834	n.a.
% of total taxes	n.a.	1.0	1.4	1.1	1.8	1.8	n.a.	0.3	0.2	0.4	2.5	6.2	n.a.

-- Not applicable
n.a. Not available
SOURCE: See Appendix B

Peruvian accounting practice does not consider indirect taxes as line items in the income statements, so reported figures underestimate transfers to the government. Figures shown in the table consist of direct taxes for most companies and indirect taxes for only a few firms.

PETROPERU paid the most, with many levies on its own operations including income and payroll taxes, corporation wealth taxes, import and export duties, and royalties. It also collected income taxes and import and export duties on the operations of its subcontractors and it acted as government agent in collecting excises and consumption taxes. In 1970 it accounted for almost 100 percent of taxes paid by public enterprises and in no year did it account for less than half. Its importance diminished over time, so that in 1982, it paid almost one fourth of total government tax revenues.

Two other resource-based companies, CENTROMIN and PESCAPERU, had large tax shares. CENTROMIN's taxes depended on international metal market prices. In peak price years it paid heavily, but during price slumps, its tax share dropped to less than 3 percent. PESCAPERU shows that companies paid taxes even if losing money. In 1981, it lost S/. 15.3 billion, but paid S/. 12.6 billion into the government coffers via indirect taxes (MEF, unpublished data).

Tax arrears were less severe than subsidy arrears. For example, although PETROPERU's tax payments lagged in 1979, it redressed the balance in 1980 by paying more than 95 percent of taxes owed, a better record than the government's in paying subsidies (BCRP, unpublished statistics). Minor discrepancies between payments and billing period led to negligible inflation effects between 1978 and 1980 amounting to S/. 2 billion, less than 12 percent of taxes payable. Some lags arose from conflicting interpretations of tax laws between government and company accountants.

Comparing subsidies to taxes not only indicates the net impact of public firms on government finance, it also reveals intra-governmental cash flows.[20] The net position differs from Short's estimate of the "budgetary burden" by deleting two components, government loans and company dividends and interest payments (1984:161). While both are necessary to get a true picture of the flows, double counting occurs if subsidy arrears force firms to borrow from government banks, a common situation in Peru. Normally, both loans and the subsidy payments figure as cash flows from the government to the public enterprise. Short's method overestimates the budgetary burden when subsidies remain unpaid. The public enterprise net position follows the period-marked behavior pattern [Table 4.7]. Firms were granted more in subsidies from government than they paid to it in taxes until 1978; thereafter, the opposite occurred. During the early 1980s, public enterprises contributed, net of subsidies, almost 30 percent of government revenue. Schydlowsky and Wicht's conclusion that "[w]hereas prior to the takeover those enterprises made profits and paid taxes; after takeover they did not," is plainly refuted (1983:106).

EMPLOYMENT

Peru's public enterprises rarely generated high levels of direct employment, providing jobs for less than 3 percent of the total labor force, according to data presented in table 4.8.[21] The low employment figures follow the standard pattern and fall between Britain's 8.1 percent average during the late 1970s and Sierra Leone's 1.3 percent in 1979 (ICPE, 1983b:5, Short, 1984:143). Since much of Peru's labor force is self employed, particularly in agriculture and in services, the 3 percent figure understates the portfolio's importance in providing modern sector jobs. However, even netting out the self-employed, public enterprises employed more than 6 percent of the non-independent labor force only in two years, 1975 and 1976.[22]

Employment effects rarely entered the decision to create a new firm or to take over an entire sector, with the notable exceptions of PESCAPERU or Moraveco [See Chapter 2]. Indeed, the government's focus on capital-intensive sectors neglected the employment dimension (James, 1983). As a consequence, public enterprises compare badly to the rest of government where 80 percent of public sector employment and more than 80 percent of new jobs during the 1970s were generated (Robles Chávez, 1985:96).

Employment in most large firms, those with more than 5,000 workers, generally increased until the late 1970s when slight declines resulted from the 1977 and 1978 government-wide austerity programs. Personnel reductions were only temporary, followed by later rises. PESCAPERU remains an exception. While absorbing the fishmeal and

TABLE 4.8
Employment of Major Public Enterprises: 1974–1982
(Thousand workers)

	1974	1975	1976	1977	1978	1979	1980	1981	1982
PORTFOLIO	113.4	136.2	136.1	126.8	120.1	121.6	131.0	126.4	145.3
as percent of:									
labor force	2.43	2.83	2.75	2.48	2.28	2.23	2.33	2.18	2.43
non-independent									
labor force	5.36	6.22	6.01	5.42	4.97	5.02	5.23	4.91	5.50
PETROPERU	6.9	7.8	8.1	8.8	8.2	8.2	8.7	10.1	8.8
ENAFERPERU	6.4	5.7	5.8	5.7	5.9	5.8	6.2	6.3	6.5
ENTELPERU	3.1	3.8	3.9	3.9	4.0	6.3	7.1	7.1	7.9
PESCAPERU	18.4	24.8	23.3	11.6	6.9	7.2	8.5	7.1	5.4
CENTROMIN	15.1	15.9	15.9	16.1	16.3	16.5	16.9	17.1	17.2
BN	n.a.	7.5	7.5	7.8	7.6	7.8	8.9	7.9	7.3
ELECTROPERU	3.9	4.2	4.9	5.4	5.3	5.6	6.3	6.7	7.2
SIDERPERU	6.0	5.2	5.1	5.1	4.9	4.8	5.1	5.0	4.9
ENAPUPERU	3.6	5.1	4.9	4.7	4.4	4.2	4.3	4.2	4.0
SIMAPERU	3.5	3.6	3.7	4.1	3.6	3.7	4.6	4.8	5.6

n.a. Not available
SOURCE: See Appendix B

fishoil sector, its employment swelled to almost 25,000, as many as 18,000 of whom were idle (IBRD, 1979:237). From 1971 to 1976, its fishing fleet and the number of processing plants were halved while its catch dropped by more than 60 percent. As PESCAPERU's operations were progressively sold, closed, or scrapped, its employment fell to less than 5,500 by 1982.

INVESTMENT

During the early 1970s, both public enterprise and public sector investment rose sharply, compensating for the stagnant private sector spending [Graph 4.2].[23] Before 1970, "government policy reflected a keen awareness that the long-term viability of the transformation in the economy demanded that it be as much as possible self-sufficient" (IBRD, 1979:227). That keen awareness later lapsed as a frenzy of company-level decisions, based on optimistic forecasts of copper earnings and oil receipts, led to 90 percent investment growth rates in 1973 and 1974, and a widening gap between savings and investment. The second half of the decade was marked by two opposite trends: central government authorities increasingly tried to impose order and rationality on the public enterprise investment process and the real

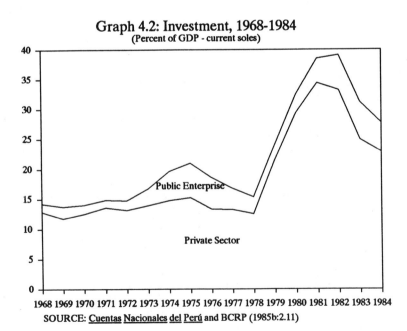

Graph 4.2: Investment, 1968-1984
(Percent of GDP - current soles)

SOURCE: Cuentas Nacionales del Perú and BCRP (1985b:2.11)

TABLE 4.9
Investment of Selected Public Enterprises: 1970-1984
(Millions of constant 1973 soles and percentages)

	1970	1971	1972	1973	1974	1975	1976	1977	1978	1979	1980	1981	1982	1983	1984[a]
PORTFOLIO															
(S/.)	4,689	4,480	5,402	10,318	19,334	23,886	20,542	13,152	10,598	10,233	10,827	15,219	20,316	18,779	16,569
% of GDP	1.5	1.2	1.6	2.8	4.8	5.8	5.2	3.5	2.8	2.5	3.1	4.1	6.0	6.2	4.8
PETROPERU															
(S/.)	850	1,327	1,433	4,025	7,538	14,133	12,790	5,418	2,480	1,218	991	2,551	3,558	2,511	2,995
% of portfolio	18.1	29.6	26.5	39.0	39.0	59.2	62.3	41.2	23.4	11.9	9.2	16.8	17.5	13.4	19.2
ELECTROPERU															
(S/.)	1,996	1,684	1,552	2,341	1,416	1,404	2,070	1,576	2,946	1,457	3,538	6,745	8,487	9,011	7,285
% of portfolio	42.6	37.6	28.7	22.7	7.3	5.9	10.1	12.0	27.8	14.2	32.7	44.3	41.8	48.0	46.8
MINEROPERU															
(S/.)	1	173	398	977	2,329	3,876	2,087	1,057	1,952	2,860	2,335	2,075	337	23	93
% of portfolio	0.0	3.9	7.4	9.5	12.0	16.2	10.2	8.0	18.4	27.9	21.6	13.6	1.7	0.1	0.6
CENTROMIN															
(S/.)	--	--	--	--	n.a.	n.a.	n.a.	n.a.	n.a.	1,355	2,335	2,032	1,659	1,078	472
% of portfolio	--	--	--	--	n.a.	n.a.	n.a.	n.a.	n.a.	13.2	21.6	13.4	8.2	5.7	3.0

a Preliminary
-- Not applicable
n.a. Not available
SOURCE: BCRP, 1985b:3.20.

value of investment persistently dropped. After 1978, a private sector-fueled investment boom returned until the economic downturn forced project retrenchment.

The public enterprise share of GFCF increased from 10 percent in 1970 to 17 percent in 1973. For the rest of the decade, that share averaged 25 percent, slightly higher than the hemisphere average of 22.5 percent (Short, 1984:121). Later, it dropped steadily, to less than 17 percent of GFCF.

Investment was dominated by a few companies whose large-scale projects were carried out for "development needs and national security" (Pinzas, 1981:87). Table 4.9 provides information on the four firms that together accounted for 72 percent of public enterprise investment.

Petroleum and electricity projects dominated. From 1973 to 1977, PETROPERU's trans-Andean pipeline project cycle reflected the initial optimism of the oil fever in the Amazon basin later tempered by low yields. By 1980, PETROPERU's real investment dropped to less than 10 percent of the portfolio total. ELECTROPERU supplanted it as the major investor to satisfy a growing electricity demand. CENTROMIN and MINEROPERU mining projects were less important although, in both 1978 and 1979, they accounted for more than 40 percent of public enterprise fixed capital formation.

The investment projects had several similarities: they had long gestation periods; were highly capital intensive; generated little new employment; had a high import content; led to the massive use of external finance; and were often provided by turnkey contracts with foreign consultants or contractors (Portocarrero, 1982:444–446). They have been criticized as having been hastily decided with scant attention paid to economic criteria and as subject to large cost miscalculations (IBRD, 1979:222–223).

FOREIGN AND LONG-TERM BORROWING

The long-term implications for the balance of payments of public enterprises' international indebtedness has aroused wide concern (Gillis, Jenkins, and Lesard, 1983:262–262; Saulniers, 1983.) However, in marked contrast to the borrowing patterns shown elsewhere in Latin America, Peru's public enterprises did not borrow heavily abroad.[24] According to data presented in table 4.10, enterprises accounted for only 30 percent of the total public external debt contracted during the 1970s. The rest was undertaken by other parts of the public sector.

Financing the large investment projects did lead to increased foreign borrowing during the early 1970s, peaking around $500 million in new loans in 1974. From 1975 to 1977, annual borrowing levels remained under $400 million annually, later dropping sharply. PETROPERU was the heaviest borrower, accounting for less than 30

TABLE 4.10
Public Enterprise External Public Debt Contracted: 1970-1980
(Millions of US dollars and percentages)

	1970	1971	1972	1973	1974	1975	1976	1977	1978	1979	1980
PUBLIC SECTOR ($m)	n.a.	n.a.	500	1,025	1,294	984	1,383	1,008	465	1,757	1,539
PUBLIC ENTERPRISE ($m)	37	87	281	301	560	380	365	399	110	787	236
(% of Public Sector)	n.a.	n.a.	56.1	29.4	43.3	38.6	26.4	39.5	23.6	44.8	15.4
PETROPERU ($m)	n.a.	n.a.	70	13	403	166	107	39	62	389	33
(% of Public Sector)	n.a.	n.a.	14	1.2	31.1	16.9	7.7	3.9	13.3	22.2	2.1
ELECTROPERU ($m)	9	6	7	90	4	14	58	71	0	257	177
(% of Public Sector)	n.a.	n.a.	1.4	8.8	0.3	1.4	4.2	7.1	0.1	14.6	11.5
BANKS[a] ($m)	n.a.	36	30	108	67	73	122	94	7	109	25
(% of Public Sector)	n.a.	n.a.	6	10.5	5.2	7.5	8.8	9.4	1.5	6.2	1.6
EPSA/ENCI ($m)	21	45	76	55	41	42	6	5	1	8	0
(% of Public Sector)	n.a.	n.a.	15.2	5.4	3.2	4.3	0.4	0.5	0.2	0.5	0

a Includes: BN, COFIDE, BI, BA, BANVIPE, BANMINERO
n.a. Not available
SOURCE: Public sector data - BCRP, Memorias; Public enterprise data - MEF unpublished statistics.

percent of public enterprise foreign loans. It relied more heavily on long-term financing than did other companies in the portfolio. ELECTROPERU also borrowed heavily, especially in 1979 and 1980. Financial institutions such as COFIDE, the BN, and the four sectoral development banks borrowed funds abroad that were earmarked for other public enterprise projects. When companies arranged loans directly, COFIDE usually acted as official government guarantor. Guarantees effectively reduced the risk premium charged the public enterprises and resulted in a lower interest rate. COFIDE'S service was not without charge. It levied a 3 percent guarantee fee on such loans (interview, 1981). EPSA and ENCI financed foodstuffs imports through short- and medium-term foreign borrowing. During the 1970s, the combined loans to these two firms amounted to $300 million, which accounted for 10 percent of public enterprise borrowing, all of which had been repaid by the end of the decade.

The public enterprise foreign debt issue is not simple. Units of measurement and time horizons play an important role in arriving at definitive conclusions. Indeed, the contribution of public enterprises to the debt burden may be spuriously overstated by ignoring the effect of exchange rate shifts on debt measured in local-currency. The telecommunications company, ENTEL, a relatively minor foreign borrower, provides an example. For 1978 and 1979, its sol-denominated debt went from S/ 8.3 billion to S/ 20.2 billion, an apparent increase of 140 percent. However, S/ 8.1 billion of the increase was due to an exchange rate adjustment for old loans.[25] With a stable currency, ENTEL's foreign debt would have risen by only 44 percent during the two years, but, measured by a rapidly depreciating sol, it jumped far more.

SHORT-TERM AND LOCAL BORROWING

Peru's public enterprises were often accused of having borrowed heavily in the short-term market during the 1970s to compensate for their inadequate internal finances.[26] Close analysis of their bank loans and overdrafts, sheds a different light on the accusation. Table 4.11 summarizes available data.

Measured in constant 1973 soles, the portfolio's short-term indebtedness rose steadily then fell, dropping in 1976 and 1980. However, the huge short-term debt increases in 1973 and 1974 did not come from a change in the borrowing patterns of the existing companies. Instead, the government created new firms with two different characteristics from earlier public enterprises: they had higher overall short-term borrowing requirements and short-term funds comprised a much higher share of their liabilities. Three firms that fit the new borrowing pattern were PESCAPERU, ENCI, and MINPECO. When PESCAPERU was created, its overdrafts accounted for

TABLE 4.11
Short-Term Overdrafts for Major Public Enterprises: 1970-1982
(Millions of 1973 soles and percentages)

	1970	1971	1972	1973	1974	1975	1976	1977	1978	1979	1980	1981	1982
PORTFOLIO	1,668	1,545	3,067	8,732	11,334	15,966	17,597	8,487	13,486	15,432	10,858	12,187	15,690
PETROPERU (S/.)	226	1,303	n.a.	525	2,339	2,301	a	a	672	122	429	129	110
(% of debt)	13.5	84.3	n.a.	17.2	20.9	22.6	b	b	6.3	1.4	10.8	3.5	2.2
ELECTROPERU(S/.)	195	n.a.	n.a.	9	10	11	13	b	48	27	58	268	62
(% of debt)	4.2	n.a.	n.a.	2.4	0.7	0.9	0.4	0.4	2.7	0.9	2.0	3.7	0.7
MINEROPERU (S/.)	a	n.a.	8	543	12	93	16	350	205	134	1,885	3,030	6,328
(% of debt)	b	n.a.	0.2	6.4	1.6	7.1	0.5	9.7	7.3	3.6	49.1	45.5	57.1
PESCAPERU (S/.)	--	--	--	5,154	3,353	3,682	7,415	2,332	1,991	238	79	171	312
(% of debt)	--	--	--	86.2	46.5	48.5	73.3	44.0	37.5	7.6	1.8	3.0	4.4
CENTROMIN (S/.)	--	--	--	n.a.	993	751	n.a.	n.a.	n.a.	n.a.	66	243	5,890
(% of debt)	--	--	--	n.a.	38.7	21.2	n.a.	n.a.	n.a.	n.a.	0.7	2.9	59.6
SIDERPERU (S/.)	942	97	37	26	17	475	260	96	136	51	110	43	16
(% of debt)	62.6	14.4	5.0	2.9	1.3	20.8	11.7	3.5	4.9	3.7	6.6	1.1	0.3
EPSA (S/.)	n.a.	n.a.	2,918	1,113	783	1,906	1,277	1,748	n.a.	5,776	--	--	--
(% of debt)	n.a.	n.a.	33.3	18.9	10.4	20.5	11.7	12.6	n.a.	34.2	--	--	--
ENCI (S/.)	--	--	a	109	313	186	a	30	a	a	a	a	7
(% of debt)	--	--	b	76.8	42.4	7.9	b	2.3	b	b	b	b	1.0
MINPECO (S/.)	--	--	--	--	1,421	1,405	1,483	1,758	3,072	5,024	4,452	1,810	2,387
(% of debt)	--	--	--	--	50.8	44.5	43.1	38.9	29.1	38.1	36.3	32.4	48.1
EPCHAP (S/.)	80	146	91	82	594	3,162	3,129	1,238	n.a.	--	--	--	--
(% of debt)	3.7	4.3	10.8	11.9	31.2	63.2	42.3	10.5	n.a.	--	--	--	--
CPV (S/.)	169	n.a.	n.a.	119	3	61	37	9	53	87	111	140	n.a.
(% of debt)	23.3	n.a.	n.a.	22.6	0.8	6.9	6.5	1.6	2.4	7.6	8.8	12.6	n.a.
AEROPERU (S/.)	--	--	--	a	23	113	37	24	40	119	28	43	a
(% of debt)	--	--	--	b	6.3	16.6	3.3	5.8	6.6	12.1	3.0	3.6	b

a   Current liabilities less than S/. 0.1 million
b   Less than 0.05 percent
-- Not applicable
n.a. Not available
SOURCE: See Appendix B

60 percent of the portfolio total. They also comprised 86 percent of its current liabilities. Similarly, ENCI's overdrafts were more than three-fourths and MINPECO's more than half of current liabilities.

The short-term requirements of established firms changed little during the mid-1970s, most of the increase in short-term indebtedness arose when the government created underfunded companies and forced them to rely on volatile bank financing. During the Belaúnde administration, the pattern reversed as the state traders' situation improved while large firms such as ELECTROPERU, became cash strapped.

Peru's public enterprises borrowed heavily at home, mostly from the BN, which throughout most of the 1970s, held monopolies on many government financial transactions.[27]   Table 4.12 summarizes BN's year-end credit position vis-a-vis its largest public enterprise borrowers. The data show a net credit position with the BN in all years that, expressed in constant 1973 soles, rose from S/. 313 million in 1973 to more than S/. 13 billion in 1977. The noticeable drop in 1978 and 1979 resulted from BN demands for prior payment in local currency for all imports of foodstuffs and industrial inputs (BCRP, 1979a:20).

From 1973 to 1976, PESCAPERU was BN's largest public enterprise net borrower and was consistently in debt. PESCAPERU's debts usually counterbalanced the positive net position of the rest of the portfolio. Of the other producers who borrowed heavily from the government financial system, PETROPERU was the most important. Initially, it had low or negative net borrowing requirements, however, controlled prices combined with treasury arrears in making subsidy payments, eroded its deposits in the BN, while its credit needs rose rapidly. The BN automatically issued loans to the company [not to the Treasury] to cover Treasury arrears. By 1979, PETROPERU's position improved with new petroleum exports and government financial sanitizing.

State traders presented a different picture. Until 1977, EPSA was the strongest net creditor to the system with its deposits in the BN exceeding BN credit. EPSA's deposits did not bear interest, although the BN charged it interest on loans or overdrafts. EPSA maintained separate accounts by product lines and any overdrawn account incurred interest charges with no mechanism provided for automatic transfers.   Excess deposits may demonstrate EPSA's poor financial planning which lowered financial income and raised financial expenses. Its overdrafts demonstrate a severe flaw in the financial system that was remedied in 1980.[28] Other state traders generally were net debtors to the financial system. MINPECO's strong credit demands arose because the government was unwilling and unable to endow it with even a minimal capital base consistent with its level of operations. Instead of paying substantial capital initially, the government merely authorized the newly-created MINPECO to overdraw its BN accounts, with the attendant need to pay interest charges.[29]   By 1980, this

TABLE 4.12

Year-end BN Position with Key Public Enterprises: 1973–1981

(Millions of constant 1973 soles)

	1973	1974	1975	1976	1977	1978	1979	1980	1981
TOTAL	313	2,985	11,697	14,186	13,337	10,233	6,550	7,252	8,339
PETROPERU									
Credits	394	4,739	4,020	4,654	6,062	5,068	419	399	859
Deposits	49	6,393	2,025	967	318	627	912	59	115
Net Credit	345	(1,654)	1,995	3,687	5,744	4,441	(493)	340	743
MINEROPERU									
Credits	1,423	1,066	868	49	106	83	578	832	330
Deposits	13	377	197	146	45	168	61	149	115
Net Credit	1,410	689	671	(97)	61	(85)	517	683	215
EPCHAP									
Credits	98	664	2,698	3,146	2,877	2,074	81	--	--
Deposits	1,189	229	1,267	1,173	990	1,624	89	--	--
Net Credit	(1,091)	435	1,431	1,973	1,887	450	(8)	--	--
SIDERPERU									
Credits	317	295	1,186	1,028	361	1,005	117	1,244	906
Deposits	289	353	102	190	208	220	126	52	89
Net Credit	28	(58)	1,084	838	153	785	(9)	1,192	817
EPSA									
Credits	2,670	3,611	3,863	4,554	4,157	5,205	6,399	491	--
Deposits	4,983	3,939	4,605	5,299	4,820	2,326	1,319	675	--
Net Credit	(2,313)	(328)	(742)	(745)	(663)	2,879	5,080	(184)	--
ENCI/ECASA									
Credits	569	2,144	2,629	1,912	1,684	2,260	1,592	3,773	6,371
Deposits	671	1,138	458	1,227	620	1,742	603	917	1,016
Net Credit	(102)	1,006	2,171	685	1,064	518	989	2,856	5,355
PESCAPERU									
Credits	2,043	2,081	3,976	6,763	4,160	2,044	587	n.a.	n.a.
Deposits	7	613	41	272	28	37	46	n.a.	n.a.
Net Credit	2,036	1,468	3,935	6,491	4,132	2,007	541	n.a.	n.a.
MINPECO									
Credits	--	1,427	1,166	1,602	1,359	406	544	2,856	1,743
Deposits	--	0	14	248	400	1,168	611	491	84
Net Credit	--	1,427	1,152	1,354	959	(762)	(67)	2,365	1,659

-- Not applicable
n.a. Not available
SOURCE: BCRP, Memorias.

situation also had improved.

In many countries, public enterprises benefit from soft loans granted by the local, often government-controlled, financial system. In Peru, the average rates charged on loans to public enterprises were comparable to those charged to private firms by government development banks. Sometimes public enterprises received favorable treatment, at other times they did not. Access to funds at zero or low rates was rare.[30] Loans for subsidies at a 4 percent interest rate only indirectly benefited the public enterprises by lowering their cost of meeting cash-flow needs caused by persistent Treasury arrears. The Treasury turned out to be the major beneficiary of the 4 percent rate by shifting its immediate borrowing requirements to public enterprises that could borrow at lower rates.

VALUE ADDED

Value added by public enterprises measures their contribution to national product. From data presented in table 4.13, the value added by Peru's nonfinancial public enterprises grew steadily until 1980, then stabilized.[31] At first, public enterprise value added doubled with the nationalization of the International Petroleum Company (IPC), rising to more than 2 percent of GDP. Later, as more sectors were swept into the public portfolio, value added increased to 4 percent of GDP following the 1973 nationalization of the important fishing sector. With existing public enterprises expanding and new firms continually added, by 1977 public enterprises accounted for almost 6.5 percent of GDP. By the early 1980s that share remained steady at close to 11 percent.[32] BCRP estimates that the largest companies account for 70 percent of portfolio value added (interview, 1985). On that basis, actual portfolio shares hover at 15 percent of GDP. Over time, value added increased in real terms, rising from slightly more than S/. 3 billion in 1968 to almost S/. 41 billion by 1980. The performance was not consistent across companies, however, and differentials provide some indication of the effect of government policies.

PETROPERU early emerged as the most important source of value added, accounting for at least half of the portfolio's contribution. Until 1978, its value added remained stable, while dropping steadily in relative terms. Following the shift to a more market-oriented pricing system in 1978, its value added jumped to a new plateau which held through the early 1980s. PESCAPERU's high value added was a measure of the substantial wages and salaries paid to a bloated labor force. In 1974, it accounted for more than 40 percent of the total, but later dropped. CENTROMIN at nationalization accounted for almost a fifth of total portfolio value added, a share maintained with slight fluctuations. SIDERPERU showed a smaller, but still credible performance with a consistent 5 to 9 percent of value added. Overall, food marketing made a negative net contribution to value added. EPSA, ENCI, and ECASA consistently absorbed more funds than they contributed.

CONCLUSIONS

This chapter employs macro data on the largest companies to gain important insights into overall portfolio behavior. It analyzes the growth and evolution of Peru's portfolio, largely accounted for by the

TABLE 4.13
Value Added of Major Nonfinancial Public Enterprises: 1968-1982
(Millions of constant 1973 soles and percentages)

	1968	1969	1970	1971	1972	1973	1974	1975	1976	1977	1978	1979	1980	1981	1982
NON-FINANCIAL TOTAL															
(S/.)	3,039	7,183	8,451	8,821	9,681	14,464	17,137	19,127	25,687	28,971	n.a.	n.a.	40,778	34,559	39,369
(% of GDP)	0.9	2.2	2.8	2.8	2.9	4.0	4.5	4.9	6.3	7.1	n.a.	n.a.	11.1	11.2	10.3
PETROPERU															
(S/.)	599	4,685	4,557	4,265	4,558	4,790	3,383	3,557	5,133	4,910	4,467	8,832	7,836	6,372	7,753
(% of total)	19.7	65.2	53.9	48.4	47.1	33.1	19.7	18.6	20.0	16.9	n.a.	n.a.	19.2	18.4	19.7
PESCAPERU															
(S/.)	--	--	--	--	--	3,505	7,075	681	4,115	5,403	5,114	n.a.	3,836	3,790	3,209
(% of total)	--	--	--	--	--	24.2	41.3	3.6	16.0	18.6	n.a.	n.a.	9.4	11.0	8.2
SIDERPERU															
(S/.)	n.a.	n.a.	n.a.	n.a.	n.a.	1,143	1,156	1,251	1,395	1,566	1,803	727	1,546	2,308	3,426
(% of total)	n.a.	n.a.	n.a.	n.a.	n.a.	7.9	6.7	6.5	5.4	5.4	n.a.	n.a.	3.8	6.7	8.7
CENTROMIN															
(S/.)	--	--	--	--	--	--	n.a.	4,247	5,521	5,526	n.a.	n.a.	7,873	9,784	6,560
(% of total)	--	--	--	--	--	--	n.a.	22.2	21.5	19.1	n.a.	n.a.	19.3	28.3	16.7
EPSA															
(S/.)	--	n.a.	1	1	1	(951)	(1,806)	(805)	(1,381)	(214)	n.a.	--	--	--	--
(% of total)	--	n.a.	0.0	0.0	0.0	-6.6	-10.5	-4.2	-5.4	-0.7	n.a.	--	--	--	--
ENCI/ECASA															
(S/.)	--	--	--	--	1	38	42	(75)	(149)	(68)	n.a.	n.a.	395	n.a.	(3,022)
(% of total)	--	--	--	--	0.0	0.3	0.2	-0.4	-0.6	-0.2	n.a.	n.a.	1.0	n.a.	-7.7
MINPECO															
(S/.)	--	--	--	--	--	--	239	340	352	430	300	n.a.	1,248	801	157
(% of total)	--	--	--	--	--	--	1.4	1.8	1.4	1.5	n.a.	n.a.	3.1	2.3	0.4

-- Not applicable
n.a. Not available
SOURCE: BCRP, CONADE, unpublished statistics.

behavior of a few significant companies, often in energy and mining.

The period framework, sketched in Chapter 3, proves remarkably robust in explaining the evolution of macro indicators. Behavior patterns differed from one period to the other and differed in a consistent fashion. Generalized growth was a portfolio hallmark during the early 1970s sweep of the commanding heights. Widespread variation in indicator levels occurred almost without exception through the mid-1970s mopping-up operations. The variations reflected both uncertainty and sharp differences at top policy levels, compounded by the effect of external factors precipitated by the 1973 oil shock and magnified by the Velasco government's staunch refusal to recognize that external forces influenced public enterprise income, growth, management, and profits.

The weight of the four to six largest firms in explaining each of Peru's principal macroeconomic indicators has important policy implications for the design of efficient monitoring systems. Such systems should be limited to monitoring those companies with the greatest indicator impact; generalized monitoring of the entire portfolio is inappropriate, costly, and inefficient both for the companies and for the government with limited resources.

The data reveal several shortcomings with Peruvian government accounting practices. Most importantly, cash flows between government and public enterprises were subject to deliberate delays or nonpayment by both the public treasury and the companies. The immediate result of government's nonpayment was to distort operating cost structures by raising the company financial costs. Had payments been made in a timely manner, the total subsidy bill would have been lowered considerably, saving money for companies and the government.[33] The tax analysis demonstrated that public enterprises often gave the government more than they received. The portfolio did not absorb massive amounts of labor; it took in only a minute portion of Peru's labor force.

The rich detail provided in the accompanying tables gives ample evidence for some of the chapter's more startling conclusions regarding profits, subsidies, taxes, and employment. These conclusions may be resumed into one that forms the basis for Chapter 6: Peru's government was responsible for many problems of Peru's public enterprises. Given the harsh operating environment that the government foisted on the companies and given the dependency relationships that the government forced on them, their successes in showing good levels of macro performance variables such as profits and taxes, indeed, must be admired.

NOTES

1. The portfolio data of Chapters 4 and 5 are more encompassing than those in official Peruvian publications because they include firms irrespective of legal status. The rare case of missing data usually does not seriously distort the broad picture and any notable omissions are mentioned in the text. Consistent accounting data for 1968 and 1969 are unavailable. Data for this chapter come from many sources including company annual reports, the principal monitoring agencies, and other government or company documents. Appendix B provides an explanation of sources and methods.

2. Flagship firms include PETROPERU, ELECTROPERU, MINEROPERU, SIDERPERU, PESCAPERU, and CENTROMIN; the utilities include all providers of water and electricity; transporters include air, land, and water.

3. Strong portfolio growth of the early military years was only a transitory phenomenon not reported in earlier writings. See FitzGerald (1976a, 1979) and Figueroa and Saberbein (1978).

4. I corrected reported figures to remove intragovernmental transfers from the operating budget by: deducting current subsidies, whether paid or promised, and restoring legal deductions, such as ENTEL's placing 25 percent of gross income into an expansion fund. During the early 1980s, as a result of such deductions, ENTEL showed losses instead of high operating profits.

5. While pre-takeover bankruptcy often relates to poor profits performance thereafter, two of the three companies that FitzGerald named as responsible for a portfolio-level deficit don't fit the case (1983:79). CENTROMIN always had an operating profit and PESCAPERU only had an operating loss in 1975. Only ENAFER showed an operating deficit each year. Accounting profit was only slightly different. CENTROMIN remained profitable; PESCAPERU ran deficits only half the time; and ENAFER showed losses.

6. Accounting profits were often based on inadequate provisions for depreciation during the late 1970s and early 1980s due to poor government policies. Depreciation allows companies to set aside funds to keep capital intact, hence, especially under inflationary situations, replacement cost is a better basis for calculating depreciation than is historical cost. Periodic revaluation of fixed assets updates historical cost figures, bringing them closer to replacement cost. Peru levied strong taxes on such revaluations. Consequently, some public enterprises postponed revaluing their assets, to lessen their tax burden, a practice which understated the basis for calculating depreciation. The largest companies reportedly maintained two sets of accounts: the nominal accounts published in the annual reports and revalued accounts that more

correctly gauged overall profitability (interview, 1985).

7. Former fishing minister Tantalean's memoirs omit PESCAPERU's losses, while including data for the profitable fishing firms (1978:342–343).

8. Not all financial expenditures corresponded to payments to the government banks, however. Interest and principal payments on foreign indebtedness are also included, as are exchange losses, which became severe in 1977 when four companies, PETROPERU, CENTROMIN, PESCAPERU and ENCI had foreign exchange losses of almost S/. 8 billion.

9. See the BCRP *Memorias* and Pinzas (1981:88–89).

10. A recent meeting took a tentative step in examining nonfinancial public enterprise management, project formulation and loan repayment (ICPE, 1983a:17–21).

11. Bylaws defined "distributable profits" as all profits less legally mandated reserves (D.S. 230-82-EFC, D.S. 091-83-EFC).

12. I concentrate on explicit subsidies, and make no estimates here of implicit subsidies whether through lower tax rates or lower return on public investment. See Gray for difficulties in measuring implicit subsidies (1984:43–47).

13. Open subsidies are recommended to cover losses resulting from specific government-imposed loss-making obligations (UNIDO,1969:5), (Bokhari 1982:26).

14. Peruvian government accounts mistakenly assign subsidy incidence to a public enterprise, instead of to their ultimate beneficiaries, usually consumers.

15. The small fisheries service company, EPSEP, received no current subsidies during its first three years and only 35 percent of those due during its first six years to cover forced losses in meeting social objectives (Tantalean, 1978:267).

16. The numbers in table 4.6, provided by the MEFC, differ slightly from BCRP figures, but the general picture remains the same. The transfer of payment from current to capital account in 1980 explains the major discrepancy between the two sets of figures.

17. Former Economics and Finance Minister Silva Ruete boasted that he left the public enterprises in economic and financial equilibrium when he left office (Silva, 1981:263).

18. Similar burdens for petroleum producers prevailed in other Latin American countries. PEMEX forwent income of $ 13 billion in 1979 through forced low price domestic sales, an amount almost double its actual receipts (Saulniers, 1981b:22).

19. Almenara provides a thorough review of public enterprise tax bases and an detailed application within the Peruvian context (1981).

20. See Jenkins for other income adjustments (1978a:10–11).

21. The indirect generation of employment opportunities, however, is not measured, neither do the employment data permit the ex-

amination of period-related changes.

22. This employment figure, based on reported data for all major firms, is less than FitzGerald's estimate of 36 percent of modern productive sector jobs during the mid-1970s (1976a:36).

23. FitzGerald provides a long term view of public and private sector investment (1979:148–155). However, he only looked at investment in the infrastructure of primary, secondary and tertiary sectors, which accounts for half to two-thirds of total GFCF (1979:150). A smaller base led him to report a larger public sector share (1983:73).

24. Green proposes criteria for governments seeking foreign funding for public enterprises (1976:20–23).

25. Data taken from ENTEL internal accounting documents.

26. Interview (1981) and Thorp (1983:52).

27. MINPECO was among the first public enterprises to move some of its financial arrangements elsewhere. By 1978, although the BN maintained the monopoly on MINPECO's foreign transactions, the formerly private associated banks handled its local currency dealings.

28. After 1978, following the EPSA merger, its net credit became positive and substantial, which reflected unpaid subsidies covered by BN loans, whose repayment awaited a treasury transfer.

29. The tripling of MINPECO's year-end deposits from 1977 to 1978 was an accounting anomaly. The BN credited MINPECO's accounts with an unusual amount of foreign transactions at the end of the year. These were withdrawn within a few days to cover MINPECO's financial obligations elsewhere within the government banking system (BCRP, 1979a:21).

30. See Shirley, (1983:29) for the standard analysis of public enterprise borrowing rates.

31. BCRP calculates value added only for the nonfinancial firms.

32. BCRP report formats changed so that aggregate 1978 and 1979 statistics were never calculated.

33. A later explanation of inter-governmental discrepancies in subsidy figures, amounting to S/. 30 billion for ECASA in 1981, was that the discrepancy represented interest on loans because the public treasury failed to pay its obligations to the company on time. At the year-end exchange rate, the interest-related discrepancy alone represented more than $60 million U.S. (interview, 1981).

5

Finances, Efficiency, and Profits

INTRODUCTION

The behavior of the few large companies examined in Chapter 4 cannot easily be extrapolated to the entire portfolio since the other firms differ in size and complexity.[1] To arrive at a more general understanding of portfolio finances, efficiency, and profits, a more general method is needed. This chapter provides it by taking data from many firms and applying the standard business tool of ratio analysis [For sources see Appendix B].

Ratios are independent of company size, which avoids the disproportional weight given to big companies when using absolute numbers. Ratio analysis is common for private firms and much of its validity for public enterprise analysis derives from its wide use by government monitoring authorities and company managers. Looking at many firms provides a richer and more detailed picture of the effects of government policies on company performance. The accompanying graphs present ratios for company groups: flagship firms; utilities; state traders; transporters; major banks; financial institutions; and other nonfinancial firms.[2]

Peru's high inflation negates the use of some measures, especially those based on the ratio of a flow variable (eg. output) to a stock variable (eg. fixed assets). Others are less valid because Peru's public enterprises often postponed the revaluations of fixed assets that should have brought historical-cost figures in line with current replacement costs.[3] However, despite their limitations, the ratios presented below are basic to appraising company performance. The chapter discerns portfolio or sectoral trends and makes some inter-group comparisons but does not evaluate specific companies' financial situation.

This chapter analyzes three aspects of behavior: financial soundness and stability, internal efficiency, and profitability. Each aspect is examined through several ratios chosen from among the most significant of a large potential set. Multiple indicators provide redundancy and allow the inclusion of companies for which some data are missing.

FINANCIAL SOUNDNESS AND STABILITY

The first priority of any company should be survival, but no law creating a Peruvian public enterprise ever stated so. Survival is generally assured if a firm is liquid and solvent: it should be able to pay its debts as they fall due and it should be likely to do so in the foreseeable future. Public enterprises often find themselves illiquid or short of working capital, placing their survival in jeopardy.[4] As shown below, some of Peru's public enterprises only survived because their bankruptcy was legally impossible. This section examines three indicators of public enterprises' financial health: current ratios, quick ratios, and the ratio of debt to assets. The patterns emerging from analysis of the three ratios are internally consistent for the portfolio and for company groups. They demonstrate that persistent and severe financial difficulties of Peru's public enterprises were externally imposed by a severely restricted financial environment, that was constrained by short-sighted and contradictory government regulations.

Current Ratio

The current ratio, which is the ratio of current assets to current liabilities, is perhaps the most widely-used indicator of short-term company liquidity. Current assets normally consist of cash and bank balances, bills of exchange receivable, listed securities held as current assets, trade accounts payable, stocks, works in progress, and any prepayments. Current liabilities comprise trade accounts payable, accrued expenses, unpaid taxes for the previous year, proposed dividends to shareholders, and bank overdrafts. The ratio is calculated from data contained in the current balance sheet.

Generally, the balance sheets of private industrial or commercial companies show a current ratio between 2.0 and 3.0. Measures much below this lower limit denote a state of inadequate liquidity, while measures much above 3.0 represent a situation of idle capital. During the financial problems of the 1970s, the acceptable lower limit dropped to between 1.7 and 1.5, to conform to the observed drop in liquidity. Whenever a current ratio drops below 1.0, current liabilities exceed current assets and the working capital is negative. Current ratios for Peru's public enterprises are not strictly comparable to those of private companies because of different accounting practices, so they cannot be used for public-private comparisons.[5]

115

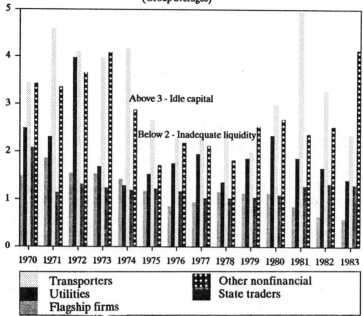

Graph 5.1: Current Ratios
(Group averages)

Above 3 - Idle capital

Below 2 - Inadequate liquidity

Transporters

Utilities

Flagship firms

Other nonfinancial

State traders

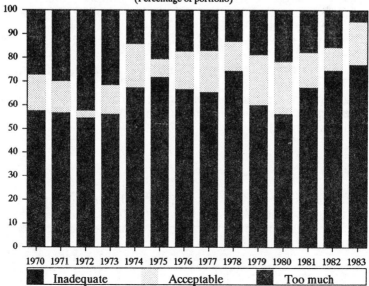

Graph 5.2: Liquidity of Public Enterprises
(Percentage of portfolio)

Inadequate   Acceptable   Too much

Current ratios from 1970 to 1983, shown in graph 5.1, reveal widespread inadequate liquidity.[6] Flagship companies, utilities, and transporters show similar patterns. Their highest ratios came at the beginning of the 1970s, followed by lower fluctuating ratios corresponding to the internal policy debates during the mid-1970s. During the late 1970s their ratios again rose, followed by sharp declines in the 1980s. Traders and other nonfinancial firms followed the same pattern until 1980, when their ratios rose. The liquidity crisis becomes apparent in graph 5.2. In the best year, 1980, only 22 percent of all firms had current ratios between acceptable limits of 2.0 and 3.0. By 1983, more than three-fourths of firms had inadequate liquidity and less than 5 percent of them had excess liquidity.

The flagship firms were distinguished by size or dominant sectoral position, but their current ratios were among the lowest for the entire portfolio. As an example of their problems, from its creation, ELECTROPERU executives lobbied government officials for sufficient capital but only a fraction of the requested funds was ever received (Wolfenson, 1981:150).

Transporters fared the best of any group. Their average current ratio fall below 2.0 in only one year. They often held idle capital, for example, until 1975, ENAPU's current ratios exceeding 5.0, indicating poor overall financial management.[7] In sharp contrast, AEROPERU usually was in dire financial straits, with ratios of 0.5 in 1975 and in 1976 and 0.14 in 1983.

State traders had the worst liquidity. Their average current ratio never exceeded 1.3. During 1975, it dropped below 1.0 when group liabilities exceeded assets. MINPECO was the group's strongest firm but, it too fell victim to the slow liquidity decline until 1979 followed by a slight recovery in 1981.

The utilities showed poor financial health through low and constantly declining ratios until 1980. The majority privately-owned Hidrandina performed the worst of the utilities, with its current ratios, until 1979, always less than 1.0, and until 1977, always less than 0.5. Other nonfinancial public enterprises, freer from government controls than the larger, more visible firms, invariably demonstrated stronger financial positions.

Quick Ratio

The quick ratio or acid test, defined as the ratio of liquid or quick assets to current liabilities, is a better measure of liquidity for firms which keep a high level of inventories. Liquid assets are defined as cash plus assets capable of being turned into cash in the ordinary course of business without substantial loss or inconvenience during the time allowed for the payment of immediate liabilities. The quick ratio measures the ability of a company to raise cash to readily meet its current liabilities in the short term, generally within one month. Liquid assets differ from current assets chiefly by excluding inventories and works in progress. Inventories are not necessarily realizable in the short run and their forced sale may produce revenues far below book value. Inventories can also deteriorate or become obsolete. A common rule of thumb is that the quick ratio for a financially sound company should exceed 1.0.[8]

The quick ratio for the flagship firms and the state traders, companies which by the nature of their business often maintain high inventory levels, is found in graph 5.3. Their quick ratios, always below the benchmark, never indicated financial soundness. Slight differences, both within sectors and over time, merit closer analysis. Flagship firms' quick ratios fluctuated around a long-term declining trend. Although they rose again at decade's end, the chilling effect of the Belaúnde administration's anti-public enterprise bias resulted in a sharp drop from 1981 to 1983. The average quick ratio of state traders varied little, even though changes can be observed at the company level. Only two firms maintained quick ratios above 1.0 for more than one year: MINPECO, at creation and during the 1980s, and EPCHAP, when restricted catches depleted inventories.[9]

Debt Ratios

The equity problems that resulted in poor current and quick ratios led to high funding requirements and financial overextension. Although there is no widely acceptable debt level for a private company, much less a public enterprise, there are some general guidelines.[10] Perhaps the most widely accepted is the ratio of total debt to total assets. Total debt includes all current liabilities plus long- and medium-term loans and any outstanding income tax liabilities. Taxes should be included in a public enterprise ratio because they represent money that, although legally due another branch of government, is being used to finance current business operations.[11] Total assets include all fixed and current assets.[12] The debt ratio lends itself to examination for several reasons. It is a convenient private sector reference point to which financial analysts already are accustomed and, more importantly, it indicates the extent of a government's undercapitalization of its public enterprises.

The rule of thumb is that the debt ratio should be close to 0.5.[13] In other words, it is generally acceptable to finance half the company's assets by debt. For private firms, if the debt ratio exceeds 0.5, creditors and other debt holders have an increased risk of not realizing their claims. Risk factors are presumed lower for public enterprises because if the company cannot pay the interest or repay the capital, it is expected that government repayment guarantees, whether explicit or implicit, could be invoked in its role as ultimate shareholder.[14]

Graph 5.3: Quick Ratios
(Average percentage by group)

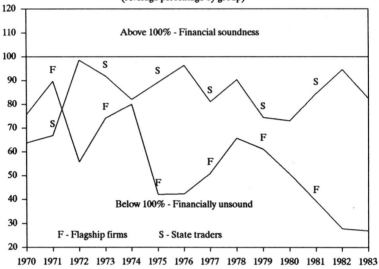

Graph 5.4: Debt Ratios
(Average percentage by group)

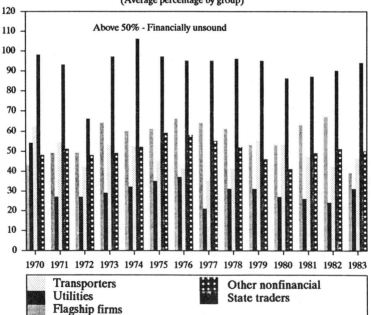

The debt ratios of Peru's nonfinancial public enterprises from 1970 to 1983 are found in graph 5.4. Most fell within the acceptable limit but some sectors showed persistent problems.

A company may be considered legally insolvent when it is unable to raise the necessary cash to pay its debts. This means that even realizing all its assets would be insufficient to meet the demands of its creditors. State traders showed unacceptable limits of debt every year and three of the four major ones were legally insolvent during the 1970s: EPSA from 1971 to 1974, ENCI in 1975, and MINPECO after 1979. The first two companies confirm Hanson's finding that an urban populist mandate often leads to deep financial crisis and irrevocable damage (1968:102). MINPECO's problems, however, were the immediate result of disaster in the silver market, but they culminated a steady upward reliance on external financing by a heavily over-leveraged company. Because Peru expected its state traders to operate without sufficient (or any) infusion of government equity, their financial situation remained problematical (MINCOM, 1978:15). Internal and external experts repeatedly recommended that the government pay its authorized equity levels, but it procrastinated.

The debt ratios of the flagship firms remained above the acceptable limit from 1973 to 1982. PETROPERU, the most heavily endebted, financed more than 90 percent of its total assets by borrowing from 1977 to 1979.[15] By contrast, the utilities only showed over-indebtedness in 1970. Thereafter, they held a stable, low ratio. Transporters showed problems in 6 out of 14 years. Other nonfinancial firms showed little variation, remaining close to the benchmark.

Conclusions

Public enterprises often have an inadequate financial base. Peru's were no exception. Broad similarities in the evolution of key financial ratios demonstrate clearly that the problems were endemic to the entire system, largely caused by the government-determined environment, not by company management.

Lack of working capital caused the poor measures of financial soundness and stability. This lack is linked to many efficiency- related problems including capacity underutilization, inflated unit costs, and, because of price rigidities, deficits. Pressures to maintain full employment also mean that lack of working capital is linked to low workloads and low productivity, adversely affecting labor costs.[16] In Peru, inadequate working capital resulted from the government's triple failures to adequately capitalize its public firms, to pay its debts to them on time, and to enforce a system of prompt and timely inter-enterprise payments. The system was at fault, not company management, and government must shoulder responsibility for the companies' insolvency.[17] Placing the blame squarely on government was belatedly recognized by a former Velasco minister of Economics and Finance, Amilcar Vargas, who stated that lack of working capital kept firms from being more efficient and created interlinkage problems between financial and nonfinancial public enterprises.[18]

Standard analytical frameworks often prescribe policies to remedy financial problems at the company level without realizing that the source of the problems lies elsewhere. For example, the 1979 IBRD report on Peru stressed three major sources of poor public enterprise performance: pricing problems, the quality of financial management, and the special situation of the fishing industry (1979:230). This section demonstrates that improved company financial management would not have solved a problem caused by the government. Some experts have also criticized public enterprises for excessive leveraging which often exceeds the company's debt capacity (Gillis, Jenkins, and Lesard, 1983:263). As shown above, Peru's public enterprises had little choice in the matter. They were forced into indebtedness as the government tried to carry out its programs with a minimum commitment of budget resources.[19]

EFFICIENCY

Efficiency comparisons between public and private enterprises almost invariably place the former in second place. More recent scholarship has found that while at times the public enterprises were more efficient than private firms, at other times the opposite was true and that any apparent differences were not statistically significant.[20] Indeed, such findings undermine the implicit assumptions of public enterprise inefficiency, on which many policy prescriptions are based.

Efficiency should be measured against defined objectives, but Peruvian public enterprises either receive multiple goals and objectives or their goals are vague and ambiguous. Consequently, any attempt to measure efficiency against stated goals or the important unstated ones is severely handicapped. Even clearly stated company objectives often interweave social with political and economic factors, thereby compounding the efficiency measurement problem.

Technical efficiency free from the effects of inflation and price controls is measured by relating physical output to employment or other inputs. However, joint or changing product mixes and missing physical output data make such measures impractical in this broad-based fourteen-year study. The INP evaluated how well firms met their planned physical output targets for one year (1979c). Its analyses, had they been maintained, would have provided invaluable technical efficiency data. Instead, the Belaúnde government dropped them.

This section measures operational efficiency using the standard ratios of one or more cost components to income received from sales.[21] These ratios better estimate corporate efficiency in the absence of restrictive government pricing policy on inputs or outputs, which certainly did not occur in Peru. Nevertheless, they are useful for examining general sectoral trends over time.

The ratios reveal any major changes in the way that public enterprises used their capital resources, raw materials, fuel and power, inventories, or overheads. Ratio analysis must be interpreted with caution: increases in ratio values do not necessarily indicate poorer efficiency. They may signal faults in coordinating company-government activities, or rising input prices over which management had no control, to cite two common occurrences in Peru.

This section does not examine efficacy, whether public enterprises contributed to the development objectives of the state. Short-term government goals often changed rapidly, but mechanisms to communicate such goal changes to the firms were inadequate. To hold the companies accountable to unknown or uncommunicated goals is unfair. Also, goals of different enterprises often conflicted, so looking at individual companies, when their good performance worsened the record of others, is unreasonable.[22]

Ratio of Cost of Goods Sold to Sales

Manufacturing and service companies undertake three basic functions: production, selling, and distribution. This section examines the evolution of the ratio of production costs, commonly known as the costs of goods sold, to sales. Production costs may be broken down into two different components: direct expenses which include materials, wages, and other costs, that can be readily identified with a specific job or process in production, and indirect expenses or overheads, which cannot be ascribed to a particular job or process, such as the rent or depreciation on a factory. Unlike the ratios examined above, no particular rule of thumb can be stated. The ratio is ideally suited for making general and tentative cross-sector comparisons about how a company or sector evolve through time.

Proper cost accounting supports competent management decisions in setting output prices as a function of input prices, for ensuring that product costs are contained, and in deciding on the introduction or abandonment of product lines. With government-determined prices, accurate cost data can justify requests for price adjustment.

The ratio of the cost of goods sold to sales can provide important information. A ratio higher than the industry average may indicate a needed improvement in cost structure. Other things being equal, a drop in the ratio may indicate increased efficiency in resource use through the adoption of cost-saving and performance-improving measures. In monopolistic or oligopolistic markets a low ratio may reflect the power of the leading firms to set high prices, while a high ratio may indicate strong government price control.

High ratios are expected for Peru for several reasons: no stated efficiency objectives, monopolistic or oligopolistic markets, and an open-ended subsidy policy. The ratios should steadily drop, however, because the ratio does not distinguish between fixed and variable costs. Other things being equal, as fixed costs vary inversely with output, so the ratio should vary inversely with sales, dropping as sales rise. A negative correlation with sales increases with inflation, since revenue and variable costs are more quickly adjusted than are fixed costs. Periodic asset revaluations raise depreciation charges, an element in the numerator, but they should not strongly influence the overall ratio.

The pattern that emerges, as seen in graph 5.5, goes counter to the hypotheses: all sectors had highly variable and unstable ratios, except the predominantly small other nonfinancial firms. During the early 1970s the ratios of the flagship firms and utilities increased while those of the other nonfinancial firms fell. During mid-decade, those of flagship firms and transporters rose then declined, while those of the state traders and utilities held steady. The late 1970s saw upward trends for the flagship firms, transporters, and utilities, while the state traders' ratio decreased. The early 1980s ratios for most groups rose, with traders' ratios exceeding 100 percent indicating that the latter sold at less than the variable cost of production.

PETROPERU's ratio reflected the rise in world market petroleum prices coupled with domestic price control which blocked any use of monopoly market power. From 1974 to 1977, with a ratio exceeding 100 percent, its costs exceeded its sales revenue. In 1980, when the government brought domestic petroleum product prices in line with those on the world market, the ratio dropped from 125 percent in 1979 to 86 percent.

Widely fluctuating ratios in key sectors stand out in sharp contrast to those in the other nonfinancial firms which remained around 65 percent. The difference indicates that managers in the smaller companies had a freer hand in controlling costs and prices than did their counterparts in the large, highly visible firms that attracted government attention.

Ratio of Sales and Administrative Expenses to Sales

Manufacturing and service companies incur costs to sell and distribute their product or service. Administration costs, usually grouped with those of sales and distribution, are considered overheads that are incurred as part of normal business activities, but cannot be directly allocated to production. Peruvian policy impeded management from minimizing sales and distribution expenses that largely consisted

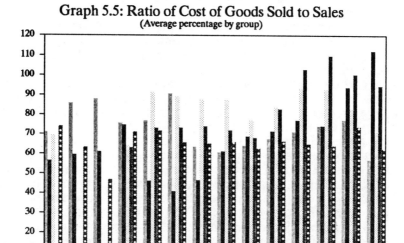

Graph 5.5: Ratio of Cost of Goods Sold to Sales
(Average percentage by group)

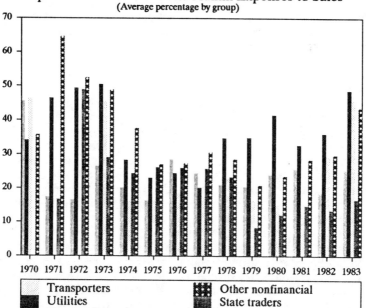

Graph 5.6: Ratio of Sales and Admin Expenses to Sales
(Average percentage by group)

Transporters   Other nonfinancial
Utilities   State traders
Flagship firms

of costs associated with the sales staff whose size was subject to government constraints on hiring and firing and whose wages required government approval. The government also expected firms to handle, without compensation, administrative duties unrelated to production and sales. For example, PETROPERU's supervisory duties included receiving and analyzing copies of all studies, seismic data, and drilling reports carried out by private oil companies and carrying out on-site visits nationwide. PETROPERU also funded two-thirds of the cost of starting a graduate program in petroleum engineering at the National Engineering University (UNI) (Stepan, 1978:268).

Analyzing the ratio of sales and administrative expenses to sales provides important information about resource use. Other things being equal, a drop in the ratio indicates more efficiency, as the same level of spending on sales or administration generates more revenue. Because the ratio is strongly correlated with real wages, government wage controls indirectly boost efficiency. Commonly used for private firms, the ratio provides clues to the complex interface between public enterprise and central government, even though other factors including advertising campaigns, changes in product lines, and changes in the sales area influence it. It too has no rule of thumb.

From graph 5.6 a generalized pattern emerges in the ratio's evolution. Sharp drops during the early 1970s were followed by stability or a slight upward trend to 1978, when austerity measures, including wage controls, took effect and forced most ratios down. The 1980s showed sharp ratio increases across all sectors under the Belaúnde administration. Patterns that are sector- or portfolio-specific once again indicate that managers had little latitude in determining expenditures. The external environment determined company finances.

Ratio of Accounts Receivable to Sales

Companies should want to get paid as quickly as possible. Translating this desire into practice often involves balancing profitability against liquidity. In a market comprised of several buyers and sellers, easy credit terms can attract sales, so the longer a firm allows its customers to delay final payment, the greater will be its sales and (usually) profits. However, easy credit increases the amount of trade accounts receivable and strains the company's liquidity, particularly during periods of high inflation.[23]

For Peru's public enterprises, the solution to the problem of balancing profitability against liquidity was uncomplicated. Imperfectly competitive markets limited the number of buyers and sellers and resolved the problem according to their relative bargaining strengths [See Chapter 6]. Poor information management also allowed buyers to delay payments with minimal follow-up. For many companies, stated goals stressed providing a service, which implicitly permitted nonpayment, since commercial objectives were either never stated or consistently downplayed [See Table 6.1].

The ratio of accounts receivable to sales indicates how easily a company collects its trade and other accounts. Other things being equal, an increase in the ratio shows increasing collection problems and vice versa. Increases can mean more sales to non-creditworthy buyers, a generalized credit crunch leading to delays in paying bills, or a shift in debtors' attitudes to prompt payment. A decrease may indicate tougher bill collection, possibly due to tighter internal control, better management information flows, possibly through introducing computerized billing, or a more effective collection system. Graph 5.7 provides information on the ratio.

With some exceptions, the portfolio followed a pattern of high ratios of accounts receivable to sales at the beginning of the 1970s, generally falling during the mid-1970s, then rising after 1978. Peru's public enterprises have high ratios. PETROPERU posed a special case, with a ratio that soared from 9 percent in 1970 to 148 percent in 1977, then fell back to 9 percent by 1982. Its current accounts receivable consisted mainly of unpaid government subsidies for petroleum products bought at high world market prices and sold cheaply at home. In 1977, PETROPERU's average bill was paid almost 18 months after it was incurred, with government non-payment of debts accounting for almost all of the delay.[24] The average collection period on trade accounts was a mere 29 days, well within standard business norms (PETROPERU, *Memoria*, 1977).

Companies depending heavily on other public enterprises or on the government had the worst collection difficulties. For example, ELECTROPERU, which sold mainly to other public electric companies for distribution, had an average collection period from 1974 to 1977 of 9 months that fell to 4 months for the 1978-1982 period. The Piura electric company, with prices so low that most of its income came from an inter-enterprise compensatory fund, had an average collection period that jumped from 18 months in 1980 to 28 months in 1983.

Some key points are illustrated by these examples. first, payment often depended less on commercial considerations than it did on the relative bargaining strengths of the two parties. Greater strength often meant longer delays in payment, so that government or a powerful public enterprise, could stall payment for years, while a weaker public enterprise could not refuse to sell to its major customers. Second, the fewer the number of customers, which economists characterize as markets with a high degree of monopsony power, the longer payments could be delayed. Thus, the numerator of the ratio, sales, was not always under management control, but instead, depended on other characteristics of the company's operating environment.

Third, companies that billed consumers after providing services had stretched-out collection periods, while companies that demanded prior payment fared much better. Thus the water and wastewater

Graph 5.7: Ratio of Accounts Receivable to Sales
(Average percentage by group)

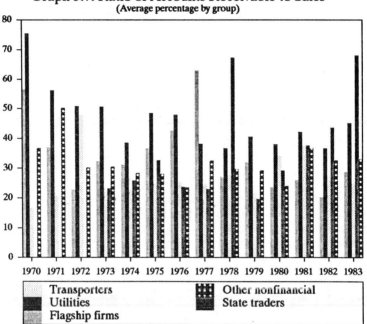

companies, ESAL in Lima and ESAR in Arequipa, generally had ratios exceeding 50 percent, which meant that their bills remained unpaid for an average of 180 days. Even with improvements after 1980, the ratio never fell below 40 percent, still almost a five month delay in payment. ENATRU, Lima's bus company, provides a surprise. Ranked worst according to most other indicators, it chalked up the lowest ratio of accounts receivable to sales of any major public company, generally less than 3 percent. Having passengers pay on boarding the busses relieved ENATRU of the need to prepare invoices and statements or to maintain customer accounts.

Inventory Management

Companies need an efficient inventory policy. Since stocks weigh heavily in total assets, improvements in inventory control can have positive financial repercussions (Sishtla, 1982:31–39). Inventories normally comprise raw materials, work in progress, and finished goods awaiting sale. As a general rule, an adequate inventory policy insulates stages in the production and distribution process from each other. For example, a finished goods' inventory acts as a cushion between production and sales; likewise, a raw materials' inventory protects against irregularities in the arrival of supplies, a cushion that is particularly necessary in developing countries where management practices and suppliers' shortfalls may make the implementation of just-in-time inventory systems impractical. During inflationary periods, inventories have a speculative element: A finished goods' inventory may be built up in expectation of a rise in prices; a raw materials' inventory rise may delay the repercussions of increasing input prices.

A common finding is that public enterprises hold excessive inventories. This has been explained by management inexperience, higher EOQs (economic order quantities) to compensate for delays in government approval, and risk aversion to downtime caused by the lack of spare parts (Ramanadham, 1974:171). This section examines two ratios to determine the influence of government-imposed environmental factors in setting inventory levels.

Inventory Turnover Ratio. The inventory turnover ratio, defined as the ratio of sales to inventory, is commonly used by management to monitor short-term trends. It can also indicate changes over a longer period. A high ratio indicates that management can move the company's inventory quickly. Low ratios indicate the opposite, i.e. that substantial resources are tied up in stocks. Because Peru's public enterprises undertake widely differing activities, only general comparisons may be made within or across groups [See graph 5.8].

The Peruvian data do not substantiate the finding that public enterprises hold excessive inventories. Approximately half the sectoral averages exceed 8.0, equivalent to an inventory turnover of only 6 weeks. The Peruvian figures better Prakash's data showing that only one Indian firm had a ratio greater than 2.3 (inventory turnover exceeding 5 months) (1971:297).

Flagship sector ratios of between 4 and 3 were among the lowest, dragged down by SIDERPERU's extraordinarily high inventory levels that, at times, exceeded sales. SIDERPERU provides an isolated example of an inadequate inventory policy. As might be expected, ratios for transporters and for other nonfinancial firms were much higher. Moreover, there is always room for improvement in inventory management. For example, PETROPERU's 1984 annual report boasted of implementing a manual inventory control system for its Talara operations while describing sophisticated economic, financial, and technical simulation models developed by its informatics division (1984:32,36). Computerizing engineering applications while keeping inventories manually obviously deprives management of a potent cost-cutting tool.

Inventory Asset Ratios. The ratio of inventory to total assets examines the relative importance of inventories in the balance sheet. Managers use the ratio to monitor changes in inventory levels. Graph 5.9 presents the data. The standard caveats about cross-sector comparisons apply.

Peru's inventory-asset ratios do not support the generalized findings about excessive inventory holdings. It confirms that holding

128

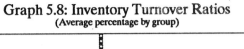

Graph 5.8: Inventory Turnover Ratios
(Average percentage by group)

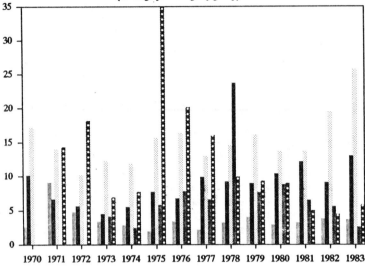

Graph 5.9: Inventory Asset Ratios
(Average percentage by group)

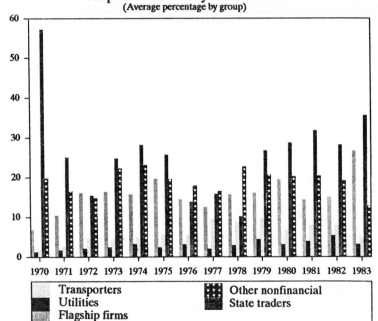

Transporters
Utilities
Flagship firms

Other nonfinancial
State traders

patterns are sector specific. Utilities and transporters have low ratios, usually lower than 5 percent of total assets. The flagship firms and state traders have higher ratios that only occasionally dip below 15 percent. Leaving aside EPCHAP's and EPSA's exceptionally high ratios at the beginning of the decade, a pattern emerges of generally rising ratios for most sectors throughout the period.

The rises were due to exogenous government policies. For example, increases in transport sector ratios largely reflected increased stocks of spare parts for the railway, ENAFER, and bus company, ENATRU, because they faced negative consequences for having vehicles immobilized. To keep their largely foreign stock rolling, managers increased inventories on imported items to cover delays of complying with more stringent foreign exchange regulation (interview, 1978).

Conclusions

Widespread portfolio or cross-sectoral similarities in efficiency ratios indicate that government authorities strongly influenced the public enterprise operating environment. The more a ratio depended on factors under central government influence, the more its movements fit the period analysis of overall government movements. Patterns in the evolution of the relation between sales and the cost of goods sold, selling and administrative expenses, and accounts receivable fit the period analysis better than do patterns in inventory ratios. Detailed analysis of the ratios indicates that efficiency did not result from government guidance of company management.[25] The less elements of a ratio depended on government directives or control, the better the ratio level and vice versa. It follows as no surprise that inventories, over which managers exercised the most direct control, showed the best ratios.

PROFITS

Profitability has re-emerged as a public enterprise criterion. Earlier writings downgraded profits as a measure of performance since the "public" dimension implies meeting non-economic objectives,[26] recent work has stressed the "enterprise" notion and returned to profits as a measure of how well costs are covered or how great a return is made on investment as well as for the sense of discipline it provides management.[27] Profitability indicators are easily extracted from financial statements. Examination of portfolio profits through two measures, the ratios of operating profits to sales and of accounting profits to net worth, leads to startling conclusions and buttresses the need for a proper working environment.

It should be emphasized that profits do not measure public enterprise efficiency. Firms can be technically efficient, yet have low profits because their prices were held down by government fiat. Alternatively, when a public enterprise enjoys a monopoly market position, earning high profits reveals nothing about technical efficiency.[28] Profits have a useful role in indicating which enterprises or sectors perform better than others as a result of their environment.

Ratio of Operating Profits to Sales

The ratio of operating profits to sales is known as the operating profit margin. It measures a nonfinancial company's success in deriving profit from its activities undistorted by financial income, by rents on properties, by interest or other financial payments, and by taxes. Because the calculation of operating profits depends on how individual companies account for profits on long-term contracts, for depreciation, and for intangibles, little cross-firm or cross-sector comparison can be justified. However, a focus on operating profits indicates where pricing controls generated insufficient revenue to cover costs of production, sales, and distribution. No benchmark ratios can be stated and the standard data caveats apply [See Graph 5.10].

A clear pattern emerges of generalized, often heavy, losses in the early 1970s, followed by widespread and moderate operating profits until 1980, and spectacular, increasing losses during the Belaúnde years.

Overall, flagship firms followed that pattern except for 1983, but each reveals the role of price setting.[29] For example, PETROPERU's ratio progressively deteriorated from 17 percent of sales in 1970 to –1 percent by 1973. The ratio plunged during the mid-1970s as rising OPEC prices exacerbated the effects of fixed domestic prices.

CENTROMIN was the sole flagship firm that did well for the entire period. Its ratio rarely dipped below 20 percent and the government did not set its prices.[30] Dore's conclusion that nationalizations, especially of the Cerro de Pasco Corporation "saddled the state with relatively unprofitable enterprises," appears unfounded because CENTROMIN generally performed better than the average government-owned firm (1977:98).

Utilities also conform to the pattern. When they showed losses, rate structures incapable of providing them with sufficient revenue to cover operating costs were usually to blame. For example, the joint venture that supplied power to the Piura region had a ratio that dropped from –69 percent in 1978 to –333 percent in 1983. The Comptroller's office blamed inadequate inter-enterprise pricing policies (CGR, 1982:I:141)

Among the state traders, food marketers were always forced to sell at a loss. By 1980, long-standing commitment to urban populism

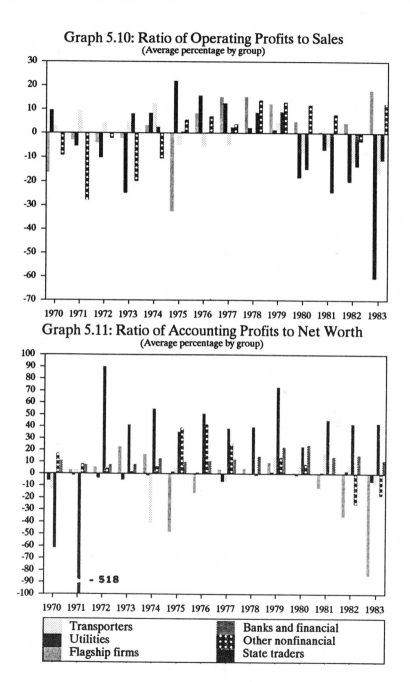

Graph 5.10: Ratio of Operating Profits to Sales
(Average percentage by group)

Graph 5.11: Ratio of Accounting Profits to Net Worth
(Average percentage by group)

Transporters
Utilities
Flagship firms

Banks and financial
Other nonfinancial
State traders

resulted in prices that covered only two-thirds of ECASA's costs in marketing rice. They also had been so low for so long that they had undermined potato's position as a staple. Similarly, the government set bus fares. The Lima bus company's ratio was persistently negative and increased to almost 50 percent by the decade's end. The other nonfinancial firms usually escaped government price controls. They showed positive ratios for every year after 1974.

Ratio of Accounting Profits to Net Worth

Return on capital employed, measured by a company's net worth, is a key indicator of economic success or failure in managing a business. It is the principal ratio that should interest the government in its role as shareholder and it sums up a firm's economic objectives in one convenient number.[31]

The portfolio yielded a positive nominal return on equity in every year until 1982, a startling finding, given the conventional wisdom about widespread losses. Nominal return on portfolio equity ranged from 1.3 percent in 1976 to 6.0 percent in 1979. The rate of return figures also fit the period analysis. The rates were generally low during the early 1970s; fluctuated during the mid-1970s, reflecting internal policy dissension; rose noticeably toward the end of the decade; and became negative under the Belaúnde administration. The sectors followed the same pattern as the portfolio. Graph 5.11 provides information on the nominal rates of return to net worth for major sectors.

Real rates of return, after removing inflationary effects, were always negative.[32] They too fit the period framework, with the greatest real loss rates from 1978 to 1983. In all fairness to the firms, it must be emphasized that neither companies nor monitoring agencies followed real rates of return.

On the basis of nominal rates of return, Peru's public enterprises may be divided into two groups: "losers" and "winners." The traditional economic losers are those companies that most fit the public enterprise popular stereotype. They showed consistent deficits from year to year, usually had heavy extra-entrepreneurial burdens, and often predated 1968. They were concentrated in food marketing and urban transport.

For example, under the Velasco administration, losses for EPSA's food marketing were staggering. In 1971, they amounted to more than 1,000 percent of net worth. From 1972 to 1974, they were not calculated because the net worth was negative and EPSA showed accounting losses. Similarly poor performance plagued the bus company, ENATRU. In 1973, its losses amounted to 1,600 percent of net worth.[33] In 1971 and 1972, both return and net worth were negative. Other transport companies showed severe losses.

AEROPERU, in 1974, lost more than 200 percent of net worth and during the following two years, it had negative net worth coupled with losses.

Winners, in marked contrast, are those companies whose nominal accounting profits were consistently positive. They do not conform to popular stereotypes, and were often formed after 1968 for the "strategic" reasons of replacing private domination of a complete sector with a monopoly public enterprise. In general, state traders were winners. EPCHAP's return on net worth was always more than 24 percent and ENCI's only twice dipped below 15 percent. MINPECO's return ranged from 57 to 102 percent from 1974 to 1978, but never recovered from the silver-induced loss in 1979. The BN, another obvious winner, had yearly profit rates that only once dipped below 27 percent.

Conclusions

Careful data analysis has demonstrated that the profitability of Peru's public enterprises is linked to two key variables: the choice of profit measure and the degree of government intervention. Because the government undercapitalized its firms and forced them to pay substantial interest on borrowed funds, the companies showed low return to net worth. Because the government forced many companies to sell at a loss, they had negative operating profit margins.

Choksi hypothesized that non-quantitative or environmental aspects of poor performance, including state intervention in the management decisions, unclear multiple objectives, and political patronage, are more robust indicators of poor social or economic performance of public enterprises than are quantitative measures of financial profitability (1979:44). This chapter qualifies two key areas of Choksi's hypothesis. First, it shows that environmental factors condition good performance as well as poor. Second, it shows strong links between financial indicators and external environmental factors.

CONCLUSIONS

The standard tool of ratio analysis applied to company-level data in this chapter reveals the effects of government policies on financial soundness and stability, internal efficiency, and profitability. Similar patterns for most ratios were found at portfolio and sector levels.

Companies were usually illiquid. They were forced to operate in a severely restricted financial environment by a government that failed to adequately capitalize its public enterprises, failed to pay its debts on time, and failed to enforce a system of prompt and timely inter-enterprise payments.

Companies were sometimes efficient. The more a ratio depended on factors under central government influence, the more they tended to be inefficient. Greater government guidance did not provide an environment conducive to efficiency; on the contrary, greater autonomy did.

The portfolio was always profitable. Many companies were, too. Because the government undercapitalized some and forced them into heavy borrowing, they earned low rates of return to net worth. Because the government forced others to sell below cost, they had negative operating profit margins.

This chapter links environmental factors to performance. To the extent that companies' problems resulted from the unhealthy environment imposed on them by government, then the system has been at fault, not management, and government must bear major responsibility for resolving the problems it created.

NOTES

1. The extrapolation of portfolio behavior from that of a few large companies is a common public enterprise problem. Trebat addresses the big company problem, but does not resolve it (1983:6).
2. Flagship firms include: PETROPERU, ELECTROPERU, MINEROPERU, SIDERPERU, PESCAPERU, and CENTROMIN; the utilities include providers of water and electricity; and the major banks are:BIP, BANVIPE, BN, BAP, COFIDE, AND BANMINERO. Service companies, such as the agricultural research institute, the official newspaper, and the government press agency are omitted from the ratio analysis.
3. Government invariably set the maximum legally-permitted revaluations at less than the accumulated inflation they were designed to compensate.
4. Similar conclusions have been reached for African public enterprises. For Nigeria, see Fubara (1983), for Senegal and Ghan, see Killick (1981:49-50).
5. In Peru, the two major accounting differences which influence the current ratio, but which are not universally applied, are that some firms consider unpaid government subsidies to be current assets and that others make inadequate provisions for bad debts.
6. Cotler claimed that the public enterprises were only underfinanced after 1974 (1983:26). Data show that the 1970s were a period of perpetual crisis.
7. In 1970, ENAPU's cash holdings were S/. 314 million, compared to total current liabilities of S/. 45 million (DGCoP, 1972?:282-283). By 1973, its cash balance exceeded S/. 500 million, and for 1974, it dropped to slightly less than S/. 400 million, representing 64.5

percent and 39.4 percent respectively of the current assets (DGCoP, 1975?:762–764).

8. As with the current ratios, during the more difficult financial conditions of the 1970s, a slightly lower quick ratio was found to be acceptable (Samuels et al., 1981:272).

9. The current value of EPCHAP's inventories fell from S/. 3.6 billion in 1970 to S/. 2.6 million in 1971 (DGCoP, 1972?:220–222, and 1973?:151).

10. A UNIDO report defined public enterprise debt as excessive when the company could not meet combined interest and repayment obligations or it was forced to neglect priority targets. Conversely, equity levels were excessive when they undermined management's financial performance incentives (1970:14–15). The report did not adopt a target debt-equity ratio, noting that countries have often adopted them in practice. Peru had no general guidelines.

11. The argument that unpaid taxes often represent disguised equity is valid only if they remain unpaid, the result when Peru converted taxes to equity in 1980. Jones proposed excluding taxes from performance criteria as they are included in overall public sector returns (1983:13–14) however, from the manager's viewpoint, they represent a claim on company resources.

12. The calculation of this ratio presumes a correct valuation of all the company's assets.

13. This is equivalent to another accepted rule of thumb, that the debt/equity ratio be close to 1.0. Having half of total assets financed by debt, means that the other half must be financed by equity. The debt/equity ratio must therefore be one if the debt ratio is one-half.

14. With a government guarantee, the lender may gauge a loan not by looking at the projected financial state of the enterprise but at that of the nation. See Jenkins (1978b).

15. Most borrowing went to cover the exchange rate differential between the time that a debt was contracted and the time of payment. The Central Bank estimated that over 75 percent of PETROPERU's financial expenditures in 1976 went to cover exchange differentials (1977:45).

16. A thorough analysis of the effects of working capital deficits on public enterprises, is found in UN, DESA (1976b:59–61).

17. Chapter 4 analyzes the effects of government failure to pay subsidies on time; Chapter 6 examines inter-company accounts payable. Fubara (1983) indicates that intra-government payment problems were widespread and the major source of working capital difficulties for Nigeria's public enterprises.

18. Tello (1983:II:229). See below, Chapter 6.

19. The Peruvian case may support Aharoni's contention that governments may deliberately undercapitalize companies to limit

managerial discretion by forcing management to repeatedly beg
funds from the government (1981:189).
20. Saulniers (1983). Others have also found little or no difference
between public and private firms. Shepherd found similar
managerial motivations and performance in the United States
and Britain (1976b:118). Marsan noted that Italy's IRI companies
outperformed private firms in 5 of 8 years from 1968 to 1975
(1981:156). Pryke found for Great Britain and for international
firms in fuel, power and transport that public companies made
significantly better technical efficiency gains during the 1960s than
did private ones (1971:433–457).
21. Sales include receipts from the activities of selling goods or
services for the year, net of any excise taxes. Taxes are important,
as some public enterprises, for example, PETROPERU and
ENATA, served as the major tax collection agencies.
22. Ivan Turk presupposes away these three thorny problems in a
proposed methodology to analyze the socio-economic efficiency
of public enterprises (1984). Because his proposed ratios employ
data not found in income statements, balance sheets, or flow of
funds statements, their practical application needs new systems of
company and government accounts.
23. Sishtla reviews major receivables problems from a management
development perspective (1982:41–50).
24. The ratio is another way of examining the average collection
period. Thus, a ratio of 25 percent means that the average
account remains unpaid for approximately 90 days, while a ratio
to 50 percent means a delay of 180 days.
25. Becker takes an opposite view based largely on government
pronouncements (1983:66).
26. See Sherif (1973:21–27) and Turk (1984) for other measures of
performance.
27. Fernandes (1986:52–56) and Ayub and Hegstad (1986).
28. Pryke argued strongly against using profit rates to examine
allocative efficiency (1971:437–442). See also Sherif (1973:15).
The standard view, that low rates of return indicate incorrect
capital allocation away from more profitable and more
productive uses in the economy, assumes that alternative
investment would have taken place, an unviable alternative in
Peru during the early military period.
29. After 1980, the MITI tried to estimate as economic cost of
production and increased accounting figures to reflect estimates
of the opportunity cost of capital and of "optimal" depreciation.
The reports stated an anti-public firm bias and did not
compensate for the income foregone by forced pursuit of non--
economic objectives, while applying judgmental factors to raise
accounting costs. See MITI (1981a to e). Gray provides a more
complete methodology for examining economic costs (1984).

30. Becker's reports lower rates of return based on a different measure, the ratio of accounting profits to sales adjusted for the effects of export taxes (1983:156).

31. Reserves and undistributed profits are included in net worth. This may cause a downward bias of ratios for Peru's public enterprises that awaited government decisions on profits disposition, for as much as six years, while the funds were not fully available for company use.

32. The year end interest rate on COFIDE type "C" bonds served as a crude measure of the opportunity cost of capital. For 1970, the interest rate payable on Agricultural Bank development bonds was employed. Although the bond rate always remained below the rise in the consumer price index or the GDP deflator, however, it indicates the public sector opportunity cost of capital. Private investors faced with a wider variety of available alternatives, had a higher opportunity cost of capital.

33. Data for ENATRU while under local government administration were deleted from the average graphed in 5.11 for reasons of visual clarity.

6

A Systems Approach to Public Enterprises

INTRODUCTION

Two different perspectives structure public enterprise management systems. The first, commonly known as the "accountability problem," addresses the design of a system that forces managers or that gives them appropriate incentives to align company operations with what the central government authorities define as the "public good." It focuses on hierarchical or instrumental control and has been widely analyzed in the public enterprise literature.[1] Chapter 3 detailed the problems that Peru faced in designing an effective strategy definition and control system.

The second perspective accepts that public enterprises are independent units with limited autonomy in planning, goals, finance, and administration. It addresses how company managers can make decisions with limited government intervention to align company operations with that same "public good." It focuses on the firm in the microeconomic sense and its policy prescriptions stress specialized management training (Ramanadham, 1974:127–181). Chapters 4 and 5 concluded that Peru's managers were stymied because their public firms faced a crippling politico-economic environment.

Both perspectives, called, for convenience, the "top-down" and the "atomistic," fail to adequately account for links between public enterprises and the central government institutions or other public enterprises that comprise a major part of the overall politico-economic environment. In practice, companies come under the jurisdiction of many different central government executive agencies concerning, for example, controls over foreign exchange, investment decisions, hiring, and firing.[2] Incompatibility among the controllers' functions, policy disagreements among them, struggles over bureaucratic territory, or slow or cumbersome procedures would have a strong impact on the financial, economic, or social viability of public enterprises. Firms also interact with each other, most commonly as purchaser and supplier, but they may also collaborate in joint ventures or projects.

Thus, many determinants of performance and profit are exogenous to the public firm, determined instead by government bureaucrats or by executives in other companies. Because managers cannot control key facets of their companies' performance, the results of increased control from a top-down perspective or of improved management training from an atomistic perspective fall short of expectations without complementary efforts to improve system relationships (Ramanadham, 1972:4).

This chapter presumes that state action was not unified, unlike most other works on Peru including government documents.[3] Earlier chapters have shown fragmented control systems and differentiated economic and financial performance, findings which support theoretical and empirical work on intergovernmental policy studies.[4]

Chapter 6 scrutinizes part of Peru's institutional environment for public enterprises, namely, relations to other functionally and legally differentiated executive agencies, as the source of external limits on management autonomy.[5] A close look at that environment leads to a systems model of behavioral constraints within a decentralized administration framework, a model which complements some public choice analyses of federal, state, or local decision making.[6]

Chapter 6 concentrates on elements of public enterprise performance, which lie beyond company management's control because they depend on decisions taken in other institutions or at different decision levels. Achieving company objectives becomes a function of company relations across levels and across functional boundaries (Hanf, 1978:2). Some elements lie beyond management's direct control because they comprise the public policy definitional basis for the entire public enterprise system and include such issues as formation of a government enterprise philosophy and its legal embodiment. Other elements lie beyond management control because they comprise the relational substructure for implementing public policy; they include direct or indirect, bilateral or hierarchical ties among central government agencies and enterprises. These links are analyzed for the Peruvian case. Understanding the framework of linkages between interdependent government units is essential to improving performance by designing adequate policy coordination mechanisms.

GENERAL GOVERNMENT ISSUES

Two issues comprise the key decision fields facing government in creating a viable environment for public firms. Philosophical issues provide the rationale for creating or liquidating companies. They include specification of company roles in society or the economy, their goals, and their strategies. Legal issues translate the philosophical basis into a working legal-institutional environment to structure public enterprise action. This section examines both types of issues.

Philosophical Issues

Defining a national philosophy concerning public enterprises or achieving a national consensus on their roles, their goals, and their strategies is essential to devising and implementing stable and successful policies.[7] Common ways of achieving a consensus include discussion, arguments, and resolutions of conflicting ideas and policies. However, Peru's government always lacked an overall public enterprise philosophy and showed no urgency in developing one. The double deficiency led to several negative consequences. Although the government amassed a portfolio of powerful companies, which accounted for a sizeable proportion of GDP, investment, and other macro indicators, it never resolved how to use them effectively to reach recognized ends. Indeed, the ends themselves constantly changed. Those at top government levels considered issues on a case-by-case basis and never confronted the need to define a coherent public enterprise philosophy.[8]

The military government's inability to define a public enterprise philosophy strongly parallels its inability to define an overall philosophy. As Villanueva put it succinctly, "[t]he military never truely [sic] succeeded in establishing an independent set of theoretical precepts to orient the transformation of society" (1982:162). Moreover, its "neither capitalist nor communist" slogan revealed an inherent ideological uncertainty (Cleaves and Scurrah, 1980:255). An informed insider in the public enterprise decision making process, Azi Wolfenson, convincingly argued that the missing consensus resulted in the government's repeatedly declaring itself an entrepreneur, while shirking entrepreneurial responsibility by depriving its companies of sufficient economic, financial, and institutional resources (1981:149).

The flurry of different draft versions of a normative law of state entrepreneurial activity, that circulated at top policy-making levels from late 1977 to mid-1979, most approached a debate on public enterprise philosophy [See chapter 2]. The drafts, several of which circulated simultaneously, were marked by a set of apparent philosophical disagreements that blocked compromise on and approval of any one particular version. However, while couched in philosophical terms, intra-governmental power disputes between CIAEF, INP, MEF, COFIDE, and the BCRP were behind some of the apparent disagreement. The relative policy differences may be summed up as a dispute between the dirigiste notions of the INP and its allies, which postulated well-defined policies and control mechanisms, and the flexible posture of CIAEF, which wanted to keep open a wide range of future policy options.[9] The disagreement led to important policy problems including confusion over company objectives, uncoordinated pricing structures, and contradictory legal bases for control.

For example, CIAEF drafts proposed centralized decision making by Silva Ruete's committee that would coordinate and recommend public enterprise policy to the cabinet, evaluate policy implementation, and represent the government on all company boards. Such a naked attempt to seize power aroused the opposition of other groups within the government including COFIDE and the BCRP, whose public enterprise roles diminished with successive drafts, and the INP which, although totally written out of early drafts, later was included as a rubber stamp for CIAEF-specified policies.

For illustrative purposes only, I shall mention the most fundamental of these philosophical cum power disagreements.[10] First, drafts showed little consensus on which public enterprises would be regulated. A version first proposed by the 1976 Multisectoral Commission would have included all government holdings, both direct or indirect, whereas drafts prepared by CIAEF limited coverage to those firms legally considered public enterprises. Second, versions clashed on the objectives for a government presence in the economy. A never-resolved controversy pitted the notion of "instrumentality," public enterprises as multipurpose instruments of a planned development policy, against "objectivity," where public enterprises are esteemed as standardbearers of a government presence. Third, versions disagreed on the scope of public enterprise activity. CIAEF favored the flexibility of having no previously fixed scope of action so that the government could undertake new ventures or drop old ones as priorities changed. INP pushed for a fixed specification of sectors subject to government monopoly or dominance. The Multisectoral Commission took an intermediate position which combined initial specification of activities with periodic redefinition by a proposed interministerial committee. Finally, versions also disagreed over shareholding patterns, control over policymaking, institutional organization, investment decisionmaking, production levels, financing, profits disposition, and budgeting. Overall, there was little policy congruence.

The post-1980 civilian government proved no better in defining a public enterprise philosophy. Although the Belaúnde administration promulgated the uniform legal code that earlier governments proved incapable of passing, some government factions refused to accept the bylaws and had them suspended [See below]. Passing D.Leg. 216, and hailing it as the long-awaited solution to many public enterprise problems only masked the blatant inability of successive administrations to reach an internal consensus.

Objectives. In Peru, deep-seated and irreconcilable philosophical or power differences led to many problems. In particular, stating objectives, whether for the portfolio or for specific companies, often served as a means of temporarily reconciling positions of conflicting intra-governmental interest groups instead of providing the companies with clear guidelines for action.[11] It must also be recognized that the portfolio's creation through hodgepodge agglomeration added to the problems of defining objectives. Moncloa rightly argued that sheer confusion explained the public enterprises' inability to fulfill their "revolutionary" social, political or economic objectives, resulting in catastrophic inefficiency (1977:118–119).

Two currents mark the general literature: public enterprises need to have clear and attainable objectives[12] and their multiple economic, social, and political objectives often conflict.[13] Close analysis of the laws creating Peru's companies reveals that, on the contrary, they rarely received clear objectives and that discernable emphasis was placed on social or political goals; economic goals, if indeed they existed, were usually left unstated.[14] In sharp contrast, private companies all have, according to Article 1 of the law of mercantile societies, "the goal of distributing profits" (L.16123). Table 6.1 lists objectives, given to selected companies, that clearly show "the state has not defined nor does it assign to its state enterprises social objectives [that are] capable of being adequately measured and evaluated" (INAP, 1978c:4). Even after reorganizing most companies in 1981, the Peruvian government never explicitly told them to earn a profit. Rather, profit became an indirect secondary goal via the law of mercantile societies. Choksi raises an issue that, based on the analysis of Chapter 2, may be valid for Peru: vague and unclear goals for public enterprises arise because desired results are vague and unclear to the goal setters (1979:42).

Three issues compounded the problem of defining objectives: explicit, but largely unmeasurable, social goals assigned at the time of company creation were inconsistent with implicit and measurable, commercial and financial goals set in response to short-term economic considerations; the ongoing processes of merger or dissolution of companies muddled or melded their goals; and short-term goals multiplied as government forced firms to take on more tasks.

For example, companies were mandated to service one or more client groups and to provide for workers' welfare; they were rarely given a market orientation. Thus, ENATA, the tobacco manufacturer, was told to produce and market tobacco and tobacco products, to purchase domestic production, to undertake research and development, and to foster the "social, cultural, professional and technical development of workers" (D.L. 18854); it was not told to earn a profit, to minimize its costs, nor to channel excises to the government. Large firms such as MINEROPERU or PETROPERU were expected to manage the government's vaguely identified sectoral interests with little clarification about other management objectives (D.L. 20035 and 20036). ENTEL's objective of providing an efficient telecommunications system was a rare exception to the overwhelmingly social or political orientation (D.L. 17881).

TABLE 6.1: Objectives of Selected Public Enterprises

OLD [Pre-1981]	NEW [Post-1981]
PETROPERU: to develop or contract for studies, works, and other ventures including exploration, production, refining, marketing, and transport of petroleum, hydrocarbons, and petrochemicals; to create subsidiaries if necessary; to promote and do research and development; to provide for its workers' social, cultural, professional and technical development. D.L.20036	to carry out state industrial and commercial activities for petroleum and related hydrocarbons, including petrochemicals; to act with economic, financial, and administrative autonomy within the goal structure fixed by the Ministry of Energy and Mines; and to preserve the environment by anticipating, controlling, and avoiding contamination. D.Leg.43
SIDERPERU: to produce and market steel and related products; to carry out planned investment, production, and promotional programs; to increase market share; to promote steel industry development; to research and develop steel and steel industry inputs; to foster its workers' social, cultural, professional and technical development. D.L.19034	to develop all steel and related or complementary manufacturing or marketing activities; with the approval of its board of directors, SIDERPERU may pursue mining, metallurgy, power supplies, and all other activities related to the production of inputs or marketing. D.S.023-81-ITI-IND
AEROPERU: to assure efficient and economical transport service which contributes to Peru's integration and socioeconomic development, as executing agency for government plans and policies. D.L.20030	to undertake national and international air transport of passengers, freight, and mail; to carry out all other air services; and to foster international tourism. D.S.158-81-EF
MINEROPERU: to carry out state entrepreneurial activities; to participate in joint ventures; to market minerals; to draw up and execute plans to promote mining. D.L.20035	to carry out state mining and related industrial activities, both directly and indirectly; to participate in joint ventures; to act with economic, financial, and administrative autonomy within the goal structure fixed by the Ministry of Energy and Mines; and to preserve the environment by anticipating, controlling, and avoiding contamination. D.Leg.42
ENATA: to make and market cigars, cigarettes, and pipe tobacco; to buy domestic tobacco production; to carry out research and development; to provide for its workers' social, cultural, professional, and technical development. D.L.18854	to make cigarettes, cigars, pipe tobacco, and other similar products, including any needed inputs; and to market those products and tobacco leaf at home or internationally. D.S.038-81-ITI-IND
EPAPRODE: to regulate, promote, and transact betting on the results of soccer matches, whether held in Peru or abroad, and to funnel the revenues obtained to the development of a national system for recreation, physical education, and sports. D.L.21091	EPADESA: to undertake and promote contests predicting the results of sporting events held both at home or abroad. D.Leg.255

EPSA clearly showed the effects of a constantly shifting and increasingly confused situation. In 1969, it was formed from bits and pieces of the SSPI and Ministry of Agriculture and given broad and diverse goals - to increase agricultural production and productivity; to develop marketing infrastructure for agricultural inputs and output; and to stabilize domestic prices (D.L. 17734). After the 1969 ministry reforms, EPSA lost jurisdiction over any fishing activities and it was stripped of guano and fertilizer operations in 1970.[15] By 1976, EPSA's directors were themselves uncertain about the company's objectives. They ranked their three goals as: consumer price regulation, assuring adequate food supplies, and producer price support (Comisión, 1977e:Anexo 1:7).

Unclear company objectives either to central government officials or to company executives resulted in unclear company operating strategies. Hanson theorized that originally vague and general goals may become clearer with an accumulation of experience and analysis (1968:98). This rarely happened in Peru, as shown by TAS top executives who, four years after their companies were created, didn't knew whether the principal objective was to assure steady food supplies or to control food prices; moreover, they didn't know whether the firms were even supposed to earn profits.[16] The example substantiates El-Namaki's finding, that "entrepreneurial objectives...are grossly misunderstood" (1979:150). Although an ECLA study stated that "clarifying objectives and making them known is often as good a promoter of efficiency as is the introduction of new techniques" (1969a:12), the Peruvian government obscured and changed objectives, which promoted inefficiency.

Lacking clear centralized direction, management repeatedly proposed an agenda of micro-entrepreneurial objectives, but government authorities placed many agenda items beyond management control. Profitability and pricing objectives depended on government pricing and product decisions [See below]. Most investment projects were subject to long, drawn-out scrutiny, but, in some cases, political authorities thrust investment on the companies. For example, SUPEREPSA was forced, over strenuous management objections, to open a new store in Southern Peru, far from its normal supply lines and without prior market survey because President Morales Bermúdez announced the headline grabbing project on a trip to the region (interview, 1979). Government authorities often vetoed improved financing. As a consequence, MINPECO, while trying to convince officials to remedy its undercapitalization, placed taxes and profits remissions into an escrow account.[17] Government authorities also controlled commercial objectives. For example, ENCI's management was only consulted once concerning changes to its product line (interview, 1979).

Confusion about objectives also provided an unstable basis for company policies because management could not accurately assign weights to specified or implied multiple objectives while government never assigned priorities. Consequently, government authorities had no firm basis to control or to evaluate companies. In addition, the government never circumscribed objectives to limit "instrumental abuse," the inefficient use of public enterprises to meet objectives better handled by other means (Boneo, 1981a:II.3). Instead, constantly changing, unclear objectives flung the enterprises into incoherence, contradiction, and anarchy. The problem grew so acute that authorities openly recommended that the government should "establish *clearly stated* objectives, goals and programs" (INAP, 1979c) [italics mine].

Control. Relations between a government and its public enterprises, codified in the control system, constitute another global issue. Some control is necessary to monitor both the macroeconomic impact of company actions and its microeconomic, social, or political results. In Peru, the missing national consensus resulted in a poorly organized control system, which led, in turn, to the erroneous view, common in top government echelons, that any public enterprise-related problem arose from inadequate government control. Government authorities tried simplistic remedies that degenerated into continually heaping ad hoc, uncoordinated, and contradictory control mechanisms on the companies that served only to hamper and frustrate management and to degrade performance [See also Chapter 3].[18] The comptroller's office, charged with enforcement, publicly referred to Peru's "cult of control" (CGR, 1978:17). Devotion to that cult typified the suggestion, made by a high-ranking MEFC official, that the only method of controlling public enterprise deficits was *fastidiarlas y crear trabas* ("to bother them and to create obstacles") (interview, November 1981).

Peru clearly fit Boneo's analysis of the general Latin American situation: "the excess of external controls tends to suffocate initiative, entrepreneurial spirit and the tendency to assume risks, which are [all] prerequisites for entrepreneurial behavior" (1981a:II.20). The results of Peru's control cult support the ECLA theory that "control procedures designed to prevent presupposed mistakes and to guard against potential irresponsibility in effect create the very carelessness they are meant to suppress" (ECLA, 1969a:15).

Prices. Price policy is a special case of the control issue. Adequate public enterprise prices are crucial to the companies' economic success, financial health, and social efficiency; adequate price setting mechanisms help assure adequate prices. Peru's government rarely fixed public enterprise prices on the basis of any rational and consistent general principles. Such principles might have included: maximize net economic benefits by considering managerial costs; break even on current costs; provide normal returns to capital; or maximize net social benefits by carefully considering the costs and benefits to various classes or income groups. Instead, the government often set prices for purely political advantage on an ad hoc basis that was inconsistent with company wellbeing and led to severe distortions in the economy.

Although the plans espoused financially independent public enterprises whose prices reflected costs, so that they generated profits and had no need for subsidies, the pricing system often produced the opposite and forced the public enterprises into subsidy dependence.[19] Setting public enterprise prices, especially those for consumer items, posed constant economic, political, and religious dilemmas for government authorities. For example, President Velasco is reported to have been adamant that the peasants should be satisfied with better access to land provided by the agrarian reform and should not press for more benefits in the form of higher farmgate prices (Schydlowsky and Wicht, 1983:104). In marked contrast, General Tantalean wrote that the only food price rises permitted by the government were those that benefited the peasants (1978:112). Religious arguments were invoked for price stability. Miguel Angel de la Flor, Minister of Foreign Affairs, relates that President Velasco opposed food price rises by reminding government officials of a verse in the Lord's Prayer (Tello, 1983:I:46).

Regime rhetoric intended for public consumption stressed concern for Peru's poor and humble majority. Consequently, raising prices may have made financial sense for companies and been healthy for the economy, but some members of the coalition felt that the effects on the poor would contradict the regime's ideological bases (Lê Châu, 1982:206). Such arguments were often erroneously based on upper- or middle-class urban consumption patterns that were extrapolated to the entire country. For example, the price of gasoline was held well below world market levels to benefit the poor. However, government analysts later found that most direct and indirect benefits of the policy were concentrated in the top 3 percent of income earners (interview, 1978). An IBRD study later concluded that gasoline subsidies were clearly regressive, those on diesel probably neutral, while those on kerosene for domestic use were slightly progressive (1981:24). Similarly, "social" electric rates, almost the lowest in Latin America (Kuczynski, 1982:71), were expected to benefit the poor. Data from Lima, the most densely electrified city, revealed that more than 25 percent of the residences lacked electricity and that the electric pricing structure was broadly regressive (Amat y León, 1977:136).

PETROPERU's pricing structure merits detailed attention [See Graph 6.1]. An early measure in June 1969 reduced the price of 84 octane gasoline by 10 percent, to boost the Velasco regime's popularity among the middle class. Prices thereafter remained fixed as the government insulated Peru from external markets and the 1973 world price hikes. In June 1975, several months before the regime shift, prices were raised. The change illustrates similarities between the late Velasco and early Morales Bermúdez regimes, which both allowed real prices to slowly drop before an abrupt price hike. It was not until 1976 that the real price of gasoline regained pre-1968 levels.

GRAPH 6.1: Index of Real Petroleum Prices: 1969-1985
(January 1974=100)   (5-month weighted moving average)

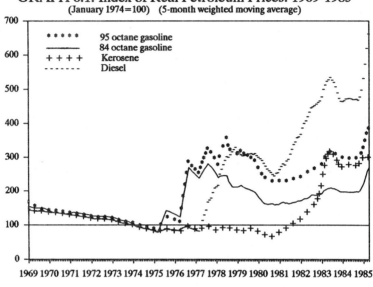

Source: 1968–1975 — IBRD, 1979:223; 1978–1979 — BCRP, 1979b; 1980 —
          BCRP, 1981; 1981–1985, BCRP, 1985a.

Comparison of monthly indexes of real prices for gasoline, kerosene, and diesel provides startling results about income distribution. President Velasco, alleged champion of the poor, let all prices slide equally, mostly benefiting the rich, who used petroleum products far more than the poor. Under Morales Bermúdez, prices of kerosene, mainly used by the poor, were held at low levels, while raising the real price of premium and regular gasoline, principally consumed by the highest income earners. Belaúnde administration officials upped the real price of kerosene, thereby taxing the poor. Although the Velasco administration's policy subsidized high income groups, the Morales Bermúdez administration's pricing policy resulted in PETROPERU becoming a de facto instrument of income redistribution via high gasoline prices. Stevens notes that stabilization measures hit the lowest income groups the hardest (1980:228), but because PETROPERU was the largest subsidy channel, the data presented above indicate that, before 1980, the upper income groups were hard hit.[20] After 1980, the poor paid more, in real terms, for kerosene than did the upper and middle classes for regular gasoline. The poor also lost out under Belaúnde from the dramatic rise in diesel prices, since diesel is a major input to urban mass transit and long-haul transport.

    Companies faced another pricing problem: the government often taxed away proceeds of price hikes, leaving little new revenue to the

TABLE 6.2
PETROPERU Prices per Gallon: 1978
(current soles and percentages)

Product		18 January 1978			31 December 1978		
		Net to PETROPERU	Taxes	Consumer Price	Net to PETROPERU	Taxes	Consumer Price
Gasoline 84	(S/.)	47.02	25.45	75.00	59.24	61.76	125.00
(% increase)		--	--	--	25.99	142.67	66.67
Gasoline 95	(S/.)	72.08	35.22	110.00	74.04	66.46	145.00
(% increase)		--	--	--	2.72	88.70	31.82
Kerosene[a]	(S/.)	9.47	0.53	10.00	12.30	2.70	15.00
(% increase)		--	--	--	29.88	409.43	50.00
Diesel 1[b]	(S/.)	16.78	13.22	30.00	45.77	27.23	73.00
(% increase)		--	--	--	172.77	105.98	143.33
Diesel 1[c]	(S/.)	25.11	21.89	47.00	57.90	38.88	98.00
(% increase)		--	--	--	130.59	77.62	108.51
Fuel Oil 5[b]	(S/.)	12.51	9.49	22.00	33.88	21.12	55.00
(% increase)		--	--	--	170.82	122.55	150.00
Fuel Oil 5[c]	(S/.)	12.51	9.49	22.00	39.65	32.35	72.00
(% increase)		--	--	--	216.95	240.89	227.27

a   Domestic use only
b   Coast and Sierra
c   Sales to large-scale mining
-- Not applicable
SOURCE: BCRP, 1979a:35.

company. Table 6.2, reports PETROPERU price changes during 1978 and shows the use of public enterprise as a convenient tax collector. For products with most direct consumer impact, gasoline and kerosene, the percentage increase in taxes far outweighed that in company revenue. Notably, for kerosene, PETROPERU's 30 percent income increase lagged far behind tax rises of more than 400 percent. Fuel oil sales to mining, then controlled by other public firms, showed the same pattern. Only new prices of diesel and fuel oil on the coast allowed company income to rise more than excise taxes. Whereas Peru's government viewed hidden taxation through pricing policy as politically acceptable, the literature criticizes the practice for causing significant economic distortions (UNIDO, 1970:17).

Peru's government had other bad price policies. In mid-1976, it tried to reduce subsidies by authorizing price rises on controlled items (D.L. 21532). Many firms requested increases under this legislation, however, ministries almost invariably scaled down requests by refusing to allow companies to cover costs plus a reasonable profit level.[21] Thus, prices bore little relation to the cost of production.

Legal Issues

Peruvian governments' reliance on executive acts often led to contradictory or incomplete laws about public enterprises. This section examines two such legal issues: problems caused by a missing overall framework and the inefficiencies resulting from the existing patchwork legal norms.

Missing Legal Frameworks. Until 1981, Peruvian public enterprises had no unified legal framework; thereafter, one was rejected, another negative result of the missing national consensus. As one noted jurist concluded after analyzing public enterprise regulations, "In Peru there are no general rules" (Monteverde 1979:1) because the civil code made firms subject to individual laws.[22] Individual laws may have suited the small pre-1968 portfolio, but over time they had a negative impact on company creation, management quality, and labor relations.[23]

The 1933 constitution did not specifically address the issue of public enterprises, however, several of its provisions governed their growth: government-owned monopolies and estancos were exempt from the constitutional prohibitions on monopolies (Article 16); all natural resources were considered government property that could be granted in concession to private individuals (Article 37); the state was empowered to nationalize all transports or public services (Article 38); and, if legally sanctioned, expropriation with just compensation was justifiable for the public good or social interest (Article 29). Thus, most experts concluded that the Constitution could be used to justify an expanded government role after 1970 (INAP, 1978a:16).

The 1979 Constitution tried to rectify the omission by providing an explicit basis for the state's entrepreneurial activity. It guaranteed economic pluralism through various types of property including public enterprises (Article 112); it stressed the role of government-owned firms to promote the economy, provide public services, and meet development objectives (Article 113); it legally grounded market reservation (Article 114); it reaffirmed that all natural resources were government property that could be granted in concession (Articles 118,119); it prohibited monopolies in industry and trade (Article 133); and it guaranteed freedom of the press (Article 134). Thus, although the 1979 Constitution mentioned public enterprises, its general and sometimes vague provisions could be used to justify either portfolio expansion or contraction.

A set of ad hoc, mutually inconsistent sectorial development laws, mentioned in Chapter 2, provided the legal basis for portfolio expansion during the early 1970s. The laws had several serious consequences for management. First, they never mandated profitability or businesslike conduct. Instead, they stressed service and social responsibility, often irregardless of cost to the company or the nation.

Second, companies had inconsistent creation and operating procedures. Statutes creating a public enterprise ordinarily specified its name, legal status, and objectives, endowed it with general and specific powers, prescribed its formal relations with government authorities, and provided it with a source of finance.[24] Monteverde lists five distinct combinations of creation laws, statutes, and regulations that the Peruvian government had employed by 1979 (1979:8–10). The inconsistent legal procedures resulted in some firms with unspecified operating procedures, while others were over-regulated; for some firms, undefined or blurred lines of responsibility left management unconstrained, while for others overbearing control systems eroded management responsibility.

Third, inconsistent legal bases weakened the companies' internal management structure. For example, boards of directors normally set top-level policy, represent government interest(s), and mediate between the government and the public enterprises, Fernandes, (1986:121–131). In Peru, boards were not mandated until February 1972, when D.L. 19603 set the composition, number, duration, and attributes for each company's board. The new legal basis led to a set of different problems.

First, the functions of some company boards were left unspecified because the company bylaws that specified them either were never issued or only appeared several years after a company's creation.

Second, board selection and appointment methods varied. Peru's system invariably named directors for too short a tenure. Most commonly, ministers named part-time board members to represent sectorial interests for a short, fixed term, usually two or three years.[25] Fernandes stressed that the stability and health of a public enterprise depend on adequate tenure for its board members, optimally between four to six years (1986:128). Peru fell far short of the optimum.

Third, additional inconsistencies marked whether members could be named for successive terms, the maximum number of terms they were permitted, and the appointment procedures involved. Short terms meant that the board composition could change each year, which forced managers to spend time in educating new board members about ongoing company operations (interview, 1979). Reducing turnover rates would have allowed operating management to concentrate more on the business of the firm and less on time-consuming didactic matters.

Fourth, high board turnover rates stymied consistent policy making. Table 6.3 presents such rates for selected companies from 1970 to 1980. The scanty available information shows that the average rate exceeded 50 percent per year. Rates exceeding 100 percent are found in almost every year. During 1980, after the government transition, most exceeded 100 percent as new cabinet ministers replaced virtually all board members, thereby confirming the precedence of political patronage over good management, a practice repeated by the García administration in 1985. Prakash indicates that a board member's key function is to ask intelligent questions (1971:180), but, by the time Peru's board members learned enough about company operations to begin asking intelligent questions, they were dropped. Other longitudinal evidence substantiates the excessive board

TABLE 6.3
Board of Directors' Turnover Rates: 1970–1980
(Percentages)

COMPANY	1970	1971	1972	1973	1974	1975	1976	1977	1978	1979	1980
BANMINERO	50	63	25	88	100	125	0	50	64	75	100
BANVIPE	n.a.	n.a.	38	13	n.a.	n.a.	50	n.a.	63	13	125
BAP	63	60	14	50	38	50	22	56	n.a.	n.a.	n.a.
BCHP	56	25	0	13	22	44	56	0	n.a.	n.a.	n.a.
BCRP	0	13	0	0	25	67	11	90	50	50	100
BIP	89	55	70	10	60	40	50	30	70	43	100
BN	33	17	17	0	33	50	43	57	133	14	100
CEMENTO ANDINO	--	--	--	--	100	0	167	71	11	50	100
CEMENTOS LIMA	--	--	--	--	n.a.	0	133	67	44	25	38
CENTROMIN	--	--	--	--	n.a.	78	89	22	78	67	67
COFIDE	--	0	117	33	8	50	15	50	17	136	100
CORPAC	n.a.	50	60	n.a.	n.a.	n.a.	29	57	43	43	100
CPV	n.a.	n.a.	n.a.	n.a.	43	0	100	67	100	43	100
ELECTROLIMA	7	33	13	100	n.a.	47	40	80	70	30	60
ELECTROPERU	--	--	n.a.	0	13	25	150	50	40	70	n.a.
ENAPU	13	n.a.	n.a.	n.a.	68	68	25	n.a.	n.a.	43	113
ENCI	--	n.a.	n.a.	n.a.	n.a.	n.a.	22	67	25	33	114
ENTEL	n.a.	n.a.	n.a.	n.a.	n.a.	n.a.	50	40	40	45	80
EPCHAP	n.a.	n.a.	29	0	43	100	75	43	n.a.	--	--
ESAL	n.a.	n.a.	n.a.	n.a.	n.a.	n.a.	n.a.	n.a.	33	50	150
ESAR	n.a.	n.a.	n.a.	n.a.	n.a.	n.a.	83	17	50	33	100
INTERBANK	n.a.	n.a.	50	n.a.	200	57	86	14	43	214	110
PETROPERU	n.a.	0	87	17	11	30	60	40	80	44	56
SIDERPERU	n.a.	n.a.	n.a.	67	78	56	67	n.a.	n.a.	n.a.	n.a.

NOTE: Number of changes in members in year divided by board membership in
      previous year times 100
--   Not applicable
n.a. Not available
SOURCE: Company Annual Reports.

rotation rates. During its first sixty years as a private company, CORSERELEC, the Ica electric company, had only three board chairmen. As a public enterprise, from 1973 to 1980, it had five, with four of those holding the position after 1977 (Wolfenson 1981:82). For comparative purposes, during 25 years, the large Italian public enterprises, IRI and ENI, had only 3 and 5 board chairmen respectively (Grassini, 1981:72–73).

Jones hypothesized, after studying Korean management, that public enterprise directors generally are competent, but that three-year appointments promote mediocrity: "given familiarization time and the natural lags in response to innovation, there is only modest opportunity for success to be recognized" (1975:179). It may be concluded that Peru's even shorter-term appointments championed mediocrity. Shepherd's observation that public enterprise executives stay around longer than do government officials (1976a:41) and Radetzki's conclusion that public enterprise managers have longer tenure than their private counterparts (1985:39) may better describe the situation in developed countries, such as Italy, better than in developing nations including Korea and Peru.

Fifth, Peru had a limited pool of potential directors with business expertise or sectorial familiarity. As the portfolio grew rapidly during the early 1970s, the high turnover rates coupled with a clearout of pre-nationalization directors generated increased demand, while the relative and absolute size of the talent pool fell. For example, in the financial sector, the number of government-named directors for the previously private banks jumped from 38 to 60 (de la Melena, 1973:133). The absolute drop occurred as individuals who might have been eligible for directorships, based on their technical competence, were either rejected as politically suspect by the incoming regime, refused to collaborate with it, or left the country (Bravo, 1979:22). Similar ideologically motivated reductions in the available pool of directors occurred in 1980 and 1985.

Rapid expansion in the number of directorships led to the naming of less competent individuals. Figueroa and Saberbein, writing from an insider's perspective, report that a stress on candidates' political credentials after 1975 accounted for the drop in average quality of directors and top managers (1978:16). APRA party members, involved in designating board members in 1985, claimed to have learned a lesson in naming most members for technical merit, with only one or two party watchdogs on every board.[26]

Sixth, high turnover rates among directors often induced similar rates among managers as new board members placed their candidates in management positions. Information on this link between legal problems and management is scanty and may be compounded by other factors, but CPV illustrates the link: during 1983 and 1984, it had 3 separate boards, 5 different general managers, 4 different marketing managers, and 3 different financial managers (Cepeda, 1985:205). Similarly, ENCI had a top management turnover (*Gerentes*) of 100 percent in 1977, 50 percent in 1978, and 30 percent in 1980; during 1980, 58 percent of its *Sub-gerentes* changed jobs. Making boards subject to a political process, and hence subject to high turnover, flies against any performance improvement policies. It merits closer attention in the public enterprise literature.

Seventh, Peru used representative boards, with members named by different ministers, to "eliminate the tendency to sectorialism" and to "enrich the management process."[27] In 1976, for example, ENCI's board consisted of nine members, four representing the Ministry of Commerce, one that of industry and trade, one from the Ministry of Agriculture, one from energy and mining, one from economics and finance, and one a company worker. Hanson criticized the idea of a representative board as "incapable of providing strong leadership or of interposing its authority between minister and enterprise" (1965:404). Peru met Hanson's expectations because sectoral representatives rarely received guidelines about how to represent ministerial interests and in practice exercised their own judgment on the basis of scanty professional management expertise.[28] Ministry bureaucrats were often named to boards in reward for faithful service or as a proxy to enable a strong minister to control a board and act as executive president (Figueroa and Saberbein, 1978:15). Although the technical qualifications for a civil service career differed from those required to guide company operation, some ministry officials were often required to do both simultaneously (See Ghai, 1983:195–198). According to data contained in a Multisectoral Commission Report on 328 board positions in 40 companies, certain ministers could better reward their own officials with board positions than could others: the Minister of Economics and Finance could place 51 individuals on boards, the Minister of Industry — 29, the Minister of Commerce — 25, and the Minister of Energy and Mines — 24 (Comisión, 1976, Appendix 14). Thus, MEF gained strategic importance as its officials rotated to company boards of directors. This may also have benefited the firms by having a friend at the MEF. There was no such rotation for INP officials.[29] Hanson argued elsewhere that top civil servants were "probably the best people" to serve on public enterprise boards because they knew ministerial policy and because part-time service would result in infrequent board meetings and thus a freer hand for the managing director or general manager (1968:67). In Peru while strong executives had a free hand, weak or uncertain ones allowed boards, even though composed primarily of civil servants, to overassert themselves (interviews, 1978, 1980).

Peru never scrapped the inefficient board system because it provided a source of patronage and political control. The early 1970s portfolio expansion created new jobs for both military officers and the regime's civilian supporters.[30] EPCHAP annual reports furnish overt indications of patronage as the board chairman had an additional attribute, "Personal Representative of the Minister of Fishing," under fisheries minister, Javier Tantalean. Philip stated "all of these positions allowed [military] officers to collect double salaries and many of them also offered considerable prestige and influence, while some less scrupulous officers may also have used them for direct personal advantage" (1978:112). He overstated the case: rarely did Peru's public enterprises have more than two military board members at a time and most of them had none. Ferner substantiates the weak link between military careers and government posting, in noting that only 10 percent of the officer corps served in the public administration system (1983:67,n.10). Post-1980 civilian administrations maintained lists of possible directoral candidates chosen largely for political loyalty (interview, 1985).

In Peru, strong ministerial power, frequent ministerial rotation, and pressures to use ministerial patronage by a hermetic military or political party system, crippled the boards as effective policy setters. Italy illustrates a totally different outcome, where short-lived governments enable public-enterprise managers to ignore ministerial "suggestions" if "they are confident that they have the support of other members of the political establishment" (Grassini, 1981:75). The shifting and conflicting political environment in Peru precluded managers' development of external power bases and contributed to greater public enterprise instability. Missing legal bases for the companies coupled with strong ministerial power, led to excessive board and management turnover and to significant talent loss.

Existing Frameworks. Among Peru's companies, existing laws often promoted inefficiency, whose correction lay beyond management control. Faulty implementation of partial legal frameworks was the reason. Procurement systems provide an excellent example of legal implementation gone awry.

During the 1970s, the government increasingly subjected public enterprise procurement practices to the excessive formality of the *Reglamento General de Licitaciones y Contratos de Obras Públicas,* RGLCOP. The regulation, approved in 1961 (D.S. 36), appropriately dealt with procurement by government agencies whose major capital expenditures consisted in building housing, roads, bridges, or schools; however, it was unable to provide the inherent flexibility needed in public enterprise operations.[31]

The RGLCOP set procedures that applied to all expenditures, not only to capital items. Accordingly, the budget set two limits: below a minimum level, purchases were made at the discretion of the purchasing agent; between that minimum and a maximum, local invited competitive bidding from three preselected bidders was necessary; and above the maximum, open international competitive bidding through a public tender system was required. Until 1972 public enterprises escaped the RGLCOP as company bylaws set their purchasing limits. During the 1972 budget discussions, firms without a legal procurement basis were subjected to RGLCOP. As the late-1970s inflation eroded company-specific limits, more firms came under RGLCOP. National budgets periodically revised procurement limits and according to the data summarized in Graph 6.2, they followed the period framework: stable until 1970, rising gradually until 1974, fluctuating until 1977; and dropping in real terms thereafter, as the procurement system came under tight austerity restrictions.

The procurement system had major flaws.[32] First, it required cumbersome and lengthy procedures that ill fit a dynamic company environment. Managers opted for a costly increase in inventories to cover the additional lead time needed to complete all the steps in the bidding process (Remy, (1985:13). Second, inflation eroded the arbitrarily low limits so that in constant dollars, by the end of 1981, any project costing more than US $9,672 fell under the protracted 90-day international bidding procedures. Third, RGLCOP forced companies to pass up some low-cost opportunities, when foreign aid made concessionary-priced equipment or supplies available for short periods, because the total price often exceeded legal bidding limits, making the

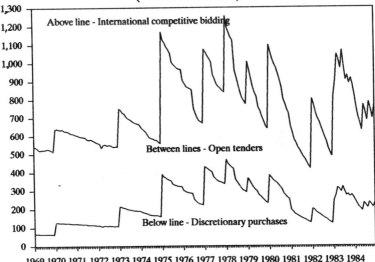

GRAPH 6.2: Procurement System Limits: 1969-1984
(Thousands of 1973 soles)

Above line - International competitive bidding

Between lines - Open tenders

Below line - Discretionary purchases

1969 1970 1971 1972 1973 1974 1975 1976 1977 1978 1979 1980 1981 1982 1983 1984
Source: Annual or biennial budget laws.

purchase subject to drawn-out international competitive bidding (interview, 1981).

Fourth, RGLCOP defined "public works" broadly enough to include normal supply operations. CPV sources claimed that it was difficult for freighters to seek out unscheduled, but often lucrative cargoes, since, in calling at a new port, following the law would have meant immobilizing the company's ships while seeking international public competitive bids for 90 days before provisioning, refueling, or undertaking major repairs (interview, 1981). Fifth, RGLCOP prohibited public enterprises from using a cost minimization strategy. Low bids could never be accepted; instead, a cumbersome procedure forced the companies to accept a bid close to the average (D.S. 002-71-VI).[33] Sixth, RGLCOP discouraged the development of local sources capable of supplying standard quality items on time, with adequate follow-up service, and an adequate inventory of spare parts. The protracted bidding process discouraged the formation of local consumer-producer relations and resulted in bids based on fictitious delivery dates, of substandard items, without backup service, and with no spare parts (Remy, 1985:13–14).

During late 1980, the Belaúnde administration, in a misguided attempt to rationalize and update the public bidding system, subjected public enterprises to even more stringent guidelines. The *Reglamento Unico de Licitaciones y Contratos de Obras Públicas*, (RULCOP) (D.S. 034-80-VC) spelled out new procedures for all majority-owned companies, irrespective of legal form, and for other agencies, whether public or private, that used government funds. RULCOP made no exceptions for emergency repairs or equipment replacement, routine purchases, maintenance, or repairs to existing installations. The government enforced inefficiency-promoting procurement practices that paid excessive attention to formal procedures and assigned a higher priority to processes than to profits.

Conclusions

Governments must make clear system-wide decisions to promote efficient public enterprise operations. These consist of defining and maintaining a national position that I call a public enterprise philosophy. The position itself is necessary, irrespective of content and irregardless of whether firms are viewed as a particular end of government policy or as just another policy instrument. The debate and the compromise leading to a national consensus help ensure the public enterprises of a stable operating environment.

Peruvian governments never clearly stated a public enterprise philosophy, nor did they come to grips with the need to define one. They placed many issues beyond management control by refusing to define some system parameters, by inappropriately defining others, and by disregarding the effects of their continued negligence on the system. As a consequence, serious difficulties continually hampered public enterprise operations and performance. Problems arose in setting and maintaining a coherent set of objectives, in setting prices, and in designing a control system. A national philosophy becomes codified in the legal system, but Peru's public enterprise never enjoyed a unified legal framework. Indeed, the few government attempts to define and codify operating procedures were marred by consistently flawed implementation.

INSTITUTIONAL RELATIONSHIPS

Introduction

Public enterprises form part of a system of interlinkages among differentiated government units. Interlinkages consist of cooperative, competitive, collaborative, or coercive relations that influence company performance either positively or negatively.[34] Others have explored links from public enterprises to the polity or to society, including political parties, trade unions, parliaments, consumers, the environment, and the community (Acosta, 1984, 1985; Fernandes, 1986:106–120). This section of Chapter 6 examines intrasystem

FIGURE 6.1
Public Enterprise System Relationships

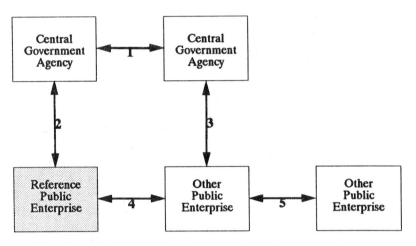

1. Bilateral relations between central government agencies
2. Direct hierarchical relations between a central government agency and a public enterprise
3. Indirect hierarchical relations between a second central government agency and another public enterprise
4. Direct bilateral relations between one public enterprise and another
5. Indirect bilateral relations between two other public enterprises

relations among executive government agencies.[35]

Some intergovernmental systemic relations that involve public enterprises have been peripherally mentioned in the literature. As employed in this book, however, they include more than the "erratic dialogue" or "structural incoherences" that Barenstein described for Mexico (1982:28–30) or the functional dichotomies found for Peru between government bureaucrat or goal setter and company technocrat and goal taker (Figueroa and Saberbein, 1978:15; INAP, 1976c). They extend far beyond the traditional top-down central government to public enterprise control model,[36] or the power links between any two public enterprises.[37]

Subsystem components possess different information, act on different objectives, pursue different (possibly conflicting) courses of action, and may represent different interests, but, in theory, they should put aside those differences to jointly pursue some public policy. Because sectarian interests often prevail, differences often result in conflicts within the intragovernmental system. This chapter analyzes the sources and effects of frictional problems in the five most important categories of system relations that strongly influence public enterprise performance [See figure 6.1].[38] Previous analysts have neglected three of these relations.

Accepting the systemic perspective leads to an important finding: many factors which influence the economic or social performance of a public enterprise are exogenous to it and beyond the control of its management. An examination of each relation shows that because Peru's government never approached its public enterprises in a coherent and systematic fashion, interlinkage difficulties often had a negative impact on their performance.[39] Examples cannot be used to overgeneralize the Peruvian case, nevertheless, they aid in understanding the nature of the intergovernmental system, as a prelude to designing adequate policy.

Bilateral Relations Between Central Government Agencies

Bilateral institutional relationships between central government agencies can have a direct impact on the financial, economic, or social aspects of public enterprise performance (shown on figure 6.1 as 1). Because companies depend on multiple government agencies, differences at the central government level, including incompatibility among the controllers' functions, policy disagreements among supervisory agencies, or struggles over bureaucratic territory, can have negative consequences for public enterprises. Alternatively, reducing friction in working relationships between central government entities can provide positive results.

Boneo describes the classic situation in developing countries as one where a government agency sets ambitious goals for a public enterprise while another severely restrains the resources necessary for it to attain those goals (1985:54). Such uncoordinated linkages sometimes appear when different agencies show different goal preferences for the same public enterprise, a state called the problem of plural principals. Jones theorized that a solution exists if tradeoff mechanisms can be adequately specified and maintained (1981:7–8). Aharoni concluded that strong public enterprise managers, compared to their multiple principals, can make the company an "agent without a principal."[40] Linkages between a public enterprise and plural agencies have been examined elsewhere, but multiple-agency analysis at the level of central government has not received any attention because of the implicit assumption that all linkages proceed in a strictly top-down fashion from government to the company.[41] This section remedies that deficiency by focusing on those links between government agencies. I conclude that everyday operating frictions between them may have strong and unintended negative repercussions on public enterprises.

A clear example may be found in the disputes over the distribution of power among central government agencies to control and monitor public enterprises. Lack of consensus, shown in the interminable delays and disagreements over a draft version of a public enterprise normative law, deprived companies of a stable working environment and enabled each new minister to assert power. At best, power plays consisted in making new appointments to the boards of directors. The new board members would often magnify the effect of the changes by imposing their hand-picked top managers on the company. In other cases, ministerial prerogatives included changing company goals, organizational structure, and management. There is no guarantee that the passage of a public enterprise law would have stabilized the ever-changing environment, however, the emergence and legal codification of a consensus on operating conditions among the controlling bodies would have gone a long way toward making major changes more difficult.

Cleaves and Scurrah report the opposition between two ministries, Housing and Agriculture, during much of the military period (1980:191–202). This dispute was based primarily on ideological differences between the two branches of the military that produced the respective ministers, which led to different staffing patterns within the ministries and which resulted in open conflict over urban expansion into agricultural land.[42] Usually the disputes opposed the interests of peasants to those of private developers. In one case, however, the state-owned BCHP held a large piece of property on which it intended to develop a housing project. The farm workers resisted and, backed by the Ministry of Agriculture, overrode the bank's plans, even though the Ministry of Housing supported the latter. Although the negligible direct cost to the bank of this decision consisted mainly of the wages or fees of staff, the opportunity cost was high, representing the difference between the property's actual agricultural use and the potential sales or rental value after development as a housing project.[43]

A company's strategic importance may negate any power due to its size, its strong corporate planning, or its financial success [see below]. After 1979, PETROPERU could sign sub-contracts for exploration or exploitation only after prior cabinet approval and with the blessing of the joint chiefs of the armed forces. In time, cabinet approval was made contingent on a favorable opinion by eight government agencies: BCRP, CGR, the National Office for Legal Affairs, the directorate general of MEM and its directorate general of hydrocarbons, MEF's directorates general of taxes and of customs, and the joint chiefs of the armed forces (Pontoni, 1981:68–69). By expanding the number of interested parties, the potential for friction between agencies also was expanded.

Peru's return to constitutional government did not resolve the problems. Indeed, the struggle for power among central government agencies continued, centered around the battle between CONADE, in its new role as policy shaper and performance evaluator, and the CGR, the traditional controliste. The struggle was couched in legal terms, with lawyers' working for opposing sides firing off briefs that contested minute points in interpreting the bylaws to the law on the entrepreneurial activity of the state.[44] It was couched in philosophical terms, pitting the CGR which operated under the hypothesis that problems, which must be rooted out and punished, exist in all public enterprises (interview, 1985) against CONADE that realized that while 100 percent management perfection was impossible, the long run goal should be gradual improvement by upgrading management practices. It was also couched in power terms as the CGR sought to retain control over many activities that the new laws had attributed to CONADE. The struggle increased the uncertainty within the company's working environment by making both organizations potential sources of sanction under the undefined control system.[45]

Information Requirements. Gathering information about public enterprise operations occupies many central government authorities but, it lacks effective inter-agency coordination. As shown in Chapter 3, many agencies periodically collected similar information, so that public enterprises faced multiple and overlapping reporting burdens. Various ministries, plus BCRP, BN, INP, and INE, among others requested information. Each had legitimate information needs that, when cumulated, resulted in massive amounts of repetitive paperwork. The acting general manager of one large company, in 1978, claimed to have received, during the previous six-month period, thirty-three questionnaires from various government agencies, which he deliberately left unanswered, citing insufficient manpower to waste time filling in redundant government forms (interview, 1978). Laws mandated compliance with information requests from controlling agencies, but *El Peruano*, the official newspaper, often reminded companies of past due reports, indicating widespread noncompliance.

Peru's central government approached information gathering from a nonfunctional perspective. Individual agencies collected incomplete and inadequate financial information, while no agency gathered the type of information needed by the government to judge performance, or needed by the company to improve performance. Monitoring agencies requested the same information on different questionnaires indicating that the government assigned a low priority to standardizing forms or to centralizing information. International conferences stressed three key elements in designing an information system: reduce the number of separate information demands on a company, standardize the flow of information, and make it relevant for management purposes ("The Focal Point," 1985:26). Peru's experience consisted in increasing the information demands on the company, complicating the information flow, and gathering data only marginally relevant for government or company purposes.

To make matters worse, low staffing levels and budgets too tight to hire new staff plagued the central government agencies that were supposed to analyze the collected data. Inadequate analyses of inadequate information by inadequately trained staff contributed to the cult of control whereby key company financial decisions became subject to even closer monitoring. Imposing more information requirements became a substitute for greater control. As more information flowed into government offices, the staffs fell increasingly farther behind so that the information problem became self perpetuating.

Although the design and implementation of a centralized information system for government would have been beneficial, there is no indication that such a system was ever proposed. Benefits to a company, including less paperwork and reduced compliance costs, would have complemented benefits to government of speedier data analysis, rapid and thorough access to information, and increased effectiveness of the few quality analysts. The simple solution with widespread benefits could not be proposed because poor bilateral relations among government agencies impeded cooperation.

Direct Hierarchical Relations between a Central Government Agency and a Public Enterprise

Direct hierarchical relations between a central government agency and a public enterprise are indicated by 2 in figure 6.1. The difficulty or ease of their administration affects company performance. The often-discussed accountability problem concentrates on those links, starting from the premise that public enterprises exist to be controlled and then searching for the most effective ways to do so.[46] Smooth implementation of control links would positively affect public enterprise performance, whereas attempting to enforce mutually incompatible or completely erroneous top-down signals can only have the opposite effect. Chapter 3 examined the evolution and imperfect functioning of Peru's control systems as a gradual rejection of accountability by public enterprise managers and their subjection to increasing government intervention in day-to-day commercial activities.

Strong public enterprises can resist control. Generally, the larger a company, the greater its relative strength, and the better it can bargain with the government (UN, ILPES, 1981:15–16), and avoid control. Observers noted that PESCAPERU so dwarfed its controlling ministry that it escaped effective control (FitzGerald, 1979:198). Consequently, a weak ministry's planning and control efforts may be limited to simply noting public enterprise planning activities.[47]

Strength also comes from other factors. In France, Anastassopoulos found that companies better resisted government demands if they had an explicit corporate strategy, a strong *esprit de corps* among company executives, or powerful and popular unions (1981:111–112). The union factor helps explain Peru's continued problems in SIDERPERU and CPV.[48] Financial success often brings strength as a profitable enterprise is likely to be subject to less interference by authorities than an unprofitable one (See Becker, 1983:229). This hypothesis may have held true in Peru, where unprofitable firms often triggered negative effects for the entire portfolio, as authorities increased interference into affairs of that firm and others as well. Imposing tighter controls, however, usually led to poorer results. Companies were caught in a no-win situation.

Other relations, the quality of which can influence company performance, may link public enterprises to central government agencies. For example, government and company often must work together or complete sequential project tasks; poor coordination can have negative results. Such a situation resulted from the conflict over ENCI's fertilizer sales program in 1977 and 1978. ENCI planned to promote increased fertilizer use among farmers, both to open new markets for itself and to boost Peru's food production. A promotional campaign was stopped because the Ministry of Foodstuffs insisted on its advertising monopoly (ENCI, 1977:3).

Coordinating several central government agencies involved in a public enterprise project only adds to relational problems. ENCI continues to serve as an excellent example. Fertilizer use in Peru is concentrated in the larger coastal farms. As part of its plans to increase and to regionally diversify fertilizer use, ENCI wanted to expand its storage network by enlarging existing warehouses and by building new ones. Coordination problems with central government agencies stymied those plans. First, two warehouses, those in Cajamarca and Ica, were to be constructed on land expropriated under the agrarian reform, but title clearing delayed construction. Second, Ministry of Housing technicians were to do the engineering studies. Inadequate ministry staffing delayed the construction of warehouses in Callao and Sullana.[49] Third, these delays, in a period of high inflation, increased construction costs, yet the INP and MEF refused to approve needed additional funds. As a result, the last two warehouses were left unfinished (ENCI, 1977:34).

Coordination problems were common. For example, they pitted ENAPU against the Customs Service whose delays in disposing of spoiled and unclaimed merchandise reportedly reduced ENAPU's warehouse capacity by 15 percent (interview, 1981). Likewise, ELECTROPERU delays in processing customs paperwork incurred demurrage charges for up to 4 years, led to involuntary abandonment of merchandise, and raised costs to cover the exchange differential. Estimates placed ELECTROPERU's coordination costs at more than S/. 1 billion from 1976 to mid-1980.[50]

**Indirect Hierarchical Relations between a Second
Central Government Agency and a Second Public Enterprise**

Relation 3 on figure 6.1 shows an indirect hierarchical link between a central government agency and a second public enterprise. Positive or negative externalities arising from that link may have an impact on the performance of the first firm.

As an example of negative externalities, Chapter 4 showed that the Public Treasury delayed payment of subsidies to public enterprise accounts at the BN. Treasury arrears forced the BN to loan funds to the companies, interest on which often remained unpaid because of disputes over responsibility: Companies claimed that they were not liable for interest on forced loans; Treasury held that the loans were taken out in the names of the companies. In most cases, agreements were worked out between the Treasury, the BN, and company representatives. Irrespective of the cause of the problem, malfunctions in the payments system resulted in increased financial costs, which in turn led to higher total subsidies that usually included the disputed interest payments. Thus, S/. 2.3 billion of the S/. 4.9 billion ($19.9 million U.S.) paid to PESCAPERU in 1979 covered interest charges on unwanted loans forced on the company following Treasury arrears in subsidy payments (D.L. 22440 and 23005). Also, by 1978 subsidy arrears to ENCI totaled S/. 1.3 billion. Even though the 1979 law approving their payment prescribed that Treasury would bear the financial costs of late payment, it refused to pay (R.M. 392-79 AA/ENCI and BN, 1980).

The interest rate on BN loans to the Treasury rose from 8 percent in early 1976 to 12 percent in 1977, while the rate charged to public enterprises to finance subsidies remained a low 4 percent. Thus, it was cheaper, in the long run, for Treasury to force the public enterprises to borrow, than to borrow needed funds itself. However, cost-minimizing forced borrowing was never a stated policy and the protracted wrangling over interest payments makes it unlikely that Treasury arrears followed such a policy. Some authors contend that public enterprises borrow heavily on the strength of the country's name and good faith (Gillis, Jenkins, and Lesard, 1983:263), Peru's government forced its public enterprises to borrow money, thereby saving the country's reputation as a borrower.

When arrears were paid with strongly devalued currency, they had other negative effects on company finance. In 1979 ENCI settled the issue of fertilizer subsidy arrears due to FERTIPERU, with which it was merged in 1974. As part of the settlement, Treasury had a two-year grace period on payment of arrears, so that the first payment on unpaid pre-1974 subsidies was not due until 30 September 1981, some seven years late, after a change of governments, and with no inflationary correction. Of the S/. 1,019 million settlement, 46 percent covered the financial costs after 1 January 1978, leaving ENCI to absorb excess financial costs of S/. 130 million (R.M. 544-79-ICTI-DM-DGA and BN, 1979). Finally, to cover the costs of the negotiated settlement, the BN lent the Treasury money at 19 percent interest when COFIDE "C" bonds were paying 35 percent interest and the inflation rate was well above 50 percent.

The examples show that high subsidy levels often resulted from incoherent government policy, not risk aversion or mismanagement by company officials. Government accounts, however, simply charged the entire subsidy to a public enterprise, which concealed Treasury's burden for not paying on time and for raising subsidies far beyond the amount needed to provide the subsidized services. Such distortions perpetuated the image of public enterprises as losers needing continual bailout by benevolent central government authorities. Although the costs of public enterprise appeared quite high, in fact those costs frequently resulted from poor government payment practices.

A different type of repeated government interference also had negative effects on performance. In early 1970, partly as a result of the personal friendship between the head of the SIMA shipyard and a top naval officer in the Ministry of Fishing, EPCHAP was made to purchase two bulk transport ships.[51] The acquisition raised two problems: it side-stepped government purchasing regulations [See above] and EPCHAP had no use for bulk transporters except to ship fishmeal, the raw material for which, the anchoveta, had just disappeared. In 1974 the Minister of Fishing forced the ships on the CPV and required it to assume EPCHAP's debt.[52] The timing was again flawed, since, as it lost the ships, EPCHAP received a monopoly on grain imports and its own demand for bulk shipping soared (interview 1981).

Direct Bilateral Relations between Two Public Enterprises

Public enterprises routinely interact with each other [shown by 4 in figure 6.1]. While the most common interaction is a purely commercial one, that of purchaser to supplier, others exist such as partners in a joint venture, or collaborators in joint projects, all of which mutually affect financial, economic, or social performance.

In the early 1970s, Peruvian experts noted negative interactions between enterprises but, although various mechanisms were tried, the problems were never remedied (ESAN, 1972:8–9). It tried horizontal and vertical coordinating committees, but they rarely solved interenterprise disputes [See Chapter 3]. Interlocking directorates among related firms are often used to coordinate policies, but Peru rarely used them, other than between parent firms and their subsidiaries.

Commercial ties raised problems that persisted, although resolvable in the courts or through arbitration. Four such ties are examined, including the pricing system, payment practices, forced contractual relationships, and the management of externalities.[53] In general, Peru bears out Hanson's finding that governments rarely foster interenterprise coordination (1968:50).

Interenterprise Pricing. Peru had no mechanisms to coordinate pricing policy for goods or services that public enterprises sold to each other. Such exchanges were common and included sales by the major utilities or by government-set monopolies to other public firms.

Often a public enterprise could only buy from or sell to another government-run firm, being legally locked into a bilateral monopoly. For example, during the seventies, the government made EPSA the sole importer of several foodstuffs, and ENCI the sole purchaser and wholesale marketer. Economic theory does not provide easy solutions to the price and quantity questions under such circumstances. Over time, however, the Peruvian government arrived at a simple pricing rule in several such cases. It was a simple rule, based on relative power, a concept to which economists often retreat when economic theory fails to provide a clear-cut answer to a theoretical problem: The public enterprise with a more powerful controlling minister set the price. When both public enterprises fell under the same ministry, as, for example, ELECTROLIMA's distribution system for ELECTROPERU's production, pricing issues remained inadequately resolved (Wolfenson 1981:149–150).

In another case, a complicated link arose between PETROPERU, and the northern electricity and water suppliers. SEDAPIURA could not supply sufficient water to PETROPERU's Talara installations because it could not generate the cash flow required to pay ELECTRONORTE for electricity to keep the pumps running. Delays in payment meant that the electric utility, in turn, could not regularly pay for needed fuel, leading to major power interruptions. The two key firms both fell under the MEM, so the solution, according to the pricing rule, was indeterminate. The impasse was finally resolved when PETROPERU agreed to pay a price for water that was six times as high as that paid in Lima; the water utility, in turn, had sufficient funds to pay its electric bills regularly; and the electric utility could then regularly buy petroleum from PETROPERU (interview, 1985).

Interpublic-enterprise pricing policy often masked hidden subsidies that never figured in the official accounts, concealing the true subsidy cost of public enterprises. Hidden subsidies contradict the generally accepted principle that "subsidization, when necessary, should be specific and open, not general and concealed" (Hanson 1968:100). Although deliberate reasons may justify hiding subsidies: governments may consider it politically expedient or desirable to conceal the full facts of a situation from the public or from the legislature (UN, DESA, 1976b:44), no such motives operated in Peru, where inadequately conceived and executed practices seem to have been the determining factors. Four examples of hidden subsidies in several sectors of the economy illustrate this widespread practice.

First, purchasing requirements forced CPV to purchase new ships from the government-run shipyards, SIMA, instead of buying them on the world market, as did the local, private, competition. CPV's extra cost, clearly a hidden government subsidy to SIMA, exceeded prevailing world prices for similar vessels by US $20 million per ship (interviews 1981). That figure excluded several items: interest on CPV-incurred loans undertaken to enable SIMA to build up the necessary preconstruction inventory, the value of CPV's no-cost freighting for imported construction materials and fittings, and CPV's foregone income while waiting for SIMA to build ships that would have been available years earlier on the world market.[54] Subsidizing transport construction is a common practice. Reasons given in the British case of forcing BOAC and BEA to buy British aircraft included defense subsidies, strong positive externalities, or a recognition that the pound was overvalued compared to the dollar (Foster 1971:106–108).[55] Only defense really applied in the Peruvian case. The needed high skill training reasons, advanced by Kuczynski, do not justify deliberately hiding the true cost of labor training behind unreported and unaccountable subsidies (1977: 82, n1).

ENCI payments to PETROPERU provide a second example of hidden subsidies. By 1980, the cost of producing urea at PETROPERU's Talara plant exceeded world market prices by 40 percent. ENCI held a legal monopsony making it the only purchaser of urea in Peru and PETROPERU set its ex-factory price to cover costs because the Minister of Energy and Mines wields more power than does the Minister of Agriculture. ENCI, thus, subsidized PETROPERU for the difference between the local and world-market prices. Because one of ENCI's goals was to provide the least expensive fertilizer to meet the needs of Peruvian farmers, hidden subsidies to PETROPERU reduced ENCI's effectiveness.

A third example of hidden subsidies was found in the lower rates charged by the CPV and ENAPU to ENCI-marketed products, including basic foodstuffs. Since the subsidy only resulted in lowered CPV and ENAPU income, it never appeared either as a government subsidy for basic foodstuffs or as a subsidy to ENCI. Hidden food subsidies took various forms: ENAPU's rate structure included port-specific loading and unloading discounts and more free storage time before incurring lowered storage charges.[56]

Fourth, the above hidden subsidies pale in magnitude, however, to that paid to financial firms by nonfinancial public enterprises that were forced to maintain cash reserves in non-interest bearing accounts while having to pay the market rate of interest on overdrafts. Taking reported year-end figures as indicative of annual balances and using the extremely low COFIDE "C" bond rate as the opportunity cost of capital, the magnitude of this hidden subsidy, from 1973 to 1981, is estimated at US $464 million in lost earnings on deposited funds. Hidden subsidies from the nonfinancial to the financial public enterprises partly explain the losses by the nonfinancial public firms reported in Peruvian central bank statistics.

Interenterprise Payment Practices. Public enterprises lagged in paying each other for services rendered. Consequently, their trade accounts receivable and accounts payable rose rapidly. As shown in table 6.4, in constant 1973 soles, trade accounts payable rose from S/. 16.5 billion at the end of 1976 to S/. 26.1 billion at the end of 1979.

TABLE 6.4: Accounts Payable and Receivable by Sector and Antiquity of Debt: 1976, 1979
(millions of 1973 soles and percentages)

	Public Sector			Private Sector			Total
	S/.	Percentages		S/.	Percentages		S/.
		Column	Row		Column	Row	
1976							
Accounts Payable							
Less than 6 months	4,306	53.8	n.a.	n.a.	n.a.	n.a.	n.a
6 to 12 months	2,598	32.4	n.a.	n.a.	n.a.	n.a.	n.a
More than 12 months	1,105	13.8	n.a.	n.a.	n.a.	n.a.	n.a
Total	8,009	100.0	48.4	8,529	100.0	51.6	16,538
Accounts Receivable							
Less than 6 months	4,059	42.7	n.a.	n.a.	n.a.	n.a.	n.a
6 to 12 months	2,564	27.0	n.a.	n.a.	n.a.	n.a.	n.a
More than 12 months	2,274	23.9	n.a.	n.a.	n.a.	n.a.	n.a
Unknown	599	6.3	n.a.	n.a.	n.a.	n.a.	n.a
Total	9,496	100.0	67.5	4,564	100.0	32.5	14,060
1979							
Accounts Payable							
Less than 6 months	7,330	40.7	69.8	3,168	39.1	30.2	10,498
6 to 12 months	5,608	31.1	59.5	3,822	47.2	40.5	9,430
More than 12 months	5,083	28.2	82.1	1,109	13.7	17.9	6,192
Total	18,021	100.0	89.0	8,099	100.0	81.0	20,120
Accounts Receivable							
Less than 6 months	3,468	35.7	63.8	1,970	40.9	36.2	5,438
6 to 12 months	3,066	31.5	75.0	1,021	21.2	25.0	4,087
More than 12 months	3,193	32.8	63.6	1,827	37.9	36.4	5,020
Total	9,727	100.0	66.9	4,818	100.0	33.1	14,545

SOURCES: CGR, 1977a and 1980.

During the same period, trade accounts receivable remained stable, only rising from S/. 14.1 billion to S/. 14.5 billion.

Changes in business practices, during the late-1970s' tight financial situation, accompanied the growth in accounts payable. First, accounts payable only grew in intrapublic sector dealings, which shifted the composition of short-term indebtedness. In three years accounts payable to other public sector entities rose more than 125 percent while accounts payable to the private sector fell by 5 percent in real terms. Thus, payments to the private sector kept pace with inflation, while those to other public agencies were allowed to slide. The strategy shifted short-run financial difficulties from one public enterprise to another.

Second, the average period of intra-public sector indebtedness grew. In 1976 only 6 percent of accounts receivable and 14 percent of accounts payable had been on the books for more than twelve months. In three years, these figures jumped to 33 and 28 percent, respectively. In 1979 the long-overdue accounts to the public sector far outweighed those due to the private sector, accounting for more than 80 percent of the total. The time shift in accounts payable not only adversely affected a company's cash flow, it created other costs in trying to collect overdue bills from government agencies. The general manager of one utility even reported political problems after cutting service to a municipal government with long overdue bills (interview, 1981).

Public enterprises repeatedly tried to shift their financial burdens, often generated by the central government's poor payment practices, to other public enterprises. The process of shifting debt burdens merits explanation. Overdrafts to cover cash-flow problems transferred the debt to the BN at a financial cost to the firm and a monetary gain for the bank. Delaying payment on commercial accounts to other public enterprises also forced them to use BN overdraft facilities. A rotating debtor association resulted as the magnitude of financial problems continually increased (See INAP, 1979a:28). Nowhere is this made clearer than for EPSA, which ranked first in accounts receivable, all from unpaid subsidies channeled through MEF, and in accounts payable. Such system-wide poor financial practices exacerbated the already poor performance of some firms.

Another example serves to illustrate that the Peruvian government did not promote efficient intrasystem payment relationships. Lima's three major utilities, SEDAPAL, ELECTROLIMA, and CPTSA, all public enterprises, proposed joint billing to reduce their administrative costs. In mid-1985, government legal experts rejected the efficiency-related move as anti-competitive, a strange decision, since each company already held a local monopoly and their products, water, electricity, and telephone service, were not substitutes (interview, 1985).

Interenterprise Forced Contractual Relationships. Government-given monopolies often forced Peru's public enterprises into contractual relationships with each other. These relationships constrained management choice and raised company costs. There are many examples where monopolies posed problems for other public enterprises. For example, the Bruce Commission cited problems posed by monopolies granted to CPV, the insurance companies, and AEROPERU (Comisión, 1977b:21).

The BN monopoly for public enterprises' local currency operations served to inflate both company financial costs and BN benefits. For example, EPSA maintained separate bank accounts by product line, such as wheat or maize, but the BN calculated charges based on individual account balances. It had no mechanism to cover temporary overdrafts in one EPSA account from a non-interest bearing surplus account.[57] BN's frequent lack of liquidity also forced companies to withdraw and store cash in advance to meet a payroll and it was unwilling to provide on-site facilities for worker payment, a service offered by competing banks (interview 1981). After the monopoly for foreign currency dealings was broken in 1978, many firms sought better banking services elsewhere.

At times, companies abused their monopoly power. The government created PUBLIPERU for the stated goal of achieving economies of scale in advertising as an intermediate step to lowering rates and to getting greater impact in advertising. Instead, PUBLIPERU became a censorship agency for ad copy. Figure 6.2 indicates PUBLIPERU's internal workings in 1977 to show that the proposed ad copy's implicit support for government policies and its explicit political content were more highly ranked than any technical content. At any stage in the internal decision process, moreover, copy could be returned for reworking and the revised copy would have to go through the whole process again.

Working with Externalities. External inefficiencies at times hampered firms, as exemplified in delayed cotton payments. ENCI paid farmers through the BAP, which deducted any outstanding loans before making final payment. Bank delays resulted from the complicated loan repayment system, but the general public and farmers interpreted delays as caused by ENCI.

Fertilizer operations also illustrate other external problems. ENCI received a substantial portion of the urea produced at PETROPERU's Talara plant in broken fertilizer sacks. ENCI officials attributed the problem to either cost-saving sack stitching by a PETROPERU subcontractor or to poor sack filling practices. The problem was the subject of bitter memoranda and acrimonious meetings, but remained unsolved seven years after ENCI first raised the issue (interview, 1985). ENCI received guano from PESCAPERU in broken sacks because PESCAPERU's cost cutting measures led it to employ used jute and polypropylene sacks, both of which had a higher tendency to break than did new ones. ENCI's costs rose because its suppliers tried to cut their own (ENCI 1978:33).

Other negative externalities existed. Discharges from CENTROMIN mines into the Mantaro River repeatedly damaged ELECTROPERU's electric turbines. Although the dispute predated the nationalization of Cerro de Pasco, after 1974 its resolution did not become any easier.[58] By the late 1970s, CENTROMIN took major steps to eliminate the mining waste discharges by constructing a water treatment plant. However, the plant was not built to accommodate ELECTROPERU's needs. Instead, by constructing it, CENTROMIN planned to recover about 7 thousand tons of otherwise unavailable copper and to reduce the level of contamination in the river water destined to meet Lima's water requirements (IBRD, 1979:368).

Not all externalities were negative. Indeed, close attention to a problem often resulted in mutual benefit, as shown in ENAPU's newsprint handling. On arrival in port, newsprint rolls had been stored in the open, which led to weather-related losses for ENCI, the importer. The two companies worked out an agreement to send newsprint to ENCI's warehouses directly after unloading, before completing all clearance procedures. ENCI's costs dropped by not incurring storage charges and by reducing losses; ENAPU, thus, had less port congestion

171

FIGURE 6.2
PUBLIPERU Control of Public Enterprise Advertising

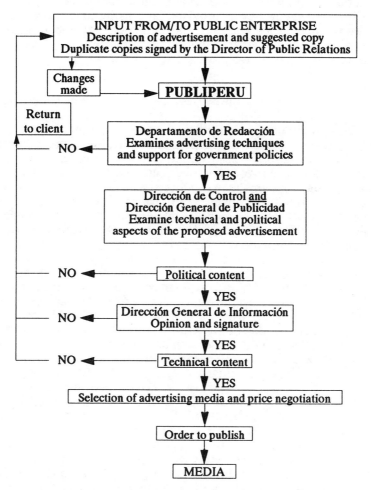

Source: Resolución de la Oficina Central de Información
No. 229-77-OCI-OAJ

(ENCI 1977:22).

The important point of examining externalities is not that inter-enterprise issues were not considered for many decisions; they were not, a fairly common finding. Far more important is the conclusion that Peru's government never provided an institutional mechanism to resolve the many frictional problems that could have been expected to arise in the normal course of business realtionships and that regularly did arise with the negative consequences detailed above.

Indirect Bilateral Relations between Two Other Public Enterprises

Fifth, indirect bilateral relations comprise another class of externalities that arise from interaction between other public enterprises [shown on figure 6.1 as 5]. Smoothly functioning ties between two companies may positively effect the functioning of third firms, whereas unharmonious relations may produce the opposite. Other researchers have neglected indirect linkages. For example, Acosta does not distinguish between direct and indirect bilateral relationships, calling all of them "horizontal" (1985:13); Sorensen mentions indirect interlinkages but does not analyze them (1985:235).

A positive externality followed a loan agreement between two firms, the Banco Popular and CENTROMIN, which had strong positive repercussions on MINPECO's financial health. Before the loan, CENTROMIN constantly pressured the dramatically undercapitalized MINPECO to pay its trade accounts to fund CENTROMIN's large cash-flow needs in meeting payrolls. CENTROMIN often needed cash long before MINPECO had received payment for minerals exports, fueling MINPECO's high short-term borrowing requirements from the BN, which led to higher financial costs for MINPECO (MINCOM 1978: 43). Through the intermediary of the Banco Popular, the Wells Fargo Bank of San Francisco provided CENTROMIN with a revolving line of credit that reduced CENTROMIN's financial pressure on MINPECO, and reduced MINPECO's demands on the BN. Widespread benefits of this transaction included: a drop in MINPECO's financial costs as its borrowing requirements decreased and a drop in CENTROMIN's financial costs because, instead of two, it had only one intermediary between it and the foreign creditor. BN revenue dropped, but that of its subsidiary Banco Popular rose. Overall, and comparing winners and losers, the result appeared positive for the entire portfolio.

As an example of a negative externality, the BN often did not honor ENCI's checks to cotton farmers because of insufficient funds resulting from Treasury arrears. In turn, farmers could not repay their BAP agricultural loans. Interest payable to one public enterprise, the agrarian bank, rose because a second one, ENCI, had not met its payments to farmers because a third, the BN, had not received Treasury payments due on subsidies.[59]

CONCLUSIONS

This chapter amply demonstrates that successful policy implementation depends on recognizing the existence of a complex interorganizational interlinkage system between central government agencies and public enterprises, an approach omitted by the standard analyses. Neglecting the systems perspective in favor of a top-down hierarchical approach or trying to better management, as warranted by the atomistic one, when key issues are beyond management control has a negative impact on public enterprise policy. Because Peru's government tried both approaches without having set the necessary bases for its public enterprise action, and without having examined the consequences of its intended actions for public enterprises, the entire system suffered.

A facile explanation of the omissions is that during the early 1970s, barely regulated portfolio expansion led to overextension of the government system. The consequent pressure on scarce government resources, including management and abundant funds, caused repeated breakdowns in administrative procedures leading to difficulties in making decisions, coordination failure, and supervisory overload (See Sherif, 1973:13). This hypothesis needs slight modification on the basis of the Peruvian case, since the period of Peru's greatest portfolio expansion was relatively calm, marked by simple and uncomplicated mechanisms. Only after major growth ceased and the portfolio had stabilized did the problems truly set in.

The Peruvian evidence presented above is partial, incomplete, and anecdotal. It has three sources of bias to negative findings. First, self-justifying company records were more likely to report negative performance by others than any successful collaboration. Second, negative effects persisted for a long time, and so were bound to be reported sooner or later. Third, managers and top executives were questioned about any problems associated with intergovernmental interlinkages. The findings of limited enterprise autonomy within a poorly functioning complex intergovernmental system provides evidence that Aharoni's finding of widespread managerial discretion in developed countries may not hold in developing nations (1981:188–189).

On the basis of these three admitted biases and partialities, several conclusions about the management of linkages to avoid confusion of authority or responsibility can be drawn. First, government and public enterprises must acknowledge that the management of interlinkages is an important field of effort. To do so, the existence of a linkage structure among multiple actors at different administrative levels within a complex intergovernmental system must be acknowledged, and those linkages must be identified and described.[60] The chapter contributes to the identification issue by detailing three links heretofore omitted in the literature: bilateral relations between central government agencies, indirect hierarchical relations between government agencies and enterprises, and indirect bilateral relations between public enterprises. Second, government and public enterprises focus on interlinkages as a conscious part of public enterprise policies. This important step will enable both government and firm to recognize the role of external constraints on improving enterprise efficiency and that government policies are often to blame for poor company performance. Third, government and public enterprises must take concrete steps to manage the interlinkages with the objective of minimizing negative effects and maximizing the positive externalities.

Learning successful interlinkage management is a major step forward from the commonly accepted evolutionary survival concepts summed up in an ECLA document: "development of these relationships [between central government and public enterprises] was, to a certain extent, an educative process in the course of which the enterprise became increasingly aware of the needs of the central government while the latter came to appreciate the necessity of giving the enterprise increasing leeway" (UN, ECLA, 1969b:4). But, evolutionary survival assumes a strong institutional memory to help avoid past mistakes. As seen in Peru, with constant personnel changes in the central government and in the public enterprises, the institutional memory was lost and mistakes were continuously repeated or needlessly perpetuated. The interlinkage system approach presented in this chapter stresses potential problem identification and is less dependent on institutional memory and continuity.

NOTES

1. See Ramanadham (1974:79–126), Commonwealth Secretariat (1982?b) especially the individual papers by El Mir, Ghai, and Motta, and the special issue of *Public Enterprise* (II:4, 1982). In this book, I concentrate on public enterprise relations to the executive; others cover parliamentary relations including Ramanadham and Ghai (1981), Commonwealth Secretariat (1982?), Marga Institute (1981), and Ghai (1981).
2. Hanson raised the issue of fitting public enterprises into a governmental systems framework "[g]overnmental co-ordination is an unknown or unexplored field" (1965:208).
3. Pease and Lê Châu both stress the notion of a unified and monolithic state while, at the same time, probing the basis for differentiated actions by minor fragments of the bourgeoisie. Pease admits the potential for friction between the state bureaucracy and public enterprises (1977:245–248) and Lê Châu mentioned latent inter-institutional conflict (1982:145), but neither considers the Peruvian state as differentiated. Some

exceptions to the standard approach include Ferner who noted divergent interests within the state apparatus (1983:63–66) and Sorj who looked at intra-ministerial divisions (1976:250).

4. For a summary of key works in the field of intergovernmental policy studies, see Scharpf (1978).

5. Portions of drafts of Chapter 6 have appeared in Saulniers (1985f, g, and h).

6. See individual chapters in Hanf and Scharpf (1978).

7. Early writers stressed the importance of consensus for public enterprise stability. See Lilienthal (1944:40–41).

8. The lack of an overriding public enterprise philosophy in Peru contrasts to pre-1964 Brazil's national consensus that public enterprises should have autonomy and that they should behave "as if private" (Trebat, 1983:80–85).

9. A set of draft laws and their commentaries provide the basis for the following discussion. These included Comisión (1977a), CIAEF (1978, 1979), INP (1979b), and INAP (1979b).

10. I lump together institutional power disputes with personal clashes among power players, both of which can generate externalities for company performance.

11. Barenstein analyzes data on Mexican public enterprise managers' perceptions of multiple objectives (1983:71–116).

12. Shirley (1983:17–21), Fernandes (1986:14–15). Even in Britain long- term objectives were either unspecified or imprecisely understood between ministers and company boards (Heath, 1983:134).

13. See Ramanadham (1974:7), Jones (1975:13–16), and Trebat (1981:46–48).

14. Stated goals are admittedly a compromise. It's obvious that public enterprises can arise out of confusion over goals whereby some parts of government "harbor one main purpose while other parts harbor another" (Vernon, 1981:11).

15. D.L. 18252 and D.S. 019-70-IC-DS.

16. Comisión (1977c, Appendix 2:2).

17. According to an unstated protocol, objectives set by management were rarely mentioned. Thus, in a report presented to the minister, MINPECO's dire need to capitalize retained earnings was not listed as an objective, but was buried in the financial analysis (MINPECO, 1979:14–15).

18. One result of the missing consensus was the 1974 EPSA scandal. There was no way of publicly admitting that the government orientation had shifted, as a result of internal strife, to a policy requiring a sharp drop in food subsidies. Uninstitutionalized mechanisms for dealing with major policy changes led to the manufacture of a food supply embezzlement scandal that distracted popular attention away from rising food bills while transmitting a clear anti-growth message to managers of other

public enterprises (Cleaves and Scurrah, 1980:216).

19. Ray applies the rule that prices should be set to avoid subsidies where public enterprises have financial objectives and targets (1975).

20. See also Pontoni who noted differential incidence of price changes for kerosene and gasoline (1983:29).

21. BCRP (1977:30) and interviews (1978, 1980, 1981).

22. Article 39, cited in INP-DESCO (1974?:8–14).

23. On management-worker relations in Peru's public enterprises, see Bustamante (1981:131–132).

24. Hanson (1965:360–366) summarizes public enterprise legal issues.

25. One-year terms were uncommon except in ENAPU. Of the public enterprises surveyed by the first Multisectoral Commission, six favored three-year terms, twenty-four favored two-year terms, and fourteen presented no information (Comisión, 1976, Appendix 14).

26. Interview, 1985. Chief executives and board chairmen repeatedly and spontaneously mentioned the inadequate preparation of other board members when interviewed (1979, 1981) and deplored appointments of political favorites. See Wolfenson (1981:310).

27. INP-DESCO (1974?b:4–5). Bonep describes the conceptual basis for representative boards (1981a:III:14–17).

28. Interviews (1978, 1981). See also CDES (1965:166) for a similar perspective on the mid-1960s government-director relations. At a higher level, Carlos Loret de Mola, as president of EPF, lamented the continual lack of guidelines from President Belaúnde (1978:16–17).

29. INP designates only sat on the boards of two public enterprises, COFIDE and INDUPERU. See Comisión (1976: Annex 14). Sorj overstates the impact of purportedly radical INP-nominated directors (1983:88).

30. Vice-admiral José Arce Larco confirmed patronage issues in CPV directorships (Tello, 1983:I:326).

31. In practice, RGLCOP had least effect in the ministry that drew it up, as procurement for housing and urban services was handled with considerably more discretion than in other ministries that were held to a greater "level of formality and detail" (Batley, 1979:22).

32. Batley analyzes qualification of proposal, bidding and payment practices for public sector agencies (1979:22–29).

33. The following procedure was observed for three or more valid bids: First, all valid bids were averaged, including the published base. Second, all bids that differed from the average by more than 10 percent were eliminated. Third, the remaining bids plus the base were averaged. Fourth, the bid closest, but not greater than,

the new average was selected.

34. Bishop examines intergovernmental relations in the U.S. (1978:22–26).
35. Fernandes' handbook for practitioners explores the nature of the links in a series of "operational exercises" aimed at managers and government officials (1986).
36. The literature comprises excessive discussions of control links, comparing the merits of sectoral ministries, ministries of public enterprises, general and sectoral holding companies.
37. Acosta (1984:39–40), Rossi (1983:2).
38. Although others have analyzed both formal or informal networks, I focus solely on formal network links (Acosta, 1984:45–47; 1985b:33). To simplify the model, I neglect all "own" relations that take place within an agency. Although internal improvements in any one system component's operating efficiency could improve the performance of a public enterprise, the impact is transmitted through one of the five standard links.
39. Acosta's interlinkage framework associates turbulence and disorder with a lack of control and monitoring mechanisms, instead of, as Peru amply bears out, with their presence (1985:19–21).
40. 1982. Raiffa provides background (1981:56–59).
41. Acosta (1985:23), Fernandes (1985:77–82), El-Namaki (1985:-110), and Sorensen (1985:235).
42. Guerra makes the point that the strong power concentration in the hands of top military officials meant that most policy conflicts could be expressed in military terms (1983:101). Agriculture was an Army Ministry, while Housing was a Navy prerogative. Officers in navy ministries were more conservative, reflecting their higher social class origins than their Army counterparts.
43. There is a fundamental difference between Cleaves and Scurrah's stress on client-dominated politics when both clients are private parties and when one of them is a public enterprise (1980:199). The first case does not involve the government at multiple levels.
44. CGR (1983a, b) CONADE (1983), and Villegas del Solar and Ansola (1982).
45. By 1983, CONADE oversaw some financial decisions, while CGR oversaw some auditing. Both fell far short of their legal potential (INAP, 1983b:83–84; 1984b:53).
46. Hanson surveys controlling links between a ministry and a public enterprise (1968:32–40); Prakash details commercial ties (1971:262–265).
47. Boneo indicates that large Latin American petroleum companies dwarfed their sectoral monitoring agencies (1981a, III:8).
48. Cepeda provides a case study of CPV problems, including the extreme politization of the labor unions (1985).
49. The Ministry of Housing was always under the more conservative

naval ministers, which suggests an alternative explanation, namely, that the delays were partly intentional.

50. "Sin necesidad tiene que pagar millones en aduana," *El Observador*, 2. Nov., 1981.
51. D.L. 18914 and Tantalean (1978:294–296).
52. Tantalean, 1978:296 and D.L. 20759.
53. Nove examines some interenterprise relationships for the British case (1973:121–131). He concludes that a only systems approach could resolve many otherwise intractable problems.
54. Although one of the ships was officially christened in 1982, by mid-1985, serious design flaws still kept it in the shipyards (Cepeda, 1985:194).
55. Similar reasons were advanced to force Air Inter and later Air France to purchase the Mercure 100. Air France successfully resisted; Air Inter did not (Anastassopoulos, 1981:100–102).
56. For a detailed breakdown of the rate schedule on port charges, see the appendix to R.M. 0191-78-TC/DS, *Reglamento de tarifas*.
57. See Revesz (1982:144–145) and Merino-Reyna (1979:18–19) for more information on EPSA's relations with banks.
58. "Centromín, una nueva versión del Cerro de Pasco Corporation: El envenamiento de las aguas del Río Mantaro," *Actualidad Económica*, Oct. 1978, pp. 5–6.
59. Revesz (1982:145) discusses the ramifications on the farming community of payments problems.
60. Fernandes details how to manage interlinkages (1985).

7

Conclusions

INTRODUCTION

This book assesses Peru's public enterprises using institutional, economic, and financial perspectives. It examines the timing, motives, objectives, and mechanisms that accompanied changes in Peru's portfolio and demonstrates the weakness of standard growth paradigms. It scrutinizes the overlapping strategy definition and monitoring systems and shows the weaknesses of standard control processes. It measures portfolio growth and deflates the notion of continued public enterprise drain on the government budget. It analyes efficiency, financial soundness, and profitability and reveals sectoral behavior patterns set outside the firms. It constructs and applies a theoretical framework to examine the structural dynamics of an inter-governmental interlinkage system. The following section reviews those contributions.

REVIEW

Chapter two detailed the evolution of Peru's public enterprise portfolio from 1968 to 1985, a period of rapid changes in the number and importance of firms. Although government policies went through five distinct periods, a constant thread prevailed: portfolio growth was incoherent and uncoordinated. Most government actions related to the portfolio responded to short-run and shifting political, social, or (rarely) economic objectives that only exceptionally coincided with perceived long-run national goals. Still other actions were accidental and unintended. The final result was a large, unwieldy, and disarticulated portfolio.

Under General Velasco, the portfolio agglomerated from

January 1970 to December 1973 as several irregular, unplanned, or proposed sector-level policies converged to sweep the commanding heights of the economy into government control. Although the Velasco government clearly intended that public enterprises occupy a powerful economic position, it did not carefully examine the implications of a large, legally autonomous portfolio on the rest of the economy or on the rest of government. Neither did it carefully plan many aspects of its public enterprise policy. In taking over a sector it aimed at undercutting bases of economic power rather than taking the necessary steps to ensure the long-term viability of the resulting firms. The growth by agglomeration reduced public enterprises to the status of incidental means to achieve sectoral goals and led to permanent crippling of their economic and financial health. By the end of 1973 the government's style in amassing more companies for the portfolio had changed from uncoordinated, but fervent, lightning-like strikes to raid the established bastions of private economic power to the duller, less exciting, and definitely sluggish mopping-up operations.

Public enterprise treatment of the late Velasco years strongly resembles that of the early Morales Bermúdez period as strident internal government policy disagreements, reinforced by a confluence of external economic and social factors, resulted in a tumultuous policy environment marked by frequent policy reversals. The policy outcomes of such a constantly changing context increased the portfolio disarticulation and worsened company problems.

From 1978 to 1980, the military leaders and their civilian advisors tried to sanitize the portfolio as it came under increased political scrutiny, in the transition to constitutional rule, and under increased government scrutiny under the widespread austerity measures. The Morales Bermúdez-Silva Ruete duo tried three portfolio strategies: privatization, reorganization, and capitalization. They succeeded in establishing the appearance of a financially healthy portfolio, but weakened the companies in the process.

From 1980 to 1985, the second coming of President Belaúnde was marked by hypocritical timidity. Downsizing the portfolio figured prominently in his party platform; real reduction escaped him, unless it benefited party insiders, while real growth occurred in his favored housing sector. Although upgrading company finances constantly marked party pronouncements, his administration featured the worst portfolio performance because the president failed to take key decisions and lacked the administrative clout to follow through on enunciated policies.

With time and experience, the government's public enterprise posture evolved from the naiveté of the early Velasco years that public enterprises would solve all the country's problems, to a later leech-like attitude that public enterprises could be bled white to support other producers, consumers, and the government. Still later, it switched to the Morales Bermúdez-Silva Ruete dual strategy: real improvement in many economic indicators coupled with manipulation of some financial statements to show the symptoms of financial health. Under President Belaúnde, the potential to tap public enterprises overwhelmed the lingering ideological repugnance to state ownership.

Chapter three examined Peru's contradictory, and mutually inconsistent ways of defining, reviewing, and monitoring public enterprise strategies. The three delicate tasks simultaneously must allow company management sufficient autonomy and flexibility to meet commercial goals, yet constrain company management to achieve any extra-entrepreneurial objectives. By these simple criteria, Peru's strategy definition, review, and control systems failed.

After 1968 Peru's INP improved but, even with improvement, it could not clearly set objectives or reconcile conflicting strategies, nor did it have the power to monitor goal attainment. The medium-term planning documents reveal that the INP never provided specific evaluation criteria that balanced economic against social or political objectives because INP left economic goals undefined while stating social or political ones imprecisely.

In the absence of a strong plan, the MEF used the budgeting system to set a policy that clearly subordinated company long-term development needs to government short-run financial requirements. It imposed increasingly complicated control and reporting systems on the firms that hindered management instead of helping it. The government belatedly realized the need to collect data to monitor performance, but the system adopted gathered late and incomplete information, insufficiently shared it among government agencies, and never fed it back to the public enterprises to improve performance.

Peru also used committees to monitor strategic and everyday affairs of its public enterprises. Their impact was limited: they had no line authority, leaving policy execution to the ministries, and they merely served as intra-governmental forums for discussing conflicting opinions without ever resolving problems. No real solutions were expected and none were achieved.

Chapter four surveyed macro indicators of Peru's portfolio. The period framework explained their evolution remarkably well. The performance of the four to six largest companies, often in energy and mining, dominated the portfolio and determined the evolution of income, profits, subsidies, taxes, employment, investment, foreign and local debt, and value added. The weight of a few large firms suggests that portfolios need parallel monitoring systems: a universal one to periodically assess portfolio performance and specialized ones to follow those firms with greatest impact on a few key indicators. As a corollary: subjecting all public enterprises to the same detailed government scrutiny is costly, inappropriate, and counterproductive.

Chapter five examined measures of financial soundness and stability, internal efficiency, and profitability to provide a richly detailed picture of how government policies can negatively influence company performance. Lack of working capital plagued the companies and was caused largely by the government's failing to adequately capitalize them, by failing to pay them on time, and by failing to enforce a prompt and timely payment system. The government created an environment hostile to efficiency. The degree of government control over variables used in constructing measures of efficiency bears a direct relationship to the measure's behavior: the more the measure's components came under government control, the more the measure's movements fit the period analysis.

Chapter six proposed an interorganizational framework to explore limits on public enterprises arising from the environment and from relations among agencies. Governments place many issues beyond management control by refusing to define some environmental parameters or by inappropriately defining others. This hampers company operations and performance by causing: confusion over objectives, uncoordinated and unsound pricing structures, and unresolved legal issues. With no stable context, stating overall strategies, whether for the entire portfolio or for specific companies, became a means of reconciling interests of conflicting governmental groups, instead of a way of providing the companies with clear guidelines for action. An unstable context also led to the fallacy that any public-enterprise problem resulted from inadequate management control. This fallacy led to the simplistic heaping of ad hoc, uncoordinated, and contradictory control mechanisms on the companies that served only to hamper management and lower performance.

Other elements are beyond management control because they comprise a formal network of relationships linking government agencies to public enterprises. Five categories of systems relationships are examined to show that the problems that resulted when Peru's government never approached the problems of its public enterprises in a coherent and systematic fashion.

MYTHS DEBUNKED, MISCONCEPTIONS CLARIFIED, MISPERCEPTIONS CLEARED

Myths, misconceptions, and misperceptions abound about public enterprises and their roles in the economy. Contemporary Peruvian folklore also contains misconstrued and distorted notions about portfolio growth after 1968. Using materials presented in earlier chapters, this section debunks five of the tenacious myths.

Supine State?

The first is the myth of a historically weak state in Latin America. To explain public enterprise formation and growth, the standard historical-stages approach postulates a series of consecutive motives which are supposed to have impelled Latin American governments to create different types of public enterprises during different, well-defined, sequential time periods.[1] For example, until the first third of this century, Latin American primary-product, export-oriented economies are said to have maintained a public enterprise portfolio to meet the needs of the foreign-owned or -dominated exporters of agricultural or extractive products. Consequently, the state supinely complemented private undertakings by providing basic infrastructure (including public utilities), forming regional or sectoral promotion agencies, and mounting rescue operations when private interests did not obtain a sufficiently high rate of return.

A major motivational change is supposed to have occurred when the Great Depression and the Second World War cut off Latin America from its traditional European or North American suppliers of manufactured consumer goods and inputs to low-level manufacturing processes. This opened the second stage, that of easy import substitution of foodstuffs, textiles, and any other industrial processes whose simple engineering technology and limited capital requirements were within reach of the traditionally conservative-investing, domestic entrepreneurs. Tariffs and quotas to protect the new domestic firms were the norm. Occasional exceptions to the general pattern were found in politically based nationalizations of public services and basic transport, and in rescue operations of foreign firms made unprofitable to their overseas owners by the expiration of government-granted concessions or by the imposition of government-imposed barriers to unfettered profit remittances.

Problems associated with the historical view have been examined elsewhere (Saulniers, 1985a:228–233; 1985c:333–335). For example, first, it simplifies the evolution of the portfolio to being linear, unidirectional, and additive, according to some inevitable historical logic. Thus, there is no logical provision for governments to have created those companies associated with late entry into the public portfolio, earlier than expected. Peru provides clear exceptions and counterexamples to the homogenized general myth (Saulniers and Revilla, 1983; Revilla, 1987). After Independence, Peru's government was the most important owner of the means of production. Its substantial colonial inheritance and the spoils from the long independence struggle resulted in a stronger state much earlier than explained by standard historical theories. Moreover, subsequent portfolio growth was not, as predicted, oriented to the external market. During the first half-century after independence, the government's new ventures either bolstered production for the local market or assured national security. The standard historical approach to public enterprises is unable to handle such common anomalies.

Second, the standard historical view assumes a broadly defined framework of development or growth, not contraction and shrinkage.

It cannot adequately explain how governments could, or indeed why they ever would want to, divest themselves of enterprises. The massive erosion of the Peruvian government portfolio during most of the nineteenth century, strongly paralleled by the recent privatization efforts in many countries, clearly contradicts the growth assumption and serves to refute the conventional wisdom. Boneo's cyclical model of state intervention in Argentina provides a better basis for historical theories by relating swings in the prevailing government ideology to portfolio composition and pricing policies (1981b).

Third, to maintain that Latin America as a whole adhered to the same inexorable development pattern oversimplifies the complexities both of development and of Latin America. Some countries created public enterprises commonly attributed to the later stages without having passed through earlier stages. In fact, stages are not sequential, their distinctions are blurred, and attributes of earlier stages often became mixed in a hybrid fashion with those of a later one. The standard historical approach cannot deal with individual countries nor does it supply the expected universalist theory of public enterprises.

The preceding diatribe against the standard historical approach should not be construed as an argument against proper use of historical method in explaining the public-enterprise phenomenon. Instead, it argues the need for a revisionist view of public-enterprise history. The standard historical approach draws analogies between the current portfolio and a bed of fossils, added to by accretion in well-defined layers, with public enterprises comprising the fossil remains of past government policies. This approach completely neglects the tumultuous policy environment wherein governments continually changed, modified, countermanded, reversed, and reinstated policies under different guises. Similarly, public enterprises were created, dissolved, merged, and allowed to deliberately atrophy. The proper analogy should be to the alluvial deposit downstream from a fossil bed instead of the bed itself. Studying the alluvial deposit (the existing portfolio) and theorizing about the nature of the intervening geological (government) processes is a useful beginning. It does not substitute for the much needed detailed examination of the original fossils in situ, through a thorough historical analysis of policies related to the entrepreneurial role of individual states as a preliminary step to generalizing about the dynamics of public enterprises in Latin America.

New Vision?

The second myth alleges that Peru's extremely rapid public enterprise growth, during the 1970s, constituted a major break with historical patterns. Misperceptions of rapid, ahistorical growth are partly due to problems in measuring public sector growth in general.[2]

First, applying a clear, agreed-on, and workable public enterprise definition consistently over time is indispensable to resolving measurement problems. Peru demonstrated that because coherent definitions don't interest governments, successive attempts to establish portfolio size often measure different things. Many countries don't maintain adequate public enterprise records. By cross-checking information on Mexico's government-owned corporations from all official sources, the Office for Public Sector Studies (OPSS) established that the Mexican portfolio was twice as large as any single government agency admitted. Because Peru legally transformed semi-autonomous government agencies to semi-independent public enterprises, analysts who have uncritically relied on faulty government data, confused apparent growth in the number of legally defined firms with real numerical growth of an economic phenomenon.

Second, data inadequacies fuel the growth misconception. Until recently, official Peruvian sources neglected to remove inflationary effects from their data. In current terms, Peruvian public enterprise income rose 4,822-fold between 1968 and 1984; carefully adjusting for inflation indicates growth closer to 24-fold, while compensating for the general growth in the economy reveals only a 15-fold increase (BCRP, 1985b). Uncritical reliance on government-provided statistics grossly exaggerates growth.

A third misperception is that Peru's public enterprise growth represented a historical anomaly. It did not in an international perspective. Nationalizing existing natural-resource based companies and transforming them into new government firms had occurred earlier in geographically and ideologically varied countries. In Latin America, Argentina's YPF, Brazil's PETROBRAS, and Mexico's PEMEX long predated PETROPERU. Moreover, Pinelo (1973) and Philip (1982) stressed the long-standing historical roots of Peru's nationalization--resolved petroleum controversy. Similarly, other CIPEC members, Zaire's GECAMINES and Zambia's ZIMCO, predated MINEROPERU, and Chile's CODELCO preceded MINEROPERU's major shift into production via the Cerro takeover. Peru's pre-1974, sector-wide takeovers simply followed patterns established earlier in other countries with similar natural-resource endowments.[3]

Fourth, the ahistorical growth myth conveniently neglects the relentless increase in public enterprises that began during the last century and that continued well into the early 1970s. Although academic neglect suffers from definitional ambiguities and the lack of accurate historical studies, strong portfolio growth under the Prado and the first Belaúnde administrations provoked angry reactions from local conservatives (CDES, 1965).

Losers?

A third myth, persistently retold in Peru, holds that public enterprises persistently lose money, so that profits are an anomaly. Peru provides an excellent rebuttal, since, for most years, both operating and accounting profits were positive. Although some large companies had severe losses during the 1970s, the myth of persistent loser suffers from four major misconceptions.

First, definitional issues make examining public enterprise finances difficult, since the legal system impeded monitoring the firms. Those for which the government had access to financial data, were often losers and their image was generalized to the entire portfolio. Peruvian authorities and other analysts based their negative image of the firms on a small subset of government-owned companies.

Second, international accounting practices bias the reported data because the commonly accepted IMF methodology records data separately for government-owned financial institutions from those of nonfinancial public enterprises. Reported data represent a partial portfolio and obscure banking practices that aid the financial firms at the expense of the nonfinancial ones.

Third, splashy losses by one or two firms catch headlines and distract notice away from widespread portfolio profitability. Small positive profits don't sell newspapers or fuel political debate as well as do horrendous losses. Detailed analysis reveals that the portfolio earned a positive return on net worth.

Fourth, dividing profits among enterprises was sensitive to inter-enterprise pricing practices. These, in turn, depended on the cabinet-level exercise of political power. Some supposedly profitable firms received hidden transfers, while some supposed losers gave up potential profits via transfer pricing mechanisms.

Parasitic Parastatals?

The fourth particularly persistent and deep-seated myth alleges that public enterprises are "parasitic parastatals" that gluttonize subsidies from the public trough. Peru again provides a starting point for debunking that myth. Although Peru's government granted substantial subsidies, many misconceptions and misperceptions surround the nature and amount of the funds transferred so that the cause for subsidies remained hidden, the subsidy process stayed obscure, and the effect of the subsidies was misconstrued. The Peruvian experience provides indications on how to design policies to lower the need for subsidies and how to target them for maximal impact.

The first misconception concerns who got the subsidies. Almost invariably, they went to the final consumer instead of to the companies. Firms merely acted as conduits to channel benefits to the consumers via the pricing mechanism. Thus, the government bore ultimate responsibility for subsidies, while the consumers were the ultimate beneficiaries.

A second misperception arose because the government transferred funds so inefficiently that no public enterprise received the subsidies expected or due. The government claimed to pay enormous subsidies but, in fact, it usually paid in strongly devalued currency and only after long delays. The net effects of its too-little, too-late policy was to weaken the companies financially and to increase their operating costs.

A third public misconception is that the government doled out subsidies to cover up companies' persistent poor management and low levels of efficiency. Confidential reports, however, indicate that most subsidies compensated for government inflexibility in refusing to permit the companies to reflect international prices in their accounting practices and pricing. Protecting the domestic market at the expense of the public enterprises meant company costs soared and with them the need for more subsidies.

Rational Governments?

A fifth myth is that of planned government action. Economists and other social scientists presume the existence of a rational government with fixed and clear objectives, constrained by the states of the world and the national economy. In this purely theoretical model, governments create public enterprises for use as policy tools to reach national objectives when the private sector is unable or unwilling to act, or when private sector action is deemed prejudicial to national interests. While useful as a theoretical simplification to order experience, planned government action rarely occurred.

First, concealed motives give rise to misconceptions. Peru's government acted in a way that subordinated long-term considerations to short-term political gains but, for reasons of political expediency, it often concealed those short-term reasons behind long-term motives. Official sources fostered the myth of government rationality.

Second, the effects of accidental or conjunctural government actions have been underrated in explaining portfolio growth. The Banco Popular nationalization doubled the size of the portfolio in sweeping many unplanned and unwanted enterprises into the public portfolio. Similar unplanned actions occur with regularity. Hanson stressed the accidental nature of the most widely discussed and imitated river valley development authority, "the creation of the TVA, in fact, was the result not so much of a principled decision as of an accidental combination of circumstances" (1965:319). Neglecting accidental nationalization feeds the myth of planned and rational action.

A third misconception comes from neglecting the experimental nature of government actions that were often taken without proper study and without adequate planning, and that led to periodic policy readjustments. Indeed, adhocracy best describes the Peruvian government's public enterprise actions. One former government official admitted experimentation, saying that if the government tried something and, it did not like the policy results, it went on to try something else (interview, 1978). Booth, referring to the press, indicates that confused and distorted policy execution marked the late 1970s, but the ad hoc nature of government actions became apparent long before (1983:141). Thus, the haphazard nature of the policy process led to government by fits and starts, not government by planned and rational action.

POLICY OPTIONS AND POLICY PRESCRIPTIONS

Governments will continue using public enterprises to carry out policy, so that improving their performance remains an important issue. To be most effective, performance improvement should occur within an interlinked system. Brown's inter-organizational conflict management perspective, that complements the theoretical paradigm developed in Chapter 6, provides one way of designing appropriate system-wide mechanisms (1983).

Brown defines the context of a system as the whole field in which different elements to the conflict are located (1983:34). Earlier chapters have shown that government authorities bear chief responsibility in designing an appropriate context for the efficient management of intrasystemic conflict. The context must provide outlets for legitimate government needs to define, review, and monitor strategies while delicately balancing those needs against equally legitimate company needs for autonomy in action. Even if government has major responsibility, the context should not stem from unilateral action. It should arise from interinstitutional cooperation within a framework of collective goals and objectives.

Both central government agencies and public enterprises should systematically devise and implement interface strategies to productively solve frictions that develop in their working relationships. Strategies should be stable enough to isolate managers and officials from the negative effects of continual change in working environments. Neglecting an interlinkage framework can lead to inappropriate government interference in management decisions, disruptive conflict among government agencies, weakened firms, and a proliferation of increasingly ineffective government controls.

Context

A smoothly functioning system needs a strong and enduring institutional context. Establishing that context becomes easier when a national consensus on the role of public enterprises permits optimal portfolio size to be reached by carefully reasoned takeover, instead of turbulent, agglomerative adhocracy. The consensus should embody broad national goals and should specify how to relate those goals to public enterprises, how to devise strategies to implement those goals, and how to use those strategies to decide whether to create or to liquidate companies, and to set company operational plans. A national consensus, subject only to periodic reassessments, enables actions to take place within stable structural contexts and on the expectation of future stability. Having stable institutional bases, clear interventionary motives, and clear and stable objectives in turn helps set the context for the types and forms of control mechanisms.

Open and frank discussion leading to a national consensus is rare in developing countries, and Peru is no exception. Its government never attempted to bring about a national consensus on public enterprises, which deprived the companies of a fixed and stable working environment and subjected them, instead, to the vagaries of regime, ministerial, or bureaucratic changes and the consequent negative effects analyzed above.

A stable and consistent legal system is a key contextual element. Peru never had one, resulting in a still-imperative need to rethink and redesign the legal system to promote public enterprise efficiency. The key to proper system redesign is to deliberately and judiciously try to anticipate various consequences of government action within the existing system, and then to redesign as needed to avoid negative effects.

Strong and stable institutional bases also come from having clear-cut motives for the creation of a public enterprise. The Peruvian case provides ample evidence that the portfolio grew more through ignorance, uncertainty, governmental self-interest, fear of the future, and sheer accident than it did through reasoned analysis. Justification for many of the takeovers was shrouded in obscurity and veiled behind carefully crafted documents prepared for public consumption. The moves often tried to preempt possible future action by a real or imagined enemy. Although creating some companies achieved a goal of strategic sectoral presence, in most instances Peruvian officials never learned what Shepherd defines as a cardinal lesson of public enterprise: "the creation of a public firm does not assure — or even define — the optimal solution for a market or problem. That solution must often be formulated and guided from outside" (1976a:40). Thus, creating a public enterprise is only the beginning; it needs a stable operating environment and clear, fixed, and stable company objectives. Continuing processes of company reorganizations, mergers, dissolutions, and re-creations obscured creation motives and muddled objectives for the company managers forced to operate in unstable environments.

In practice, public firms pursue both social and commercial goals.

The context must specify the goal mix against which success or failure of company action is evaluated. In a badly designed context, companies often are expected to conform to a folkloric public enterprise model that encompasses bad performance and overstaffing. Imprecise goals foster inefficiency because commercial losses caused by poor management are disguised as costs of meeting social objectives. To compound the problem of imprecisely stated goals, governments often expect companies to fulfill some unstated, but implicit, objectives including: promoting consumer welfare, being a model employer, conserving foreign exchange, promoting exports, and developing the local community (Sherif, 1973:19). Lack of priorities, conflicting objectives, or mixed priority rankings from different policy makers lead to lowered performance (Shirley 1983:17). Governments must help stabilize the context by arbitrating goal-setting and priority assignment processes to reconcile the interests of the plural principles. As owners of equity, government agencies help define goals. As political mediators, government agencies reconcile the interests of the various governmental and extra-governmental parties.

In setting and ranking clear, attainable company objectives, governments must guard against instrumental abuse by discarding goals for which public enterprises are inappropriate policy tools. Generalizing from Peru, Boneo indicated that instrumental abuse characterizes governments undergoing rapid revolutionary change (1981a:II:5). Shirley backed that contention in reporting that the government inaptly required one of Peru's fishing plants to run a hotel (1983:53). Floyd proposed three basic criteria to guide the government's goal ranking: whether goals are mutually consistent or whether there exist tradeoffs between conflicting goals; whether goals are attainable by public enterprises given available resources; and what is the estimated fiscal impact on the company, the consumer, and the government (1984:8). Peru's government failed those criteria by providing poorly specified, often conflicting, objectives without looking at potential tradeoffs, whose attainability was never questioned, and which were fixed irregardless of fiscal impact.

In the larger context, external goals, which often have a national or regional character, are set outside the company by government authorities, political parties, consumers, labor unions, or other interest groups (See El-Namaki 1979:141). Each group tries to impose its own control and monitoring systems to assess goal compliance. Unless those systems account for factors beyond management control, they show limited success in improving public enterprise performance. Internal goals consist of management's specification of company objectives, often stressing the company's economic or financial viability or the operational performance of company units. They are more flexible than external goals, often respond rapidly to changes in the external environment, and are less subject to external review.

The context should provide explicit and attainable performance criteria for both types of goals. It is futile for central government authorities to require company profitability while setting prices below average cost levels. Likewise, it is inadvisable for company management to plan for major expansion at a time of externally decreed belt tightening.

Managers should also have a role in setting the context. In doing so, they specify a maximization problem: how to reach certain objectives, constrained by company capabilities and external factors. A swiftly shifting context may mean that external objectives are unknown, ill-specified, or conflicting even when internal objectives are precise. But, even without clear external guidelines, company managers must still try to interpret the decision makers' unknown or partly known preferences to combine them with internal priorities.

In general, the context is insensitive to the efforts of management to set goals and objectives. Insensitivity undermines management morale and reduces management motivation for improving performance. Sherif provides three practical considerations as a proxy for success: keep out of the red; be able to regularly pass an audit; and avoid politically questionable acts (1973:19). This approach, called success through expediency, presupposes that management already has a viable context and can control key variables that determine performance. In the Peruvian case. that assumption rarely held true.

Successful public enterprise operation should be free from structural handicaps. Peru's was not, witness: initial underfinancing, dependence on price-rising imported raw materials, persistent foreign exchange shortages, inadequate technical or managerial skills, under-utilized plant capacity, inopportune siting decisions, and excessively high cost structures. Structural handicaps hinder managers trying to keep companies afloat and running smoothly. Companies should not be held accountable for most structural handicaps, particularly those resulting from inadequate study when creating or supervising the company.

In Peru, government officials lacked the management capacity to accurately assess the costs and benefits of public enterprises (Saulniers, 1981a). They did not recognize or consistently underrated flaws in the context. Sherif warned that government must limit public enterprise activity based on its own present and projected supply of administrative capability and the extent that managerial talent can be attracted to the companies (1973:10–11). He ranked managerial shortages over such scarce resources as capital, foreign exchange, and technological know-how, but, in Peru, the warning appears to have gone unheeded. One concludes that the entire public sector's management capacity must form part of the context for prior evaluations of public enterprise creation and for later reviews of their proposed projects (Shirley, 1983:52).

Setting the operational context must not be confused with total subordination of public enterprises within the larger public administration system. That possibility only asphyxiates the firms, making them more vulnerable to bureaucratic practices and political pressures. Both central government agencies and public firms should systematically work together to devise and implement the context for mutually productive operations.

Managing Interorganizational Interfaces

Interorganizational transactions produce conflict that can have positive or negative repercussions on companies. Correctly managing interface conflict to maximize benefits and to minimize costs of public enterprises to the nation should be assigned a high priority. A key step in correctly managing the interface is to comprehend the nature of the interface itself, the parties to the interface, and the representatives of the party (Brown, 1983:20).

Interfaces involving public enterprises generally fall under what Brown has defined as underorganized interfaces (1983:28–30). Key characteristics include unclear or conflicting authority patterns; unclear or multiple and conflicting goals; openness to disruptive inputs of information, resources, and people; and resource poverty at less than survival levels. Peru's firms fit the description well.

Parties to the interface have different interests but are forced to interact (Brown, 1983:31). Interests visible to insiders often vary from those considered important by outsiders. The enduring theoretical debate on the role of the state, which fails to account for the functional differentiation within the government apparatus that has the most direct impact at the company level, serves as an example. Any differences between perceived and possible mixes of common and conflicting interests allow for changing the interface. Constructive interface management also depends on the relative importance of the interface to the parties.

Individuals, as representatives of parties, interact at the interfaces. The autonomy, power, or discretion permitted them by the parties or by the broader institutional context bear on possible conflicts. So, too, do their personal characteristics (Brown, 1983:33). Peru provides the example of excess exercise of ministerial power, whereby some ministers sought to impose themselves on the public enterprises. Circumscribing that power by changing the context to limit ministerial prerogatives or by changing the characteristics of the representatives in choosing ministers who had strong management skills, not political or military clout, would free firms from excessive ministerial dependence.

The interface between public enterprises and the planning system generates conflict and, consequently, merits major efforts at conflict management. A conclusion can be drawn from the Peruvian case that reformulating the interface boundaries by redesigning organizational characteristics can help reduce conflict. This would involve reducing the planning system's impact on public enterprises by recognizing that its two main contributions are setting overall policy directions and assisting in strategic planning. Any other role, including that of controller, needs retraction. Central government authorities should set up a formal mechanism to reconcile conflict between public enterprises and the planning system.

Parliamentary control has escaped any specific analysis. Nevertheless, the need to circumscribe parliamentary power over operational decisions is inescapable, yet has long been unheeded (Hanson, 1965:355). Peru's congress remained suspended from 1968 to 1980. Thereafter, its members paid lip service to the myth that government equity ownership means that all aspects of a public enterprise belong to the public. However, they often succumbed to the irresistible temptation to use firms for personal gain in grabbing headlines and increasing their political visibility by exposing or by drumming up a new public enterprise "scandal." Excessive scapegoatism exemplifies another type of interface conflict to be managed. Recent Peruvian experience also substantiates that companies must be buffered from direct parliamentary interference. Time spent by company officials in mediating conflict at the parliamentary interface could be more productively employed in managing production. Buffering should not mean isolation, however. Developing better ways to provide parliament with better and more reliable information should alter the communications interface and reduce conflict.

Internal company goals should be the prerogative of company executives, but underorganized interfaces of many agencies lead to heavy-handed government interference in company affairs that negates the effects of good management and reduces incentives for improvement. Peru fit Sherif's contention that disorderly portfolio expansion resulted in a top-heavy supervisory structure and overinflated supervisory layers (1973:13). Monetary costs of an inadequate supervisory structure pale, however, compared to the welfare costs of mediocre competence, poor coordination, interorganizational conflicts, and other resource misallocations.

Some centralized control and monitoring arrangements must be maintained over macro variables because nonsectoral ministries, such as finance or treasury, need performance forecasts and results for imports, foreign exchange requirements, prices, and product lines. However, the right to information is not synonymous with the right to control. Attempts to direct operational policy should be curtailed, thereby altering interfaces by carefully redefining functions. Firms have the right to expect timely decisions that respect company independence. Governments should explicitly recognize company needs as a legitimate component of the interface and scrap excessive delays and complicated clearance procedures.

Governments need good information systems to generate regular flows of reliable data within an overall framework of evaluating and improving performance. Peru's minimal system could not even track the number of public enterprises. Even after the Belaúnde government reforms, government insiders admitted that untraceable firms still existed (interview, 1983). Information systems should have the dual purpose of externally controlling managers and of serving as managerial control tools. Such an external monitoring system, carefully integrated into an internal management information system, should also provide managers with information for improving internal policy.

To reduce interface conflict brought about by poorly designed information systems, altering information relationships as a function of the costs of government regulation becomes necessary. A two-tier system should combine a basic system that gathers periodic information on key variables for all public enterprises with specialized monitoring systems for a few companies. The two-tier system provides benefits of lowered reporting and compliance costs to most firms with little data or control loss to the government.

Uncoordinated information demands by different agencies multiply organizational interfaces, increase the potential for conflict, and burden the companies. Centralized data gathering should distribute information among all interested agencies to reduce interfaces, lower companies' reporting costs, and provide timely and more accurate statistics.

Organizational characteristics form part of the interface structure which characterizes an institution. As shown in the Peruvian case, counterproductive management incentive structures blocked efficient system operation. They should be dismantled and replaced with structures that link incentives to results. Incentives should provide what managers seek, including power, prestige, and pecuniary rewards. Instead, the system often gives them denunciations and denigration. As one Peruvian executive lamented, the manager's poor public image hindered his company's recruiting efforts and slowed down improvement (interview, 1981). Recognition must be linked to performance, which means that performance must be measured and firms and their managers must be evaluated. Design and implementation of a system that quantifies performance and compares it against goals or targets is essential to redefining the organizational characteristics to better manage conflict.

Designing a good recognition system must correct past shortcomings. Company accountability strongly relates to efficiency, but managers were rarely held accountable for their decisions. Indeed, with control over many decisions removed from them, Peru's managers had little responsibility. A good incentive structure strongly relates to efficiency, yet management was not motivated to improve performance. Performance standards and indicators were often implicit, while explicit ones were often countermanded. Moreover, politics, parentage, or patronage, not performance, often determined promotion. Overbearing control systems inhibited competent decision making. Indeed, managers were often demoralized by the three missing keys to proper decision making: autonomy, incentives (particularly pecuniary ones), and a specification of consistent and attainable goals. Sherif stated the problem succinctly: "a public enterprise can perform ineffectively despite the greatest contribution of good management. But the reverse is seldom true" (1973:34).

Some market imperfections may persist, for example, a company's unregulated monopoly power may have adverse consequences both for customers and for proper resource allocation. Regulating a government monopoly similarly to a private one should be done. The policy of breaking up monopolies is not feasible for most LDC companies with small domestic markets and limited export possibilities (Shirley 1983:44). To replace a national monopoly with regional ones does not help solve the allocation problem; removing unnecessary government barriers to efficient resource use does.

This book has repeatedly stressed issues beyond management control, but the traditional advice to improve management skills must not be neglected. It, too, can result in better portfolio performance. Management development is a priority, and should be linked to a reward structure to ensure that executives stay with the company. Public managers should be paid similarly to those in the private sector to reduce losses of competent executives. The issue remains, nonetheless: performance improvement from management development can be overestimated unless major improvements occur throughout the system.

Both the context and the interfaces must be redesigned to provide companies with the standard business operational autonomy. Flexibility, fast response, innovation, and the ability to make mistakes are prerequisites to successful business operation. Chapters 3 and 6 concluded that Peru's government authorities continually interfered in company affairs to enforce rigidities, deaden response, stifle innovation, and rigidly censure even the slightest mistake.

Central government organizations must not escape scrutiny. government influences company efficiency, yet Peruvian bureaucrats were not always held accountable for their decisions. For example, the CGR's excessive zeal in misapplying its mandate disheartened company management. The power of comptrollers to intervene into standard operating details must be curbed and performance audits should be substituted for "propriety audits" (Fernandes, 1979:55). Moreover, the tone of comptroller interventions must shift from undue negativism to positive support to aid companies meet their objectives.

Top-level government confusion between "managing the managers and managing the enterprise themselves" (Sherif, 1973:34) must give way to a more productive managing of the interface conflicts. By so doing, governments will be forced to carefully set the desired objectives, adhere to them, and evaluate how well they were achieved.[4]

CONCLUSIONS

The policy environment needed for proper public enterprise functioning differs little from that needed by a private firm. Public enterprises need stability, autonomy, motivation, and feasible goals. In many countries, including Peru, difficulties in coordinating a fragmented intergovernmental system mean that firms always face instability; government interference always overshadows autonomy; the government imparts counterproductive motivational structures; and companies receive unknown or unrealistic goals.

The model of the Peruvian state that emerges from the heavy empiricism of this book is one of well-intentioned, inexperienced bungler. The policy prescriptions detailed above, if applied, require it to shift to being a well-intentioned, sophisticated adept. The transition from one to the other is never simple, but it is possible. Should it prove impossible, i.e. should the state prove unable to effectively manage inherent structural conflicts, drastic portfolio sanitizing measures will become necessary.

Company liquidation or privatization is the ultimate sanitizing measure. Firms should be purged from the public portfolio, not because they are bad, but because the governments have continually abdicated their responsibilities as public owner. In this respect, I differ sharply from other analysts who advocate privatization to reduce the public enterprises' managerial and fiscal burden on government[5] or who view continual rolling privatization as the logical sequence to the public sector's temporary stewardship over firms.[6] I also differ from those who favor distressed privatization when "a constellation of problems impels the state to move toward divestment" (Glade, 1983:91). Instead, I stress it because the government is responsible for much of its own burden, so that streamlining the portfolio may relieve its management burden, simplify its interlinked system, and aid in the transition to a sound government.

The privatization or liquidation decision, however, should be taken only after careful, objective analysis of benefits and costs. Even though public sector growth never resulted from a carefully planned scheme, maintaining the public portfolio or reducing its size and importance, must be carefully thought out to avoid introducing further sources of systemic bias (Saulniers, 1981a).

Privatization of equity, whether total or partial, is only one option for pruning the public portfolio. Privatization of management, by granting management contracts to private national or foreign groups, provides an alternative course of action. Private managers may be better able to resist the encroachments of government officials and be more effectively isolated from political pressures that reduce a company's autonomy than public managers. Joint ventures between government and domestic or foreign capital can combine equity and management privatization by bringing in otherwise unattainable new equity, providing access to technology, and incorporating management skills.

Activity privatization by reducing supernumerary functions is another possibility. For example, by 1980, CPV maintained a navy yard, warehouses, and substantial repair facilities, none of which were held by competing firms (interview, 1981). If the resulting activity set of the public enterprise matches that of its private counterparts, improved performance and heightened competition may result. Activities may be hived off as independent subsidiaries, leased or sold to the private sector.

Finally, privatization by objective must be considered. This entails giving the public enterprise the goal of operating as a private business concern. Major behavioral changes in management should result from increased autonomy, price setting ability, and access to capital markets.

This book undertook a systematic interorganizational policy study of Peru's public enterprises after 1968. I have heavily emphasized identifying and explaining past failures of the Peruvian public enterprises as an aid in the design of better interorganizational systems approaches in LDCs. The key contribution of this book has been to shift the focus of research and policy action away from the single enterprise or the public enterprise portfolio to the set of interlinkages, both direct and indirect, that constitute the entire system. The system, not the company nor the portfolio, must be the basis for future reform to improve public enterprise performance.

NOTES

1. See FitzGerald (1974, 1976c) and UN, ECLA (1971).
2. Valuable contributions to solving some of the public sector measurement problems appear in contributions to Taylor (1983).
3. See Radetzki (1985:23–24). Some authors have emphasized the conjunction of nationalizations, which gave rise to the perception of ahistorical growth. For background, see, Akinsanya (1980), Baklanoff (1975), Ingram (1974), and Sigmund (1980).
4. Sherif (1973:43) used the term "cult of results." Peruvian public enterprise managers continually complained that they were never evaluated on their results. Jones found similar complaints in Pakistan (1983:5).
5. Choksi (1979: 71), Shirley (1983:70).
6. Glade (1983:88–89) develops the historical basis for rolling privatization in Peru's industrial sector.

Public Enterprise Definitional Issues

WHAT NUMBERS?

Peru never kept accurate count of its public enterprises. Peru's negligence complicates assessment of the portfolio's performance, since both size and composition were never accurately determined. This appendix examines definitional, conceptual, and institutional issues of inadequate recordkeeping and uses standard definitions to enumerate Peru's portfolio.

NUMBERS USED AND NUMBERS ABUSED

Peru's principal problem is that its public enterprises have usually been politically defined. Similar figures for the 1960s justify this conclusion. For example, the conservative Centro de Documentación Económico-Social (CDES) castigated excessive public enterprise growth after 1950. Several of the 20 firms mentioned in 1965 were aggregations, such as the grouping of five sectoral development banks or the lumping together of all regional development corporations (CDES, 1965:211). Taking a pro-government perspective, the INP estimated 22 companies for 1966, but erroneously omitted regional development corporations while disaggregating the banks (INP, 1980a:98).

Two approaches mark assessments of portfolio growth during the military period. The first, clearly anti-statist, indicts the military for the extraordinary growth by comparing the small portfolio in 1968 to a greatly expanded one in 1980. The second, more pro-statist, focusses on the reorganization of diffuse entrepreneurial holdings by demonstrating that many public enterprises in 1980 were already present in 1968 under other legal forms, which reduces the growth rate.

Prime Minister Manuel Ulloa upheld the anti-statist position in his first address to Congress in claiming only 18 public enterprises in 1968, compared to more than 170 in 1980 (Ulloa, 1980:7). His figures followed those presented by the 1976 Multisectoral Commission (Comisión, 1976:Appendix 9).

The 1981 Multisectoral Commission on the Government's Entrepreneurial Activity sustained a more moderate position. Its report recognized that in 1968 approximately 40 entities, including corporations, institutes, firms, and central government agencies carried out activities that, by 1981, were done by public enterprises (Comisión, 1981:4). The INP estimated 24 firms in 1968 and 171 in 1980 (1980b:79), while a more thorough academic survey claimed only 29 firms in 1968 (Gallegos et al., 1985:97).

Peruvian economist Luis Gutiérrez Aparicio took a strong pro statist-position, by claiming that, in 1968, 53 public entities, existing under different legal forms, exercised activities being carried out by public enterprises in 1981 (Gutiérrez, 1982:iv). The same figures appeared in a long-term comparison of 48 firms in 1980 with 53 in 1968 in an unsigned article in *El Diario*'s economic supplement, which was under Gutiérrez' direction (*Economía*, 1981:12–13).

Low estimates of the number of firms in 1968 resulted from a focus on legal forms of economic organization in 1968, while high estimates result from a focus on later legal forms. Neither approach consistently applies a definition of public enterprises to Peru.

PUBLIC ENTERPRISE DEFINITIONS

In chapter one, I provided an interim definition for the term "public enterprise" as an enterprise in the economic sense of the term, that produces and/or sells goods and services with a separate legal personality and with its capital wholly- or majority-owned by the state, whether directly, or indirectly. Although public enterprises appear, in theory, to be subject to precise and consistent definition, in practice, the opposite is true. This section explores terminology used by various Peruvian authorities. For broad surveys of Latin American usage, see Boneo (1980, 1981a).

Peruvian writings never defined the term "public enterprise" except for an undergraduate thesis presented at the Engineering University (UNI) in 1978 and an academic study done at the graduate school of business (ESAN) and published in late 1985 (Talavera and Villar, 1978; Gallegos et al., 1985). Neither influenced either mainstream writings or policy behavior during the period examined in this book. Rather, authorities used different implicit definitions based on percentage of government ownership and company legal form. A January 1971 definition of "Empresa Estatal Asociada" went further in restricting shares not held by the government to Peruvian nationals and in giving government a management role (D.L. 18748).

Peru's government explained the lack of interest in definitions as due to having no explicit guidelines for government entrepreneurial activity; a focus on short-run considerations that usually marked public enterprise creations; and the lack of sufficiently detailed technical/-economic studies on the subject (Comisión, 1976:10).

The nature of government holdings provides a basis for differentiating among types of public enterprises. The commonly accepted categories during the late 1970s were:

Public Enterprises — 100 percent government ownership and the legal status of public enterprises.

State Enterprises with special status — 100 percent government ownership and private legal status (Mercantile Society) with special provisions. These are also called enterprises of direct state property and generally undertook activities which were reserved to the state.

Enterprises with state participation — the legal status of a private sector firm and indirect government ownership through another public enterprise, a municipal council, benevolent society, public works programs, or other firms with state participation. These are further broken down:

those that are 100 percent state owned;
those with a majority state share;
and those with a minority state share.

Most authors have employed minor variations on the above legal definitional taxonomy. No one posed a more general definition or applied one based on economic or other non-legal variables (Figueroa and Saberbein, 1978:10–11; Monteverde, 1978:6; INP, 1978a:2; INAP, 1978a:23, 1978b; Comisión, 1976:10; Comisión, 1977b:Appendix 2).

The 1981 Commission, simplified the categories into a two-way breakdown, by type of ownership, direct or indirect, and by legal basis for participation — public law; private law (100 percent), private law mixed company (25 percent to more than 99 percent of shares) and private law diffused shareholding (less than 25 percent) (Comisión, 1981:36). Its breakdown parallels that found in the defunct normative law of state entrepreneurial activities (D.Leg. 216). Even greater simplification appeared in an INAP work that divided public enterprises into only two types: those with 100 percent state owned capital, organized under public enterprise law, and all of whose directors, except workers' delegates, represent a government agency; and mixed firms that associated the state with foreign or domestic private capital, irrespective of the size of the government share (INAP, 1979a:25–26).

An unpublished report done for the DESCO research center tried to delineate all forms of government productive activity, in addition to the types mentioned above, including: central government agencies with no separate legal existence, such as repair and printing services, research institutes, and investment or project agencies; and private companies without state equity under state control (Cabrera, Gutiérrez, and Giesecke, 1981:40–42). The latter companies abounded in the agricultural sector and included state-managed cooperatives and social property firms with worker-owned capital both of which totally depended on the government for financing, marketing assistance, and technical help. Although the approach gives the best picture of government direct economic activities, it is barely operational in practice and not cost-effective for overall monitoring.

The implicit definitions of public enterprise, found in government reports, make portfolio monitoring extremely difficult. The legal distinction between firms organized under public law or under private mercantile law is a major contributing factor. The two were different. Private-law firms had fewer central administration controls, less stringent reporting requirements, and fewer restrictions on management decisions. As a consequence, government controlling agencies had little information on them and sometimes lacked the names of their subsidiaries or the extent of their portfolio holdings, an omission which hindered tracing indirect government ownership.

A closely related problem is the relation between ownership and control. The government exercised little effective control over those firms with a state equity share less than 50 percent (N−31 in 1976). It may well be argued that such companies and their subsidiaries should not be listed as government-owned corporations given the lack of any effective control but, because they represent a potential budgetary claim, they should be included.

Autonomy, as a definitional criterion, is often reduced to having a separate legal existence. However, subunits of larger agencies sometimes exercised distinct entrepreneurial functions, as in the marketed production of coinage or commemorative medals by the Mint, Casa de la Moneda. All the Mint's activities had been administered by the Central Bank since 1944 but legal merger only occurred in 1977 (D.L. 21945). Although it was legally separate and, by most definitions, a distinct public firm for a 33-year span, its accounts were indistinguishable from those of the Bank in government documents.

Finally, many autonomous agencies did not market their production, relying instead for income on central government transfers or earmarked taxes. This is the case with a variety of agencies ranging from the government munitions factory to the benevolent societies called *Sociedades de Beneficencia Pública*.

PERU'S INSTITUTIONAL PROBLEMS

Peru's government organization in 1968 hindered precise definition and enumeration of its public enterprises. This section explains two institutional sources of definitional ambiguity.

The Independent Public Sub-Sector

Most public enterprises were grouped under the Independent Public Sub-Sector, SSPI, a set of legally separate agencies engaged in diverse activities and with various degrees of autonomy. All SSPI agencies were organized under a ministry, but their income depended on earmarked taxes or other direct transfers. The SSPI included: universities, regional development corporations, benevolent societies, development banks, and other diverse organizations, including the Automobile Club of Peru. Only a fraction of their revenues came from sales. For the entire SSPI in 1968, 65 percent of current income came from government transfers, 22 percent from sales, and 9.4 percent from rental income (CGR, 1970?:II:12–13).

Central Government Agencies

Other non-autonomous government agencies produced goods and services, further blurring the company-government boundary. Many of them became public enterprises as part of the public administration reforms in 1969, but in 1968 they were a part of general government. These included the modern versions of the old colonial monopolies that sold denatured alcohol, matches, imported wines and liquors, salt, and tobacco. The military controlled other income-generating activities, some of which were later incorporated into public enterprises, including the military hospital, a set of commissaries, a uniform factory, training centers, and the mapping agency.

Separate classifications in government accounts were provided for the postal, telegraph and radio telegraph services, the manufacture and sale of license places, the government-run rail lines, the printing and sale of mining sector legal codes and documents, a trout hatchery, and a fish-drying operation. Their income from sales was only S/. 512 million in 1968, equivalent to 22 percent of total SSPI sales during that year (CGR, 1970?:I:19, 26).

The government also maintained specialized warehouses for dangerous items, as inflammables and explosives, and for the controlled storage of foodstuffs. The warehouse chain only accounted for S/. 2 million in earnings in 1968 (CGR, 1970?:I:21). Specific government departments also administered programs, such as ports or hospital services. These generated S/. 523 million in 1968 (CGR, 1970?:I:20–21).

In total, the sale of goods and services by all categories of central government agencies, excluding normal licenses and fees, provided an amount equivalent to 44 percent of total SSPI sales. Central government agencies did not retain all their revenues, nor did they always transfer funds to the public treasury. Rather, at times, they collected earmarked taxes and transferred them to their intended beneficiaries.

AN ATTEMPT AT STANDARDIZING DEFINITIONS

If the fruitful approach to any concept depends on the existence of an shared body of data, and vice versa, the study of public enterprises is far from fruitful. Currently there is no single definition of the term on which scholars and practitioners agree. Lack of an acceptable public enterprise definition may have broad impacts on estimates of total public sector size, as shown by Peters and Heisler (1983:188–191). The ICPE has begun the process of reconciling and standardizing definitions (Böhm, 1981).

This section broadly surveys different approaches to two key elements in any public enterprise definition: specification of the meaning of "public" and of "enterprise." Other authors provide more detailed coverage, notable Sicherl and Fernandes (1980), Ramanadham (1984), and Fernandes (1986).

Public Enterprise

Definitions of the "public" element of the term may be grouped into four categories. First, an enterprise may be public because it has a public purpose. Analysts have devised creation taxonomies of motives for initial state ownership and permanence taxonomies of motives for which existing firms remain in the public portfolio [See Chapter 2]

Second, an enterprise is public if the government owns it, generally through a share of equity. Different definitional categories and different degrees of public interest may be based on the government's percentage of equity. For example, two companies, with government equity of 100 percent and 0.1 percent respectively are public in different ways. The argument may be made that because of potential call on government's budgetary resources, a company with any public equity should be included in the definition of public enterprise. Shepherd separates "public cost" from ownership, such cost including both current and capital subsidies, each of which could be positive or negative (1976a:36). Alternatively, because the ability to direct company policy in a public direction is contingent on a minimum equity share, only companies which have a "substantial" government equity, held directly or indirectly, are commonly called public enterprises.

Third, an enterprise may be public if the government can control or manage its internal decision making, whether or not the government chooses to exercise its prerogative. This case also occurs when the government intervenes a private company and exercises control and management without having any equity share. For example, in 1983, the Chilean government ran more than fifty private industrial concerns following the failure of the Cruzat/Larrain and Javier Vial groups.

Fourth, an enterprise is public if there is some public accountability. Usually accountability entails a post-hoc review of enterprise performance, finances, and management.

Public Enterprise

The second part of the term is the "enterprise" dimension, which indicates the production of goods and services for sale. Two approaches to narrowing the definition are commonly employed. First, an enterprise requires autonomy, which is often understood as having a separate existence. This omits any government offices or institutions that may qualify under an alternate definition. However, the autonomy requirement is not absolute, witness Peru's Mint.

Second, an enterprise requires market orientation by selling its goods and/or services. Often there is an expectation that, as a business venture, the revenues from those sales will cover a "substantial proportion of costs." (Short, 1984: 113) Market orientation is meant to specifically exclude many providers of public goods, such as national defense, or merit goods, such as low-cost housing. In practice, however, many countries do include such providers in the public portfolio. Alternatively, government authorities may provide a specific focus on investment and returns when setting up the firm and in defining its objectives.

Macro Decision

Another dimension complements the two key elements: should the definition be comprehensive or should it be operational? The distinction strongly influences the selection of a universe for analysis (Jones, 1975:26). A comprehensive definition results in a bigger portfolio than does a narrow one.

HOW MANY IN 1968?

This section applies different definitions of public enterprise to the standard government accounts, *Cuenta General de la República* (CGR, 1970?) to estimate the Peruvian portfolio size in 1968.

A restrictive definition encompasses three elements: legal autonomy, government equity participation high enough to guarantee control, and sales accounting for more than 50 percent of current income. This definition is operational and leads to an easily analyzed set of companies. Legal autonomy is presumed if the entity formed part of the SSPI in 1968, which also, with few exceptions, assured government control. Thus, the determining variable is the ratio of sales of goods and services to current income. Using information from the

1966 through 1968 accounts, table A.1 lists the seventeen entities that qualified as public enterprises:

TABLE A.1
Peru's Portfolio in 1968: Most Restrictive Definition

1. Autoridad Portuaria del Callao - Port authority
2. Banco Central de Reserva del Perú - Central reserve bank
3. Banco de la Nación - National bank
4. Banco de Fomento Agropecuario - Agricultural development bank
5. Banco de la Vivienda del Perú - Housing sector bank
6. Banco Industrial del Perú - Industrial development bank
7. Casa Nacional de la Moneda - National mint
8. Compañía Hotelera del Perú - Hotel firm
9. Corporación de Saneamiento de Arequipa - Water and wastewater
10. Corporación de Saneamiento de Lima - Water and wastewater
11. Corporación Nacional de Abastecimientos - Food supply firm
12. Corporación Nacional de Fertilizantes - Fertilizer firm
13. Corporación Peruana de Aeropuertos y Aviación Comercial - Airport authority
14. Corporación Peruana de Vapores - Shipping firm
15. Empresa Petrolera Fiscal - Petroleum producer
16. Imprenta del Ministerio de Hacienda y Comercio - Ministry printer
17. Laboratorios Fiscales de Industrialización de la Coca y Derivados - Cocaine

This list, consists of financial institutions, public utilities, the steamship firm, petroleum firm and cocaine laboratories. Notable omissions include the steel mill, all three major electric companies, and the mining sector development bank, that lacked market-orientation because less than 50 percent of their current income came from sales of goods or services. The restricted definition that gave rise to the list leads to a portfolio similar in size, although vastly different in composition, to most estimates presented above.

Employing a broad, ICPE-adopted definition results in a bigger portfolio: "A public enterprise is a productive organizational entity which engages in activities of a business character and markets any of its output and which is publicly owned to the extent of 50 percent or more" (Böhm, 1981:74). Because market orientation is less important in this definition, applying it to the 1968 SSPI list, increases the portfolio by forty, to a total of 57 public enterprises. As shown in table A.2, the portfolio additions are varied in scope and consist mainly of regional development corporations, benevolent societies, utilities, a bank, and universities. They include the noteworthy omissions from the first list.

Under a still broader definition, other entities could be considered public enterprises, particularly central government agencies which sell a good or service. It is difficult to accurately estimate their numbers because the Peruvian government accounting documents are vague and do not report always income by source. Further, many smaller agencies are lumped together in a general "etc." entry. Several of these agencies later became public enterprises. Many

TABLE A.2
Additions to Peru's Portfolio in 1968: Broad Definition

18. Automóvil Club Peruano - Peruvian automobile club
19. Banco Minero del Perú - Mining development bank
20. Caja Municipal de Crédito Popular - Savings association
21. Corporación de Desarrollo Económico y Social del Departamento de Piura - Regional development
22. Corporación de Energía Eléctrica del Mantaro - Electric firm
23. Corporación de Fomento y Desarrollo del Departamento de Lambayeque - Regional development
24. Corporación de Fomento y Desarrollo Económico del Departamento de Tacna- Regional development
25. Corporación de Fomento y Promoción Económica y Social del Departamento de Puno - Regional development
26. Corporación de Fomento y Promoción Social del Departamento de La Libertad - Regional development
27. Corporación de Reconstrucción y Fomento del Departamento de Cuzco - Regional development
28. Corporación de Rehabilitación y Desarrollo Económico del Departamento de Moquegua - Regional development
29. Corporación de Turismo del Perú - Tourist promotion agency
30. Corporación Peruana del Santa - Regional development
31. Instituto de Normas Técnicas Industriales y Certificación - Bureau of industrial standards
32. Instituto Nacional de Cooperativas - Cooperative promotion agency
33. Instituto Nacional de Promoción Industrial - Industrial promotion agency
34. Instituto Peruano de Rehabilitación - Rehabilitation agency
35. Irrigación y Colonización San Lorenzo - Colonization scheme
36. Junta de Control de Energía Atómica - Atomic energy commission
37. Junta de Obras Públicas del Callao - Public works program
38. Junta de Rehabilitación y Desarrollo de Arequipa - Regional development
39. Junta Nacional de la Vivienda - National housing commission
40. Oficina Nacional de Planeamiento y Urbanismo - Urban planning office
41. Oficina Nacional de Reforma Agraria - Agrarian reform office
42. Servicio de Empleo y Recursos Humanos - Labor studies center
43. Servicio Especial de Salud Pública - Public health agency
44. Servicio Forestal y de Caza - Forest service
45. Servicios Eléctricos Nacionales - Electric holding firm
46. Sociedad de Beneficencia Pública de Arequipa - Benevolent society
47. Sociedad de Beneficencia Pública de Callao - Benevolent society
48. Sociedad de Beneficencia Pública de Cuzco - Benevolent society
49. Sociedad de Beneficencia Pública de Concepción - Benevolent society
50. Sociedad de Beneficencia Pública de Huaraz - Benevolent society
51. Sociedad de Beneficencia Pública de Ilo - Benevolent society
52. Sociedad de Beneficencia Pública de Loreto - Iquitos - Benevolent society
53. Sociedad de Beneficencia Pública de Motupe - Benevolent society
54. Sociedad de Beneficencia Pública de Santiago de Chuco - Benevolent society
55. Sociedad Siderúrgica de Chimbote - Steel mill
56. Universidad Nacional Agraria - La Molina - University
57. Universidad Nacional de Huamanga - University

met the broad enterprise criterion of deriving some income from the sale of goods or services and they had a formally recognized accounting identity which indicates some autonomy. As indicated in table A.3, twenty additional agencies qualify under an expanded definition of public enterprises:

TABLE A.3
Further Additions to Peru's Portfolio in 1968: Broadest Definition

58. Bazares del Ejército - Military post exchanges
59. Cartografía Nacional - Mapping service
60. Centro Agropecuario - Agricultural extension
61. Centro Industrial de Confecciones Militares - Military uniform maker
62. Centros de Entrenamiento Vocacional, Ministerio de Guerra - Vocational training
63. Diario Oficial "El Peruano" - Official newspaper
64. Estanco de la Sal - Salt monopoly
65. Estanco de Naipes - Playing card monopoly
66. Estanco de Tabaco - Tobacco monopoly
67. Fabricación de Placas de Rodaje - License plate manufacture
68. Ferrocarriles del Estado - Railroad
69. Hospital Militar - Hospital
70. Monopolio Fiscal - Alcohol Desnaturalizado - Denatured alcohol monopoly
71. Monopolio Fiscal - Vinos y Licores Importados - Liquor imports
72. Pescado Seco Salado - Salt fish sales
73. Reglamento, Código de Minería y Ejemplares de Jurisprudencia Minera - Printer
74. Restaurantes Populares - Subsidized restaurants
75. Revista de Leyes y Resoluciones - Printer
76. Servicio de Pesquería - venta de truchas - Trout hatchery
77. Servicio de Telecomunicaciones - Telecommunications

Other broadly defined enterprises could not be separated from the government accounts data. Several of these were local subsidiaries of regional development corporations that produced cement, fertilizers, electricity, and foodstuffs. Most of them later became either separate public enterprises, or were merged into existing ones, such as INDUPERU or ELECTROPERU.

Other non-autonomous agencies were not separated in the accounts, but were criticized, during the mid-1960s, as public ventures (CDES, 1965: 128–130). As shown in table A.4, they included:

TABLE A.4
Gray Companies for Peru's Portfolio in 1968

1. Bazares - each ministry maintained a tax-free store for the benefit of its employees. Only that of the Army (No. 58 above) had a separate account.
2. Imprentas - approximately 20 printshops were found in ministries and the major existing public enterprises. Only that of the Ministry of Finance and Trade was separated (No. 16 above).
3. Workshops - motor vehicle and building repair workshops and crews were maintained by individual ministries and large public enterprises.
4. Building maintenance - separate crews were maintained in each ministry or government dependency for cleaning and routine maintenance.

In conclusion, Peru's most broadly defined public enterprise portfolio exceeded 75 separate entities in 1968. Although many did not meet the Peruvian legal criteria, they met the wider economic criteria detailed above. They exclude a "gray area" consisting of 80 or more stores, printshops, repair centers, and maintenance agencies. Other estimates of portfolio size in 1968 clearly underestimated the government's role.

HOW MANY IN THE 1980s?

Controversy continues about the size of Peru's portfolio. The 1981 Multisectoral Commission listed 140 firms including 46 held directly and 94 indirectly. The figure differed marginally from that presented in a background document for the Commission prepared by COFIDE, which listed 47 direct and 89 indirect holdings (COFIDE, 1981?). The commission encountered problems in counting the number of firms in 1980. According to one source, many firms were untraceable, since although they figured on government lists, the authorities lacked vital information about them including: company address, phone number, and executive roster. It was later found that many of the untraceable firms had folded years earlier and their assets had either been sold or absorbed into other firms (interview, 1981).

"Hidden" public enterprises posed another, potentially more serious, problem. They appeared on lists of firms for sale or figured in government decisions about inappropriate spheres of action, but no accurate count of them was ever made and there was no indication of their importance. They usually entered the portfolio as a result of accidental nationalization, having been found in the portfolios of other nationalized companies. The most notorious example was government movie houses which showed soft-core pornography. Other examples included a PETROPERU holding in a company that manufactured gas stoves and HIERROPERU's inheriting a customs agency (IBRD, 1979:II:207).

According to Gallegos, for 1982, the development finance corporation, CONADE, counted 153 firms; MEF had 156; CGR totalled 123; and the ESAN project found 192 (1985:71). The ESAN figures are the most comprehensive and include several second-degree indirect holdings where the government share was excessively diluted. None of these estimates include "gray area" firms.

In conclusion, Peru's public enterprise portfolio went from a vague and undefined initial state in 1968, comprising between 17 and 75 firms, to a vague final state in the 1980s, with between 150 and more than 200 firms. There was no overall understanding of the nature and complexity of public enterprises in 1968; thereafter, only minor improvement was made.

Notes on Data Sources and Methods

The company-level public enterprise data analyzed in this book came from a variety of sources. This appendix examines sources, data reconciliation methods, and inflation correction techniques.

DATA SOURCES

The working definition of public enterprise employed in this book, that a public enterprise is a government sole- or majority-owned company, whether directly or through other agencies, is already broader than that used by official Peruvian sources. In gathering data, it was expanded to include firms in which the government held a minority share, resulting in a data base of about 180 companies. The three electric producers, CORMAN, CORSANTA and SEN were treated as one, even prior to their merger into ELECTROPERU. Not all data were obtainable for all companies for all years, however, the effect of missing data is relatively insignificant.

Company annual reports provided accounting data and complementary materials. These were often supplied on request through the good will of top company officials. The Benson Latin American Collection of the University of Texas at Austin has strong holdings in serial publications of Latin American public enterprises, including Peruvian firms.

Data also came from reports of government monitoring agencies, including the *Cuenta General de la República*. The reporting formats for the Cuenta varied over time. After 1970, they shifted from annual to biennial reports, to coincide with the budget period, and included more information. The 1973-1974 Cuenta's public enterprise section totalled 900 pages, four times the size of the previous volume. Public enterprise statistics were sharply curtailed with the 1975-1976 accounts only presenting company-level data aggregated over the two-year period. The change in reporting format hindered examination of accounts, a change made worse by deliberately omiting data for key companies. A top ministry official claimed the government acted out of concern for secrecy, placing the data *"bajo siete llaves,"* (under seven keys) (interview, 1978). Beginning with 1977, the Cuenta no longer reported yearly income statements and balance sheets; it only provided flow-of-funds statements. While the move generally was praiseworthy, it made gathering time-series data more difficult. With the return to democratically-elected government in 1980, Congress exercised its power of approval by repeatedly delaying final accounts' approval, often for several years.

The variously-titled evaluations of public sector performance done by the National Planning Institute were also useful. They only began coverage for 1973-1974, and hence, do not span as long a period as do the MEF publications. As the INP monitoring and coordination role dwindled by the end of the decade, the lags in document publication stretched. Both INP and MEF publications suffered from a major defect: they reported data only for firms legally defined as public enterprises, limiting coverage to approximately one third to one fourth of a broadly defined government portfolio. Data provided by other monitoring agencies, the Superintendency of Banks and Insurance for the financial firms and the Comptroller's Office for nonfinancial companies filled in gaps.

Broader, but inconsistent, company coverage was available in the strategic reviews of the three multisectoral commissions. The report of the 1976 commission provided the best statistics. The 1981 commission's covered the largest number of companies, including many firms organized under mercantile society laws.

The BCRP usually obtained data from the other monitoring agencies or from the companies themselves and reworked them into consistent formats. The BCRP published some public enterprise information in its annual reports. The Bank coverage was not always limited to firms with the legal status of public enterprises.

The annual reports of the Lima stock market provided information on those publicly-quoted, mixed enterprises.

A wide variety of qualitative information was obtained through interviews with company executives, monitoring agency officials and others, conducted on eight trips to Peru from 1978 to 1985.

METHODS OF DATA SELECTION

Although most sources agreed on the value of any one variable for one company during one year, there were some conflicts. Methods used to reconcile conflicting information need explanation. Some data differences stemmed from institutional differences in reporting procedures. Tracing inconsistencies proved onerous because, in many cases, methodological documents detailing procedures used to report or reconcile information were either unwritten or not readily available. Peruvian government officials proved exceedingly patient in answering countless questions to clarify obscure points.

Some data inconsistencies arose when monitoring agencies reported preliminary figures in place of finalized ones, which often occurred when companies had not provided needed data by printing deadlines. Preliminary figures came from a variety of sources, including preliminary or unaudited financial statements and unrevised budgets. Careful comparative checking led to reconciling differences.

Other inconsistencies arose through slipshod proofreading and report preparation. These included rounding and typographical errors, both of which were common with typewritten, unpublished data for internal circulation. Transposed digits and misaligned columns were simply revealed by verifying arithmetic.

When all the above measures had been exhausted I chose between conflicting numbers according to the following preferential rankings. Other things being equal:

1. Audited data were always chosen over unaudited data;
2. Company-provided data were chosen over central-government sources;
3. Company audited annual reports were preferred to other company sources;
4. Central government year-end accounts data were chosen over other central government sources;
5. Central government monitoring agency data were chosen over data from other central government agencies.

Government reporting procedures meant that relatively complete information exists for the firms incorporated under public enterprise law, than for firms incorporated under other legal forms.

INFLATION CORRECTION

The effects of inflation were removed from the data. Peru had no official method of inflation correction although a Canadian-funded and Argentine-staffed mission had proposed a methodology to adjust financial records in the late 1970s (DGCoP, 1977).

I corrected for inflation by applying the implicit sectoral GDP deflators calculated by the national statistical office, ONE, to the principal monetary variables such as income, sales, etc., with separate deflators applied to investment. Thus, the deflator for fishing was used for PESCAPERU, while that for petroleum applied to PETROPERU. Inasmuch as possible, tabular data were expressed in constant 1973 Soles. Table B.1 provides the sectoral deflators.

TABLE B.1: Implicit GDP Deflators by Sector: 1970-1982
(1973=100)

SECTOR	1970	1971	1972	1973	1974	1975	1976	1977	1978	1979	1980	1981	1982
Agriculture, forestry	72.8	74.9	84.0	100	115.7	151.9	184.4	259.7	344.4	543.5	846.7	1,403.1	1,945.9
Fishing	78.8	84.9	90.3	100	123.1	178.7	179.9	229.0	383.1	528.9	694.9	1,136.9	1,925.6
Petroleum	80.9	84.1	90.2	100	112.4	186.9	339.5	516.5	1,160.2	3,623.4	4,084.1	7,058.1	10,841.3
Metallic minerals	70.9	61.5	62.8	100	112.5	97.4	143.5	207.5	404.0	756.4	1,141.7	1,281.4	1,722.4
Food manufacturing	67.6	73.9	83.6	100	112.1	132.7	182.0	255.0	456.4	761.2	1,194.4	2,031.2	3,001.1
Wood industry	75.3	82.4	89.4	100	125.3	150.7	239.5	320.1	552.1	968.8	1,596.4	2,685.6	4,680.9
Paper	76.9	84.8	93.7	100	113.3	147.1	211.6	288.5	598.0	998.0	1,553.6	2,450.1	4,206.1
Chemicals	80.1	85.7	90.9	100	115.2	112.4	150.6	240.2	456.7	749.5	1,110.9	1,814.9	3,362.9
Non-metallic minerals	83.4	89.3	95.4	100	113.0	134.4	178.6	215.3	437.1	729.3	1,106.2	1,983.3	3,941.0
Basic metals	61.6	63.1	72.1	100	153.0	126.8	181.8	257.1	475.2	1,063.8	1,551.3	1,705.5	2,600.9
Metal products	80.0	87.4	91.6	100	121.5	146.0	209.5	278.2	500.2	882.8	1,418.0	1,990.3	3,252.0
Other manufacturing	72.2	82.8	92.8	100	117.5	128.6	192.0	241.0	389.0	789.5	1,568.2	2,886.5	5,311.5
Electric energy	88.6	89.7	90.5	100	99.1	128.0	171.0	222.0	402.3	653.6	884.5	1,509.3	2,883.8
Water supply	74.9	89.6	99.3	100	112.5	165.5	203.4	303.5	360.4	657.7	1,204.3	1,804.6	2,760.0
Commerce	76.6	81.7	88.8	100	126.3	162.2	218.0	297.3	498.8	914.5	1,526.5	2,601.9	4,296.0
Restaurants, hotels	79.4	81.7	89.3	100	120.0	151.0	221.4	307.8	483.8	826.8	1,669.9	3,181.4	6,176.9
Land transportation	81.5	85.8	90.6	100	120.9	166.9	223.2	335.4	440.8	715.0	1,115.5	1,987.4	3,311.7
Transportation-water	76.5	81.6	85.9	100	131.0	143.6	164.1	227.1	355.5	679.3	890.3	1,639.8	2,735.0
Transportation-air	80.7	89.3	93.1	100	128.5	132.3	168.6	208.1	350.5	580.3	861.3	1,813.9	3,802.0
Communications	86.5	87.3	97.4	100	100.1	101.3	113.3	222.7	336.2	539.2	731.5	1,106.8	1,539.6
Financial institutions	62.0	67.6	81.2	100	124.8	134.5	170.2	262.1	413.5	721.6	1,005.2	2,125.0	3,024.4
Insurance	71.8	76.5	94.4	100	126.5	137.1	201.3	225.5	284.4	523.1	939.4	1,642.2	2,181.5
Business services	79.6	84.9	91.1	100	117.1	141.3	183.3	251.6	439.6	663.5	1,023.5	1,632.4	2,773.6
Other services	80.1	85.5	91.6	100	116.4	143.0	190.5	264.4	423.8	709.3	1,122.9	1,921.5	3,160.0
Education	68.3	74.9	91.6	100	99.9	127.8	158.8	192.0	349.4	582.9	1,002.5	1,830.9	3,172.4
Investment	82.2	85.6	91.9	100	114.6	134.8	195.1	289.5	507.6	885.2	1,413.1	2,312.9	4,094.8

SOURCE: ONE (later INE), Cuentas Nacionales del Perú.

APPENDIX C

Introduction to Peru's Legal Terminology

The text cites many Peruvian laws. This appendix provides a basic
introduction to Peru's hierarchical legal system; Furnish gives a fuller
English-language treatment (1968).

Peruvian laws follow a strict hierarchy. This helps to resolve
conflicts between provisions of any two laws: the law with the higher
ranking prevails. When laws of the same rank conflict, the more recent
prevails. In general, Peruvian laws fall into three categories: the
Constitution; Legislation; and Executive acts. Although most laws
promulgated from 1968 to 1980 were executive acts, based on the
traditional power to legislate by decree, the military enacted some laws
in place of Legislation. Law types appear below in hierarchical order.

Ley - *L.* Basic legislation consisting of a law enacted by both chambers
of congress after the necessary study in committee and debate in open
session. The president has a fixed period to either approve and
promulgate the law or to return it to congress. Congress may
reapprove the law over presidential objection by a simple majority.

Decreto Ley - *D.L.* The Decree-Law takes the place of legislation, *Ley*,
but is enacted by a military or any other de-facto government. The
Decree-Law must be signed by the president and by the ministers
following discussion at a cabinet meeting.

Decreto Legislativo - *D.Leg.* The Legislative Decree takes the place of
legislation, *Ley*, but is enacted by a president under powers delegated
by congress.

Decreto Supremo - *D.S.* The Supreme Decree is the highest ranking
executive act. It is signed by the president and by the ministers
involved in executing the policies. Prior to signature, the Supreme
Decree is submitted to the full cabinet for discussion and approval.

Resolución Suprema - *R.S.* The Supreme Resolution is a lower-ranked
executive act. It need not be brought to the attention of the entire
cabinet. The president need only initial the copy before it is signed by

the responsible minister.

Resolución Ministerial - **R.M.** The Ministerial Resolution requires only the signature(s) of the minister(s) involved. The subject matter is not necessarily less important than in a Supreme Resolution.

Resolución Directoral - **R.D.** The Directoral Resolution is promulgated by directors, who are lower ranked ministerial executive officers. These generally deal with everyday or administrative matters. No one above the directors need sign the Directoral Resolution.

Numbering: Beginning in 1968, all executive acts followed a standard numbering system that consists of four main parts: 1) the type of act (D.S., R.S., R.M. or R.D.); 2) the ministry-specific serial number; 3) the two-digit year abbreviation; and 4) the ministerial abbreviation. Some executive acts have an additional designator, for the ministerial subdivision that is most directly affected by the law. As an example, ENCI's monopoly on rum imports was granted by the government via D.S. 011-74-MINCOM, which is read as the eleventh Supreme Decree issued during 1974 by the MINistry of COMmerce.

Abbreviations

AEROPERU - Empresa de Transporte Aereo del Perú
AGEPSA - Administración y Gerencia EPSA
ALMACENA - Almacena, S.A.
ANDINA - Agencia Peruana de Noticias y Publicidad
APRA - Alianza Popular Revolucionaria Americana
APSA - Aerolineas Peruanas, S.A.
APTL - Administradora Paramunicipal de Transporte
ASARCO - American Smelting and Refining Company
BANMINERO - Banco Minero del Perú
BANVIPE - Banco de la Vivienda del Perú
BAP - Banco Agrario del Perú
BCHP - Banco Central Hipotecario del Perú
BCRP - Banco Central de Reserva del Perú
BEA - British European Airways Corporation
BIP - Banco Industrial del Perú
BM - Banco de Materiales
BN - Banco de la Nación
BOAC - British Overseas Airways Corporation
CAEM - Centro de Altos Estudios Militares
CAG - Compañía Administradora de Guano
CDES - Centro de Documentación Económico-Social
CENTROMIN - Empresa Minera del Centro del Perú
CERPER - Empresa Pública de Certificaciones Pesqueras del Perú
CGR - Contraloría General de la República
CIAEF - Comisión Interministerial de Asuntos Económicos y
     Financieros
CINEPERU - Empresa Cinematografica del Perú
CIUP - Centro de Investigación de la Universidad del Pacífico
CIPEC - Conseil Intergouvernemental des Pays Exportateurs de Cuivre
COAP - Comité de Asesoramiento de la Presidencia

CODELCO - Corporación Nacional del Cobre de Chile
COFIDE - Corporación Financiera de Desarrollo
CONADE - Corporación Nacional de Desarrollo
CONSEPEM - Consejo de Empresas Públicas de Energia y Minas
CORDE - Corporación Dominicana de Empresas Estatales
CORMAN - Corporación de Energía Eléctrica del Mantaro
CORPAC - Corporación Peruana de Aeropuertos y Aviación Comercial
CORSANTA - Corporación Peruana del Santa
CORSERELEC - Compañía de Servicios Eléctricos, S.A.
COTURPERU - Corporacion de Turismo del Perú
CPTSA - Compañía Peruana de Teléfonos, S.A.
CPV - Compañía Peruana de Vapores
DAASA - Deshidratadora de Alimentos de Arequipa, S.A.
DESA - United Nations Department of Economic and Social Affairs
DESCO - Centro de Estudios y Promoción del Desarrollo
DGAE - Dirección General de Asuntos Económicos
DGAF - Dirección General de Asuntos Financieros
DGCoP - Dirección General de Contabilidad Pública
DGCP - Dirección General de Crédito Público
DGPP - Dirección General de Presupuesto Público
DGTP - Dirección General del Tesoro Público
D.L. - Decreto Ley
D.S. - Decreto Supremo
ECASA - Empresa Comercializadora de Arroz, S.A.
ECLA - Economic Commission for Latin America
EDITORAPERU - Empresa Editora del Diario Oficial *El Peruano*
ELECTROLIMA - Empresas Eléctricas Asociadas
ELECTRONORTE - Empresa Eléctrica del Norte del Perú
ELECTROPERU - Empresa Pública de Electricidad del Perú
EMADIPERU - Empresa de Administración de Inmuebles del Perú
EMATINSA - Empresa Estatal Minera Asociada Tintaya, S.A.
EMSAL - Empresa de la Sal
ENACO - Empresa Nacional de la Coca
ENAFER - Empresa Nacional de Ferrocarriles del Perú
ENAPU - Empresa Nacional de Puertos
ENATA - Empresa Nacional del Tabaco
ENATRU - Empresa Nacional de Transporte Urbano del Perú
ENCI - Empresa Nacional de Comercialización de Insumos
ENI - Ente Nazionale Idrocarburi
ENRAD - Empresa Nacional de Radiodifusión del Perú
ENTEL - Empresa Nacional de Telecomunicaciones del Perú
ENTURPERU - Empresa Nacional de Turismo
EOQ - Economic order quantity
EPADESA - Empresa Peruana de Apuestas Deportivas
EPAPRODE - Empresa Pública de Administración de Prognósticos
    Deportivos
EPCHAP - Empresa Peruana de Comercialización de Harina y Aceite

del Pescado
EPF - Empresa Petrolera Fiscal
EPPA - Empresa Peruana de Promoción Artesanal
EPSA - Empresa Pública de Servicios Agropecuarios
EPSAP - Empresa Pública de Servicios Agropecuarios y Pesqueros
EPSEP - Empresa Pública de Servicios Pesqueros
ESAL - Empresa de Saneamiento de Lima
ESAN - Escuela de Administración de Negocios para Graduados
ESAR - Empresa de Saneamiento de Arequipa
ESAT - Empresa de Saneamiento de Trujillo
ESI - Empresa de Servicios de Informaciones
FERTIPERU - Empresa de Fertilizantes
FERTISA - Fertilizantes Sintéticos, S.A.
FETSA - Fábrica de Equipo de Telefonía, S.A.
FIEL - Fundación de Investigaciones Económicas Latinoamericana
FNDE - Fondo Nacional de Desarrollo Económico
FUNAPER - Fundición Andina del Perú, S.A.
GDP - Gross Domestic Product
GECAMINES - Générale des Carrières et Mines du Zaire
GFCF - Gross Fixed Capital Formation
HELITUBCA - Helicoidales y Tubos
HIDRANDINA - Empresa Hidroeléctrica Andina
HIERROPERU - Empresa Minera del Hierro del Perú
IBRD - International Bank for Reconstruction and Development
ICPE - International Centre for Public Enterprises in Developing
    Countries
ICSA - Inversiones COFIDE, S.A.
ILPES - Instituto Latinoamericano de Planificación Económica y Social
IMEF - Imprenta del Ministerio de Economía y Finanzas
IMF - International Monetary Fund
INAP - Instituto Nacional de Administración Pública
INCA - Empresa Pública Industria de Cachimayo
INDAER - Empresa Pública de Industria Aeronautica del Perú
INDUMIL - Empresa Pública Indústrias Militares del Perú
INDUPERU - Indústrias del Perú
INE - Instituto Nacional de Estadística
INP - Instituto Nacional de Planificación
INTERBANK - Banco Internacional del Perú
INTERBRAS - Petrobrás Comercio Internacional
IPC - International Petroleum Company
IRI - Instituto per la Ricostruzione Industriale
ITT - International Telephone and Telegraph
JAC - Junta de Acuerdo de Cartagena
LGI - Ley General de Indústrias
MA - Ministerio de Agricultura
MEF - Ministerio de Economía y Finanzas
MEFC - Ministerio de Economía, Finanzas y Comercio

MEM - Ministerio de Energía y Minas
MGP - Ministerio de Gobierno, Policía, Correos y Telecomunicaciones
MHASA - Máquinas y Herramientas Andinas, S.A.
MHC - Ministerio de Hacienda y Comercio
MIC - Ministerio de Industria y Comercio
MICTI - Ministerio de Industria, Comercio, Turismo é Integración
MINEROPERU - Empresa Minera del Perú
MINPECO - Minero Perú Comercial/Empresa Pública de
    Comercialización de Productos Mineros
MITI - Ministerio de Industria, Turismo é Integración
MODASA - Motores Diesel Andinos, S.A.
MTC - Ministerio de Transportes y Comunicaciones
MV - Ministerio de la Vivienda
NAFINSA - Nacional Financiera
ONE - Oficina Nacional de Estadística
ONI - Oficina Nacional de Información
OPEC - Organization of Petroleum Exporting Countries
PEMEX - Petróleos Mexicanos
PEPESCA - Peruana de Pesca, S.A.
PESCAPERU - Empresa Pública de Producción de Harina y Aceite de
    Pescado
PETROBRAS - Petroleo Brasileiro
PETROPERU - Petróleos del Perú
PICSA - Picsa Astilleros
PPC - Partido Popular Cristiano
PROCASA - Procesamientos Callao
PUBLIPERU - Agencia de Publicidad del Estado
QUIMPAC - Química del Pacífico, S.A.
R.D. - Resolución Directorial
RGLCOP - Reglamento General de Licitaciones y Contratos de Obras
    Públicas
RULCOP - Reglamento Unico de Licitaciones y Contratos de Obras
    Públicas
R.M. - Resolución Ministerial
R.S. - Resolución Suprema
SATCO - Servicio Aereo de Transportes Comerciales
SEAL - Sociedad Eléctrica de Arequipa
SEDACUZCO - Servicio de Agua Potable y Alcantarillado - Cuzco
SEDALAMBAYEQUE - Servicio de Agua Potable y Alcantarillado -
    Lambayeque
SEDALORETO - Servicio de Agua Potable y Alcantarillado - Loreto
SEDAPAL - Servicio de Agua Potable y Alcantarillado - Lima
SEDAPAR - Servicio de Agua Potable y Alcantarillado - Arequipa
SEDAPAT - Servicio de Agua Potable y Alcantarillado - Trujillo
SEDAPIURA - Servicio de Agua Potable y Alcantarillado - Piura
SEDATUMBES - Servicio de Agua Potable y Alcantarillado - Tumbes
SEN - Servicios Eléctricos Nacionales

SENAMA - Servicio Nacional de Maquinaria Agrícola
SENAPA - Servicio Nacional de Abastecimiento de Agua Potable y
Alcantarillado
SERPESA - Servicios de Pagos y Encargos Diversos
SIDERPERU - Empresa Siderúrgica del Perú
SIMA - Servicios Industriales de la Marina
SINAMOS - Sistema Nacional de Apoyo a la Movilización Social
SOGESA - Sociedad de Gestión de la Planta Siderúrgica de Chimbote y
de la Central Hidroeléctrica del Cañon del Pato, S.A.
SPCC - Southern Peru Copper Corp.
SSPI - Sub-Sector Público Independiente
SUPEREPSA - Empresa de Supermercados EPSA, S.A.
SURMEBAN - Banco Regional Sur-Medio y Callao
TAEPSA - Tiendas Afiliadas EPSA, S.A.
TAS - Holding company for TAEPSA, AGEPSA and SUPEREPSA
TASA - Tractores Andinos S.A.
TVA - Tennessee Valley Authority
UNCTAD - United Nations Conference on Trade and Development
UNI - Universidad Nacional Ingeniería
UNIDO - United Nations Industrial Development Organization
YPF - Yacimientos Petrolíferos Fiscales
ZIMCO - Zambia Industrial and Mining Corporation Ltd.

Bibliography of Works Cited

Acosta, Ricardo. 1984. "A Conceptual Approach to Interlinkages." *Public Enterprise.* 4(3):33–48.
———. 1985. "Towards Management of Interlinkages." In *The Management of Interlinkages*, edited by Ricardo Acosta, pp. 12–37. Ljubljana, Yugoslavia: International Center for Public Enterprises in Developing Countries.
Actualidad Económica. Oct. 1978, 1(9), "Centromín, una nueva versión del Cerro de Pasco Corporation: El envenamiento de las aguas del Río Mantaro."
Aharoni, Yair. 1977. *Markets, Planning and Development: The Private and Public Sectors in Economic Development.* Cambridge, Mass.: Ballinger.
———. 1981. "Managerial Discretion." In *State-Owned Enterprises in the Western Economies*, edited by Raymond Vernon and Yair Aharoni, pp. 184–193. New York: St. Martin's Press.
———. 1982. "State-owned Enterprise: An Agent without a Principal." In *Public Enterprises in Less-Developed Countries*, edited by Leroy Jones et al., pp. 67–76. New York: Cambridge University Press.
Ahmad, Muzaffer. 1982. "Political Economy of Public Enterprises." In *Public Enterprises in Less-Developed Countries*, edited by Leroy Jones et al. pp. 49–64. New York: Cambridge University Press.
Akinsanya, Adeoye. 1980. *The Expropriation of Multinational Property in the Third World.* New York: Praeger Publishers.
Almenara, María. 1981. "Tax Links between Public Enterprises and the Central Government: Case of Peru." Master's Thesis. University of Texas at Austin.
Amat y León, Carlos. 1975. "Incidencia de los subsidios en los ingresos de las familias en el Perú: Situación actual." Lima: MEF. Mimeo.
———. 1979. "Anatomía de un fracaso teórico." *Socialismo y Participación.* (8):44–59.

Amat y León, Carlos, and Héctor Léon Hinostroza. 1977. *Estructura y niveles de ingreso familiar en el Perú*. Lima: MEF.

Anastassopoulos, Jean-Pierre. 1981. "The French Experience: Conflicts with Government." In *State-Owned Enterprises in the Western Economies*, edited by Raymond Vernon and Yair Aharoni, pp. 99–116. New York: St. Martin's Press.

Andean Air Mail and Peruvian Times. Various issues.

Arnold, Victor, and John Hamilton. 1978. "The Greene Settlement: A Study of the Resolution of International Disputes in Perú." *Texas International Law Journal*. 13:263–287.

Autogestión '79: Directorio de las empresas asociativas del Perú. 1979. Lima: Servicios Profesionales EPS.

Ayub, Mahmood Ali, and Sven Olaf Hegstad. 1986. *Public Industrial Enterprises: Determinants of Performance*. Washington: World Bank Industry and Finance Series. vol. 17.

Baer, Werner, and Adolfo Figueroa. 1981. "State Enterprise and the Distribution of Income: Brazil and Peru." In *Authoritarian Capitalism: Brazil's Contemporary Economic and Political Development*, edited by Thomas Bruneau and Phillipe Faucher, pp. 59–84. Boulder, Co.: Westview Press.

Baklanoff, Eric. 1975. *Expropriation of U.S. Properties in Cuba, Mexico, and Chile*. New York: Praeger Publishers.

Ballantyne, Janet Campbell. 1976. "The Political Economy of Peruvian Gran Minería." Ph.D. dissertation. Cornell University.

Barenstein, Jorge. 1983. *Algunas cuestiones relevantes para la gestión de empresas públicas en México*. Mexico City: Centro de Investigación y Docencia Económicas.

Bassino, Aldo, and Guillermo Cruz. 1975. "Regimen legal en el país en el sub-sector electricidad." Lima: ELECTROLIMA. Mimeo.

Batley, Richard. 1979. *The Allocation of Public Contracts: Studies in Peru and Venezuela*. Birmingham: University of Birmingham, Institute of Local Government Studies, Development Administration Group, DAG Occasional Paper 5.

BCRP, Banco Central de Reserva del Perú, División de Estudios Económicos. 1977. "Empresas públicas no financieras: Evaluación del II semestre y año: 1976." Lima. Unpublished.

———. 1979a. "Evaluación empresas públicas: 1978." Lima. Unpublished.

———. 1979b. "Evolución de precios de los productos bajo control y regulación, 1977–1979." Lima. Unpublished.

———. 1981. "Evolución de precios de los productos bajo control y regulación, 1979–1981." Lima. Unpublished.

———. 1985a. "Evolución de precios de los productos bajo control y regulación, 1981–1985." Lima. Unpublished.

———. 1985b. *Perú: Compendio estadístico del sector público no financiero, 1968–1984*. Lima.

———. *Memorias*. Various issues.

Becker, David. 1983. *The New Bourgeoisie and the Limits of Dependency: Mining, Class and Power in "Revolutionary" Peru.* Princeton: Princeton University Press.

Bejar, Hector. 1976. *La Revolución en la Trampa.* Lima: Ediciones Socialismo y Participación.

Bigler, Gene E. II. 1981. *La política y el capitalismo de Estado en Venezuela.* Madrid: Editorial Tecnos.

Bishop, Robert. 1978. "Intergovernmental Relations in the United States: Some Concepts and Implications from a Public Choice Perspective." In *Interorganizational Policy Making: Limits to Coordination and Central Control,* edited by Kenneth Hanf and Fritz Scharpf, pp. 19–38. Beverly Hills, Calif.: Sage Publishers.

BN, Banco de la Nación. 1979. "Informe al Directorio: obligaciones por subsidio de la Empresa de Fertilizantes, 'FERTIPERU' en liquidación." Lima. Unpublished.

———. 1980. "Informe: Regularización de Subsidios de las Empresas Públicas ENCI y FERTIPERU." Lima. Unpublished.

Boeninger, Eduardo, and Eduardo Palma. 1978. "Empresas estatales: el caso chileno y un análisis general." Paper presented at the seminar on the Planning Process in Latin America and Public Enterprises. Lima. Mimeo.

Böhm, Andreja. 1981. "The Concept, Definition and Classification of Public Enterprises." *Public Enterprise.* 1(4):72–78.

Bokhari, Riyaz. 1982. *Subvention Policies and Practices for Public Enterprises.* Ljubljana, Yugoslavia: International Centre for Public Enterprises in Developing Countries, ICPE Monograph Series, no. 4.

Boloña, Carlos. 1977. *Las importaciones del sector público en el Perú: 1971–74.* Lima: Universidad del Pacífico, Trabajo de Investigación, no. 5.

———. 1978. "Las importaciones del Estado: Aspectos téoricos y el caso peruano, 1971–1976." *Apuntes.* 4(8):99–130.

Bolsa de Valores de Lima. *Vademecum Bursatil.* Lima: various issues.

Boneo, Horacio. 1980. *Saber Ver las Empresas Públicas.* San José, Costa Rica: Editorial Universitaria Centroamericana (EDUCA).

———. 1981a. "Las Empresas Públicas en el proceso de desarrollo: Algunas notas introductorias a la discusión." Paper presented at the seminar on Public Enterprises and Development Planning in Central America and the Caribbean, San José, Costa Rica.

———. 1981b. *Political Regimes and Public Enterprises.* Austin: University of Texas, Institute of Latin American Studies, Office for Public Sector Studies, Technical Papers Series, no. 31.

———. 1983. "Government and Public Enterprise in Latin America." In *Government and Public Enterprises: Essays in Honor of Professor V.V. Ramanadham,* edited by G. Ram Reddy, pp. 157–180. New Delhi: N.M. Tripathi Private.

———. 1985. "Interlinkages: Concept, Characteristics, and Determining Factors." In *The Management of Interlinkages,* edited by Ricardo

Acosta, pp. 38–71. Ljubljana, Yugoslavia: International Center for Public Enterprises in Developing Countries.

Booth, David. 1983. "The Reform of the Press: Myths and Realities." In *Military Reformism and Social Classes: The Peruvian Experience, 1968–1980*, edited by David Booth and Bernardo Sorj, pp. 141–184. New York: St. Martin's Press.

Borrani, Jorge. 1982. *Empresas públicas en el Perú*. Austin: University of Texas, Institute of Latin American Studies, Office for Public Sector Studies, Technical Papers Series, no. 37.

Bourque, Susan, and David Scott Palmer. 1975. "Transforming the Rural Sector: Government Policy and Peasant Response." In *The Peruvian Experiment: Continuity and Change under Military Rule*, edited by Abraham Lowenthal, pp. 179–219. Princeton: Princeton University Press.

Branch, Brian. 1981. "Change and Continuity in the Peruvian Public Sector." Master's Thesis. University of Texas at Austin.

———. 1982a. "Report on the Peruvian Public Enterprises." Lima: U.S. Agency for International Development. Unpublished.

———. 1982b. *Public Enterprises in Peru: The Perspectives for Reform.* Austin: University of Texas, Institute of Latin American Studies, Office for Public Sector Studies, Technical Papers Series, no. 37.

Bravo, Jorge. 1979. "La evaluación de la empresa estatal." Paper presented at the second seminar on Company Management by the State. Lima. Mimeo.

Bronstein, Arturo. 1981. "Las relaciones laborales en las empresas estatales de América Latina: Estudio comparativo." In *Las relaciones laborales en las empresas estatales de América Latina*, edited by Arturo Bronstein, pp. 1–103. Geneva: International Labor Organization.

Brown, L. David. 1983. *Managing Conflict at Organizational Interfaces.* Reading, Mass.: Addison-Wesley Publishing Co.

Bustamante, Luis. 1981. "El sistema de relaciones laborales en las empresas del sector público en el Perú: Cuatro casos." In *Las relaciones laborales en las empresas estatales de América Latina*, edited by Arturo Bronstein, pp. 107–133. Geneva: International Labor Organization.

Caballero, José María. 1977. *Agrarian Reform and the Transformation of the Peruvian Countryside.* Cambridge, England: Cambridge University Centre of Latinamerican Studies, Working Paper, no. 29.

———. 1980. *Agricultura, reforma agraria y pobreza campesina.* Lima: IEP Ediciones.

Cabrera, César, Luís Gutiérrez, and Jaime Giesecke. 1981. "Estado y empresas públicas." Lima. Unpublished.

Campos, Jorge. 1977. *Las exportaciones del sector público en el Perú: 1972–1975.* Lima: Universidad del Pacífico, Trabajos de Investigación, no. 6.

Camprubí, Carlos. 1957. *Historia de los bancos en el Perú, 1860–1879.*

Lima: Editorial Lumen.
———. 1960. *El Banco de la Emancipación*. Lima: Talleres Gráficos P. L. Villanueva.
———. 1963. *Bancos de rescate*. Lima.
Carey Jones, N.S., S.M. Patankar, and M.J. Boodhoo. 1974. *Politics, Public Enterprise and the Industrial Development Agency: Industrialization Policies and Practices*. London: Croom Helm.
CDES, Centro de Documentación Económico-Social. 1965. *Las empresas estatales en el Perú*. Lima.
Cepeda, Rodrigo. 1985. "Sistéma peruano de empresas públicas: Necesidad de cambio y conceptos para su reorganización: Los casos de Pescaperú y CPV." In *Las empresas públicas en el Perú*, edited by Alfred H. Saulniers et al., pp. 137–270. Lima: Centro Peruano de Investigación Aplicada.
CGR, Contraloría General de la República. 1970?. *Cuenta General de la República: Año 1968*. Lima.
———. 1977a. "Información sobre 'Deudas entre entidades del sector público' presentada ante el Consejo de Ministros." Lima. Unpublished.
———. 1977b. "Las empresas del Estado y el sistéma nacional de control." *Perú Control*. 19(5):13–46.
———. 1978. "Gestión y control en la actividad empresarial del Estado." Paper presented at the second seminar on Company Management by the State. Lima. Mimeo.
———. 1980. "Informe situacional al 30.May.80 de la acción de control 'Cuentas por cobrar y pagar entre entidades del Estado al 31 Dic.79'." Lima. Unpublished.
———. 1982. "Informe: Las empresas del Estado." Lima. Unpublished.
———. 1983a. "Articulos del D.S. 375-82-EFC implicantes directamente con la competencia y jurisdicción de la Contraloría General de la República." Lima. Unpublished.
———. 1983b. "Función de una entidad fiscalizadora." Lima. Unpublished.
Choksi, Armeane. 1979. *State Intervention in the Industrialization of Developing Countries: Selected Issues*. World Bank Staff Working Paper, no. 341.
CIAEF, Comisión Interministerial de Asuntos Económicos y Financieros. 1978. "Ante proyecto de ley sobre nueva organización de las empresas públicas." Lima. Mimeo.
———. 1979. Draft of "Ley sobre organización y funcionamiento de las empresas de propriedad del Estado." Lima. Mimeo.
CIUP, Centro de Investigación de la Universidad del Pacífico. 1980. *Perú — elecciones y planes de gobierno*. Lima.
Cleaves, Peter, and Henry Pease. 1983. "State Autonomy and Military Policy Making." In *The Peruvian Experiment Reconsidered*, edited by Cynthia McClintock and Abraham Lowenthal, pp. 209–244. Princeton: Princeton University Press.

Cleaves, Peter, and Martin Scurrah. 1980. *Agriculture, Bureaucracy and Military Government in Peru*. Ithaca: Cornell University Press.
COFIDE, Corporación Financiera de Desarrollo. 1974?. *Memoria 1973*. Lima.
———. 1981?. "Empresas de propriedad estatal directa e indirecta." Lima. Mimeo.
Comisión Multisectorial. 1977a. "Ante proyecto de ley normativa de la actividad empresarial del Estado." Lima. Mimeo.
———. 1977b. "Primer informe sobre normas operativas para agilizar la actividad empresarial del Estado." Lima. Mimeo.
———. 1977c. "Informe." In report by the Subcommission on industry. Lima. Mimeo.
———. 1977d. "Sub-Comisión de Mineria." Lima. Mimeo.
———. 1977e. "Generalidades." In report by the subcommission on domestic trade. Lima. Mimeo.
———. 1977f. "Informe de la subcomisión encargada de proponer recomendaciones sobre normas operativas para mejorar la eficiencia y agilizar el funcionamiento de las empresas del Estado." Lima. Mimeo.
———. 1977g. "Subcomisión encargada de proponer recomendaciones sobre normas operativas para mejorar la eficiencia y agilizar el funcionamiento de las empresas del Estado en el campo del comercio internacional." Lima. Mimeo.
———. 1981. "Informe de la comisión multisectorial sobre la actividad empresarial del Estado." Lima. Mimeo.
Comisión Multisectorial de Empresas del Estado. 1976. "Informe final.' Lima. Mimeo.
Commonwealth Secretariat. 1982?a. "Relationships between Parliament and Public Enterprises." Report of a seminar held at Colombo, Sri Lanka, 15–19 June 1981. London.
———. 1982?b. "Government Executive and Supervisory Control over Public Enterprises." Report of a workshop held in New Delhi, India, 4–8 June. London.
CONADE, Corporación Nacional de Desarrollo. 1983. "El D.S. 375-82-EFC y sus implicancias con la competencia de la Contraloría General de la República." Lima. Unpublished.
Cotler, Julio. 1975. "The New Mode of Political Domination in Peru." In *The Peruvian Experiment: Continuity and Change under Military Rule*, edited by Abraham Lowenthal, pp. 44–78. Princeton: Princeton University Press.
———. 1983. "Democracy and National Integration in Peru." In *The Peruvian Experiment Reconsidered*, edited by Cynthia McClintock and Abraham Lowenthal, pp. 3–38. Princeton: Princeton University Press.
Couriel, Alberto. 1979. "Estado y estrategias de desarrollo en el Perú." in *Economía de América Latina*. (3):125–143.
de la Melena, Germán. 1973. *La reforma financiera, Octubre 1968 —*

Octubre 1973. Lima: MEF.
de Pierola, Nicolás. 1870. "Memoria del Señor Ministro de Hacienda Don Nicolás de Pierola a la Legislatura de 1870." In P. Emilio Dancuart, *Anales de la hacienda pública del Perú*, tome 7. p. 81. Lima: Imprenta, Libreria y Encuadernación de Gmo. Stolte, 1906.
DGAE, Dirección General de Asuntos Económicos. 1972. "Análisis financiero de las empresas públicas del Perú: (1970–1971), documento de trabajo." Lima. Mimeo.
DGAF, Dirección General de Asuntos Financieros. 1978. "Diagnóstico de la actividad empresarial del Estado: 1968–1978." Lima. Mimeo.
———. AFS, Area de Financiamiento Sectorial. 1978. "Gestión empresarial del Estado." Lima. Unpublished.
DGCoP, Dirección General de Contabilidad Pública. 1972?. *Cuenta General de la República: año 1970*. tome 2. Lima.
———. 1973?. *Cuenta General de la República: 1971–1972*. tome 4. vol. 3. *Empresas públicas*. Lima.
———. 1974. *Evaluación económica y financiera de las empresas públicas: (Metodología)*. Lima.
———. 1975?. *Cuenta General de la República: 1973–1974*. tome 5. vol. 4. *Empresas públicas*. Lima.
———. 1977. "El ajuste de los estados contables de las empresas públicas financieras para evaluar la incidencia de la perdida del poder adquisitivo de la moneda." Lima. Mimeo.
DGCP, Dirección General de Crédito Público. 1972. "Directivas técnicas para la formulación del presupuesto del sector público correspondiente al bienio 1973–1974." Reprinted in *Presupuesto bienal*. vol. 9. tome 3. *Biblioteca "ESEDAL" de la legislación peruana*. Lima: Ediciones ESEDAL, 1973.
Dore, Elizabeth. 1977. "Crisis and Accumulation in the Peruvian Mining Industry, 1968–1974." *Latin American Perspectives*. 4(3): 77–102.
Echenique, José. 1952. *Memorias para la historia del Perú (1808–1878)*. Lima: Editorial Huascarán.
Economía. Economic supplement to *El Diario*. 8 June 1981. "La obra de Belaúnde: Entregar el Perú al capital extranjero."
Einaudi, Luigi. 1969. "The Peruvian Military: A Summary Political Analysis." Testimony before the Subcommittee of Western Hemisphere Affairs of the Committee on Foreign Relations, U.S. Senate. *United States Relations with Peru*. 91st Congress, First Session. 14 April.
———. 1972. "U.S. Relations with the Peruvian Military." In *U.S. Foreign Policy and Peru*, edited by Daniel Sharp, pp. 15–56. Austin: University of Texas Press.
Einaudi, Luigi, and Alfred C. Stepan III. 1971. "Latin American Institutional Development: Changing Military Perspectives in Peru and Brazil." Report prepared for the Office of External Research, Department of State. Santa Monica, Calif.: Rand Corporation.

Elguera, Juan. 1868. "Memoria del Ministro de Hacienda señor don Juan Ignacio Elguera a la Legislatura Ordinaria de 1868." In P. Emilio Dancuart, *Anales de la hacienda pública del Perú*, tome 8. p. 144. Lima: Imprenta del la Revista, 1906.

El Mir, Ali. 1982. "Government Control over Public Enterprises: Current and Relevant Forms." In Commonwealth Secretariat. "Government Executive and Supervisory Control over Public Enterprises." Report of a workshop held in New Delhi, India, 4–8 June. London. pp. 101–117.

El-Namaki, M.S.S. 1979. *Problems of Management in a Developing Environment: The Case of Tanzania (State Enterprises between 1967 and 1975)*. New York: North-Holland Publishing Co..

———. 1985. "Patterns of Strategic Behaviour and Models for Strategic Planning in State Enterprises in Some Developing Countries." In *The Management of Interlinkages*, edited by Ricardo Acosta, pp. 107–137. Ljubljana, Yugoslavia: International Center for Public Enterprises in Developing Countries.

ENCI, Empresa Nacional de Comercialización de Insumos. 1977. "Evaluación del plan de trabajo ENCI: 1977." Lima. Mimeo.

———. 1978. "Evaluación de los principales factores determinantes en la gestión de la empresa durante el primer semestre de 1978." Lima. Mimeo.

ESAN, Escuela de Administración de Negocios para Graduados. 1972. "Integración de las empresas públicas del Perú. Estudio Preliminar." Lima. Mimeo.

Estenós, Felipe. 1825. "Felipe Santiago Estenós to José Gregorio Paredes y José Joaquin Olmedo." Letter of 30 Oct. 1825. In *Gaceta del Gobierno del Perú*. 22 Dec. 1825. (fac. ed.). 1967. Caracas: Fundación Eugenio Mendoza. 3:217–218.

Faucher, Philippe. 1981. *L'entreprise publique comme instrument de politique économique*. Montréal: University of Montréal, Department of Political Science, Working Paper, no. 2.

Fernandes, Praxy. 1979. "The Accountability of Public Enterprises: Some Thoughts on the Rationale and Spirit of External Control Systems." Paper presented at the workshop on Control Systems for Public Enterprises in Developing Countries. Ljubljana, Yugoslavia: International Centre for Public Enterprises in Developing Countries.

———. 1985. "The Management of Interlinkages." In *The Management of Interlinkages*, edited by Ricardo Acosta, pp. 72–106. Ljubljana, Yugoslavia: International Center for Public Enterprises in Developing Countries.

———. 1986. *Managing Relations between Government and Public Enterprises: A Handbook for Managers and Administrators*. Geneva: International Labour Office. Management Development Series, no. 25.

Fernández Maldonado, Jorge. 1983. Address delivered at the seminar "Peruvian Mining and Government Policy." *Balance y Perspectivas de Minero Perú*. Lima: Sindicato de Trabajadores de Minero Perú.

Fernández Moreno, Héctor. 1983. "Experiencias y planteamientos para la planeación y control de las empresas del sector público." Paper presented at the ECLQ seminar on State Control and Planning of Public Enterprises, Brasília, 15–17 June.

Fernández, Luis. 1977. "Algunos aspectos metodologicos y empiricos sobre la gestión empresarial del Estado." Undergraduate Thesis. Pontificia Universidad Católica del Perú.

Ferner, Anthony. 1983. "The Industrialists and the Peruvian Development Model." In *Military Reformism and Social Classes: The Peruvian Experience, 1968–1980*, edited by David Booth and Bernardo Sorj, pp. 40–71. New York: St. Martin's Press.

Figueroa, L., and G. Saberbein. 1978. "Empresas del Estado en el Perú: Una primera aproximación para su análisis." Paper presented at the CEPAL-ILPES seminar on the Planning Process in Latin America and Public Enterprises. Lima. Mimeo.

FitzGerald, E.V.K. 1974. *The Public Sector in Latin America*. Cambridge, England: Cambridge University, Centre of Latin-american Studies, Working Paper, no. 18.

———. 1976a. *The State and Economic Development in Peru since 1968*. Cambridge: Cambridge University Press.

———. 1976b. "The Political Economy of Peru 1968–1975." *Development and Change*. 7:7–33.

———. 1976c. "Some Aspects of the Political Economy of the Latin American State." *Development and Change*. 7:119–133.

———. 1979. *The Political Economy of Peru, 1956–1978: Economic Development and the Restructuring of Capital*. Cambridge: Cambridge University Press.

———. 1983. "State Capitalism in Peru: A Model of Economic Development and its Limitations." In *The Peruvian Experiment Reconsidered*, edited by Cynthia McClintock and Abraham Lowenthal, pp. 65–93. Princeton: Princeton University Press.

Floyd, Robert H. 1978. "Some Aspects of Income Taxation of Public Enterprises." *IMF Staff Papers*. 25(June):310–342.

———. 1979. *Income Taxation of State Trading Enterprises*. Montreal, Ecole des Hautes Etudes Commerciales, Les Cahiers du CETAI, no. 79–05.

———. 1984. "Some Topical Issues Concerning Public Enterprises." In Robert H. Floyd, Clive S. Gray, and R.P. Short. *Public Enterprise in Mixed Economies: Some Macroeconomic Aspects*. Washington: IMF. pp. 1–34.

"The Focal Point: A Proposal for the Improvement of Relations between Government and Public Enterprises." 1985. In *Essays on Relations Between Government and Public Enterprises*. Ljubljana, Yugoslavia: International Center for Public Enterprises in Developing Countries.

Fortune. Various issues.

Foster, C.D. 1971. *Politics, Finance and the Role of Economics: An*

Essay on the Control of Public Enterprise. London: George Allen & Unwin.

France, Groupe de Travail du Comité Interministeriel des Entreprises Publiques. 1967. *Rapport sur les entreprises publiques.* Paris.

Fubara, Bedford. 1983. "Negative Profitability Performance of Public Enterprises in Developing Countries: A Business Policy Anatomy." *Public Enterprise.* 4(3):61–72.

Furnish, Dale. 1968. *An Economic Developer's Guide to Peruvian Legal Dispositions.* Lima: Iowa-Peru Program, Special Report no. 1.

Gaceta del Gobierno del Perú. 10 July 1825. "Razon de las haciendas, minas, ingenios y casas citas en el Cerro de Pasco que el Estado da en arrendamiento." 3:38–39. (fac. ed.). Caracas: Fundación Eugenio Mendoza, 1967.

Gallegos, Armando. 1985. "Comentarios a la exposición del Doctor Saulniers." In *Las empresas públicas en el Perú,* edited by Alfred H. Saulniers et al., pp. 67–77. Lima: Centro Peruano de Investigación Aplicada.

Gallegos, Armando, et al. 1985. *Mapa económico-financiero de la actividad empresarial del Estado peruano.* Lima: Escuela de Administración de Negocios para Graduados, Departamento de Investigación, Proyecto de Gestión Pública.

Garner, Maurice. 1983. "The Relationship Between Government and Public Enterprise." In *Government and Public Enterprises: Essays in Honor of Professor V.V. Ramanadham,* edited by G. Ram Reddy, pp. 3–23. New Delhi: N.M.Tripathi Private.

Ghai, Yash. 1981. "The Legislature and Public Enterprise." In Commonwealth Secretariat. "Relationships between Parliament and Public Enterprises." Report of a seminar held at Colombo, Sri Lanka, 15–19 June. London. pp. 53–75.

———. 1982. "Alternative Systems of Executive Control over Public Enterprises and their Impact on the Performance of Public Enterprises." In Commonwealth Secretariat. "Government Executive and Supervisory Control over Public Enterprises." Report of a workshop held in New Delhi, India, 4–8 June. London. pp. 161–167.

———. 1983. "Executive Control over Public Enterprises in Africa." In *Government and Public Enterprises: Essays in Honor of Professor V.V. Ramanadham,* edited by G. Ram Reddy, pp. 181–219. New Delhi: N.M. Tripathi Private.

Gillis, Malcolm, Glenn Jenkins, and Donald Lesard. 1982. "Public Enterprise finance: Toward a Synthesis." In *Public Enterprises in Less-Developed Countries,* edited by Leroy Jones et al., pp. 257–277. New York: Cambridge University Press.

Glade, William P. 1983. "The Privatization and Denationalization of Public Enterprises." In *Government and Public Enterprises: Essays in Honor of Professor V.V. Ramanadham,* edited by G. Ram Reddy, pp. 67–97. New Delhi: N.M. Tripathi Private.

Goodwin, Richard. 1969. Testimony before the Subcommittee of

Western Hemisphere Affairs of the Committee on Foreign Relations, U.S. Senate. *United States Relations with Peru*. 91st Congress, First Session. 14 Apr.

Graham, José. 1974. "La Revolución Peruana y la Empresa." Speech given at the annual executives' conference. In *Anales de la XII Conferencia Anual de Ejecutivos CADE '74*. Lima: Instituto Peruano de Administración de Empresas. pp. 204–210.

Grassini, Franco. 1981. "The Italian Enterprises: The Political Constraints." In *State-Owned Enterprises in the Western Economies*, edited by Raymond Vernon and Yair Aharoni, pp. 70–84. New York: St. Martin's Press.

Gray, Clive. 1984. "Toward a Conceptual Framework for Macroeconomic Evaluation of Public Enterprise Performance in Mixed Economies." In Robert H. Floyd, Clive S. Gray, and R.P. Short. *Public Enterprise in Mixed Economies: Some Macroeconomic Aspects*. Washington: IMF. pp. 35–109.

Green, Reginald. 1976. "Public Enterprise Finance and National Development Goals: Some Aspects of Coordination, Articulation and Efficiency." In UN, Department of Economic and Social Affairs. *Financing of Public Enterprises in Developing Countries: Co-ordination, Forms and Sources*, pp. 1–32. New York.

Grisolle, Javier. 1983. "Rol promotor del Estado." Lima. Unpublished.

Guerra García, Francisco. 1983. *Velasco: Del Estado oligárquico al capitalismo del Estado*. Lima: Centro de Estudios para el Desarrollo y la Participación.

Guerrero, Maritza Amalia. 1981. "Las empresas públicas en la República Dominicana." Paper presented at the seminar on Public Enterprises and Planning in Central America and the Caribbean, San José, Costa Rica, 1–3 July.

Gutiérrez Luís. 1982. "Las cifras en el debate de las empresas públicas." *El Observador, (Proceso económico)*. 16 July.

———. 1983. *A dónde va SIDERPERU?* Lima: Instituto Proceso.

Hanf, Kenneth. 1978. "Introduction." In *Interorganizational Policy Making: Limits to Coordination and Central Control*, edited by Kenneth Hanf and Fritz Scharpf, pp. 1–15. Beverly Hills, Calif.: Sage Publishers.

Hanf, Kenneth, and Fritz Scharpf, eds. 1978. *Interorganizational Policy Making: Limits to Coordination and Central Control*. Beverly Hills, Calif.: Sage Publishers.

Hanson, A.H. 1965. *Public Enterprise and Economic Development*. 2d ed. London: Routledge & Kegan Paul.

———. 1968. "Report of Preliminary Study." in UN, Department of Economic and Social Affairs. *Organization and Administration of Public Enterprises: Selected Papers*. New York.

Harding, Colin. 1975. "Land Reform and Social Conflict in Peru." In *The Peruvian Experiment: Continuity and Change under Military Rule*, edited by Abraham Lowenthal, pp. 220–253. Princeton: Princeton University Press.

Havens, A. Eugene, Susana Lastarria-Cornheil, and Gerardo Otero. 1983. "Class Struggle and the Agrarian Reform Process." In *Military Reformism and Social Classes: The Peruvian Experience, 1968–1980*, edited by David Booth and Bernardo Sorj, pp. 14–39. New York: St. Martin's Press.

Heath, John B. 1983. "Public Enterprise in Britain Today." In *Government and Public Enterprises: Essays in Honor of Professor V.V. Ramanadham*, edited by G. Ram Reddy, pp. 127–139. New Delhi: N.M. Tripathi Private.

Holland, Stuart. 1972. "The National Context." In *The State as Entrepreneur: New Dimensions for Public Enterprise: The IRI State Shareholding Formula*, edited by Stuart Holland, pp. 56–91. London: Weidenfeld and Nicolson.

Hopkins, Jack. 1967. *The Government Executive of Modern Peru*. Gainesville: University of Florida Press.

Hunt, Shane. 1975. "Direct Foreign Investment in Peru: New Rules for an Old Game." In *The Peruvian Experiment: Continuity and Change under Military Rule*, edited by Abraham Lowenthal, pp. 302–349. Princeton: Princeton University Press.

IBRD, International Bank for Reconstruction and Development. 1979. *Peru: Long-Term Development Issues*. Washington.

——. 1981. *Peru: Major Developmental Policy Issues and Recommendations*. Washington.

——. 1982. *The Management and Sale of State-Owned Enterprises*. Washington. Report no. 4088-PE.

——. 1983. *World Development Report*. New York: Oxford University Press.

ICSA, Inversiones COFIDE, S.A. 1984. "Inversiones COFIDE, S.A. y sus filiales." Lima. Mimeo.

ICPE, International Centre for Public Enterprises in Developing Countries. 1983a. "The Role of Public Enterprise Banks/Financial Institutions and their Relationships with other Public Enterprises: Report of an Expert Group Meeting." in *Public Enterprise*. 4(1):7–21.

——. 1983b. "The Role of Public Enterprise in Employment Generation in Developing Countries: Report of an ICPE Expert Group Meeting." *Public Enterprise*. 4(2):5–16.

IMF, International Monetary Fund. 1976. "Peru: Recent Economic Developments." Washington. Mimeo.

INAP, Instituto Nacional de Administración Pública. 1976a. *Empresas Públicas: Organos de dirección, mecanismos de participación y aspectos laborales*. Lima. Documento de Trabajo, no. 1.

——. 1976b. "Las empresas públicas Arequipeñas: Informe de Investigación." Lima. Mimeo.

——. 1976c. "Empresas públicas y burocracia empresarial del Estado." Lima. Mimeo.

———. 1978a. "Bases para la normatividad de la gestión empresarial del Estado en el Perú." Paper presented at the round table on Public Enterprises in Latin America, Mexico City. Mimeo.

———. 1978b. "Reforma de la actividad empresarial del Estado: Fundamentos y modelo funcional." Lima. Mimeo.

———. 1978c. "Conclusiones y recomendaciones del seminario 'Gestión empresarial del Estado'." Lima. Mimeo.

———. 1979a. "La actividad empresarial del Estado en el Perú: Política global." Paper presented at the second seminar on Company Management by the State. Lima. Mimeo.

———. 1979b. "Anteproyecto de decreto ley normativo de la actividad empresarial del Estado." Lima. Mimeo.

———. 1979c. "Conclusiones y recomendaciones del II seminario sobre gestión empresarial del Estado." Lima. Mimeo.

———. 1983a. "Vinculos de las empresas de derecho público con los sistémas administrativos." Lima. Mimeo.

———. 1983b. "Diagnostico actualizado de la actividad empresarial del Estado 1983 — Informe final." Lima. Mimeo.

———. 1984a. *Organismos del Estado: Naturaleza, finalidad, base legal, funciones generales.* Lima.

———. 1984b. "Diagnostico de la actividad empresarial del Estado 1984 — Informe final." Lima. Mimeo.

INAP, Instituto Nicaragüense de Administración Pública, Centro de Instrucción para la Dirección Estatal. 1981. "Los problemas de las empresas públicas en un proceso revolucionario." Managua. Mimeo.

INE, Instituto Nacional de Estadística. 1982. "Cuentas nacionales del Perú: Anexo." Lima. Mimeo.

Ingram, George M. 1974. *Expropriation of U.S. Property in South America: Nationalization of Oil and Copper Companies in Peru, Bolivia, and Chile.* New York: Praeger Publishers.

INP, Instituto Nacional de Planificación. 1968. *Perú, estrategia del desarrollo nacional a largo plazo, resumen.* Lima.

———. 1971. "Anteproyecto de decreto ley sobre participación estatal en las empresas." Lima. Mimeo.

———. 1975?. "Análisis económico-financiero de las empresas públicas, año 1973." Lima. Mimeo.

———. 1975. "Evaluación del presupuesto de inversión del sector público nacional — bienio 1973–1974." Lima. Mimeo.

———. 1976a. "Instituciones y empresas del Estado: Normas y funciones básicas." Lima. Mimeo.

———. 1976b. "Remuneraciones y redistribución de ingresos." Lima. Mimeo.

———. 1978a. "Apreciaciones generales sobre la problemática de las empresas públicas." Lima. Mimeo.

———. 1978b. "Evaluación de la gestión del sector público nacional en el bienio 1975–1976." Lima. Mimeo.

———. 1978c. "El Estado y su participación empresarial en las ac-

tividades productivas de comercialización y de servicios básicos."
Lima. Mimeo.
——. 1978d. "Estudio de base sobre la actividad empresarial del
Estado en el período 1969–1977: Concepción global y objetivos del
estudio." Lima. Mimeo.
——. 1979a. "Evaluación de la gestión del sector público nacional en
el año 1977." Lima. Mimeo.
——. 1979b. "Hoja informativa: Proyecto de decreto ley sobre la organización y funciones de las empresas de propiedad estatal." Lima.
Mimeo.
——. 1979c. "Informe del Instituto Nacional de Planificación en
relación a la Cuenta General de la República correspondiente al
ejercio presupuestal del año 1977." Lima. Mimeo.
——. 1980a. "Diagnóstico de la realidad nacional." Lima. Mimeo.
——. 1980b. "Logros del Instituto Nacional de Planificación
1968–1975." Lima. Mimeo.
——. 1982. "Formulación de planes de las empresas del Estado."
Lima. Mimeo.
INP-DESCO, Instituto Nacional de Planificación and Centro de Estudios
y Promoción del Desarrollo. 1974?a. "Hacia un enfoque integral de
la actividad empresarial del Estado." Lima. Mimeo.
——. 1974?b. "La estructura organizativa de las empresas públicas."
Lima. Mimeo.
——. 1974?c. "La participación de la colectividad de los trabajadores
en las empresas estatales." Lima. Mimeo.
INP-UNI, Instituto Nacional de Planificación and Universidad Nacional
de Ingeniería. 1978. "Caracteristicas del empleo estatal, 1970–1975."
Lima. Mimeo.
JAC, Junta del Acuerdo de Cartagena. 1976. "Estudio sobre compras
estatales en el Perú." Lima. Unpublished.
James, Jeffrey. 1983. "Public Enterprise, Technology and Employment
in Less Developed Countries." *Public Enterprise.* 4(2):37–49.
Jaquette, Jane. 1972. "Revolution by Fiat: The Context of Policy-
making in Peru." *Western Political Quarterly.* 25(4):648–666.
——. 1975. "Belaúnde and Velasco: On the Limits of Ideological
Politics." In *The Peruvian Experiment: Continuity and Change under
Military Rule,* edited by Abraham Lowenthal, pp. 402–437. Prince-
ton: Princeton University Press.
Jenkins, Glenn. 1978a. *Performance Evaluation and Public Sector
Enterprises.* Cambridge, Mass.: Harvard Institute for International
Development, Development Discussion Paper, no. 46.
——. 1978b. *An Operational Approach to the Performance of Public
Sector Enterprises.* Cambridge, Mass.: Harvard Institute for Interna-
tional Development, Development Discussion Paper, no. 47.
Jones, Leroy. 1975. *Public Enterprise and Economic Development: The
Korean Case.* Seoul, Korea: Korea Development Institute.
——. 1981. "The Linkage between Objectives and Control

Mechanisms in the Public Manufacturing Sector." Paper presented at the expert group meeting on the Changing Role and Function of the Public Industrial Sector in Development, Vienna, Austria, 5–9 Oct. UNIDO. Mimeo.

———. 1983. "Towards a Performance Evaluation Methodology for Public Enterprises with Special Reference to Pakistan." Paper presented at the ECLA seminar on State Control and Planning of Public Enterprises, Brasília, 15–17 June.

Jones, Leroy, and Edward Mason. 1982. "Role of Economic Factors in Determining the Size and Structure of the Public-Enterprise Sector in Less-Developed Countries with Mixed Economies." In *Public Enterprises in Less-Developed Countries*, edited by Leroy Jones et al., pp. 17–47. New York: Cambridge University Press.

Killick, Tony. 1981. "The Role of the Public Sector in the Industrialization of African Developing Countries." Paper presented at the expert group meeting on the Changing Role and Function of the Public Industrial Sector in Development, Vienna, Austria, 5–9 Oct. UNIDO. Mimeo.

Kilty, Daniel. 1967. *Planning for Development in Peru*. New York; Praeger Publishers.

Klitgaard, Robert. 1971. "Observations on the Peruvian National Plan for Development, 1971–1975." *Inter-American Economic Affairs*. 25:3(Winter 1971):3–22.

Kuczynski, Pedro-Pablo. 1977. *Peruvian Democracy under Economic Stress: An Account of the Belaúnde Administration, 1963–1968*. Princeton: Princeton University Press.

———. 1982. *Memoria de energía y minas 1980–1982*. Lima: Ministerio de Energía y Minas.

Lanatta, Romulo. 1944. *Legislación sobre la industria del guano*. Lima: Compañía Administradora del Guano.

Latin American Regional Reports: Andean Group. 1982. "Developing an Aerospace Plan." RA-82-01(22 Jan.):3.

Lauer, Mirko (moderator). 1978. *El reformismo burgués (1968–1976)*. Lima: Mosca Azul Editores.

Lavergne, Néstor, and Dante Caputo. 1979. "Para una evalorización de las políticas de comercio exterior." Paper presented at the first Latin American seminar on Public Policy, São Paulo: FUNDAP/CLACSO.

Lê Châu. 1982. *Rol del Estado, reforma estructural y crisis en el Perú, 1967–1977*. Lima: Editorial Horizonte.

Lilienthal, D. 1944. *TVA–Democracy on the March*. New York: Harper.

Loret de Mola, Carlos. 1978. *La página once*. Lima: Libre 1 Editores.

Loring, David. 1972. "The Fisheries Dispute." In *U.S. Foreign Policy and Peru*, edited by Daniel Sharp, pp. 57–118. Austin: University of Texas Press.

Llosa, Luís. 1972. "Critique of Mr. Loring's Paper." In *U.S. Foreign Policy and Peru*, edited by Daniel Sharp, pp. 118–124. Austin:

University of Texas Press.

Lowenthal, Abraham. 1975. "Peru's Ambiguous Revolution." In *The Peruvian Experiment: Continuity and Change under Military Rule*, edited by Abraham Lowenthal, pp. 3–43. Princeton: Princeton University Press.

———. 1983. "The Peruvian Experiment Reconsidered." In *The Peruvian Experiment Reconsidered*, edited by Cynthia McClintock and Abraham Lowenthal, pp. 415–430. Princeton: Princeton University Press.

Luttwak, Edward. 1968. *Coup d'Etat: A Practical Handbook.* Greenwich, Conn.: Fawcett Publications, Inc.

Marga Institute. 1981. "Issues in the Relationship between Parliament and Public Enterprise." In Commonwealth Secretariat. "Relationships between Parliament and Public Enterprises." Report of a seminar held at Colombo, Sri Lanka, 15–19 June. London. pp. 37–52.

Marsan, V. Ajmove. 1981. "The State Holding System in Italian State Development." In *Public and Private Enterprise in a Mixed Economy*, edited by William J. Baumol, pp. 138–157. New York: St. Martin's Press.

McClintock, Cynthia. 1983. "Velasco, Officers, and Citizens: The Politics of Stealth." In *The Peruvian Experiment Reconsidered*, edited by Cynthia McClintock and Abraham Lowenthal, pp. 275–308. Princeton: Princeton University Press.

El Mercado de Valores. Various issues.

Mercado, Edgar. 1964. "El ejército de hoy y su proyección en nuestra sociedad en período de transición, 1940–1965." *Revista Militar del Perú.* 59:1–20. Cited in Frederick M. Nunn. 1976. "Professional Militarism in Twentieth-Century Peru: Historical and Theoretical Background to the *Golpe de Estado*." *Hispanic American Historical Review.* 59(3):391–417.

Meriño-Reyna, Amador. 1979. "La comercialización de los productos agropecuarios y la participación del Estado." Paper presented at the first seminar on Agriculture and Foodstuffs. Lima. Mimeo.

MINCOM, Ministerio de Comercio. 1978. "Análisis de las actividades y relaciones financieras de las empresas estatales de comercio exterior." Lima. Mimeo.

MINPECO, Minero Perú Comercial. 1979. "Exposición al Ministro de energía y minas." Lima. Mimeo.

MITI, Ministerio de Industria, Turismo é Integración, Oficina Sectorial de Planificación, Sector Industria. 1981a. *Evaluación económica de la Empresa Siderúrgica del Perú, SIDERPERU.* Lima.

———. 1981b. *Evaluación económica: Industrial Cachimayo S.A. INCA.* Lima.

———. 1981c. *Evaluación económica: Fertilizantes Sintéticos, S.A. FERTISA.* Lima.

———. 1981d. *Evaluación económica: Cementos Yura, S.A..* Lima.

———. 1981e. *Evaluación económica: Empresa de Alcohol Industrial,*

S.A.. Lima.

Moncloa, Francisco. 1978. *Perú: Que Pasó? (1968–1976)*. Lima: Editorial Horizonte.

Monteverde Bussaleu, Juan-José. 1979. "Informe preliminar sobre la regulación de la empresa pública en el Perú." Paper presented at the seminar on Regulation of Public Enterprise, Mexico City. Mimeo.

Motta, Paulo. 1982. "Rationale for Government Control over Public Enterprises." In Commonwealth Secretariat. "Government Executive and Supervisory Control over Public Enterprises." Report of a workshop held in New Delhi, India, 4–8 June. London. pp. 181–194.

MTC, Ministerio de Transportes y Comunicaciones. 1974. "Evaluación de las empresas públicas del sector transportes y comunicaciones: Evaluación económico-financiero, año 1973." Lima. Mimeo.

Muhammad, Faqir. 1978. "Public Enterprise and National Development in the 1980's: An Agenda for Research and Action." Paper presented at the round table on public enterprise of the Tenth General Assembly of the Latin American Association of Public Administration, Mexico City. Mimeo.

Murphy, Ewell E. Jr. 1985. "The Mexican Bank Expropriation in Retrospect." *The Mexican Forum*. 5(3):15–19.

Nickson, Robert. 1978. "Descripción de las principales empresas transnacionales que proveen las importaciones del gobierno peruano." *Apuntes*. 4(8):131–141.

North, Liisa. 1983. "Ideological Orientations of Peru's Military Rulers." In *The Peruvian Experiment Reconsidered*, edited by Cynthia McClintock and Abraham Lowenthal, pp. 245–274. Princeton: Princeton University Press.

Nove, Alec. 1973. *Efficiency Criteria for Nationalized Industries*. London: George Allen & Unwin.

Ocampo, Tarcisio. comp. 1970. *Perú: IPC Limited; reacciones de prensa*. Cuernavaca, Mexico: Centro Intercultural de Documentación, Dossier 26.

Ondarts, Guillermo, and Carlos Correa. 1982. *Compras estatales e integración económica*. Buenos Aires: Instituto para la Integración de América Latina; Banco Interamericano de Desarrollo.

ONE, Oficina Nacional de Estadística. 1979. *Cuentas nacionales del Perú*. Lima.

Ortíz de Zevallos, Felipe. 1985. "La actividad empresarial del Estado peruano." In *Las empresas públicas en el Perú*, edited by Alfred H. Saulniers et al., pp. 99–136. Lima: Centro Peruano de Investigación Aplicada.

Palacios, Marcos. 1983. "Social Property in the Political Context of the Military Regime." In *Military Reformism and Social Classes: The Peruvian Experience, 1968–1980*, edited by David Booth and Bernardo Sorj, pp. 117–140. New York: St. Martin's Press.

Peacock, Alan, and Jack Wiseman. 1961. *The Growth of Public Ex-*

penditure in the United Kingdom. Princeton: Princeton University Press.

Pease, Henry. 1977. *El ocaso del poder oligarquico: Lucha política en la escena oficial, 1968–1975.* Lima: Centro de Estudios y Promoción del Desarrollo.

———. 1979. *Los caminos del poder: Tres años de crisis en la escena política.* Lima: Centro de Estudios y Promoción del Desarrollo.

El Peruano. Various issues.

Perú económico. Various issues.

PESCAPERU. 1981. *Que ha hecho y adonde va PESCAPERU?* Lima. Mimeo.

Peters, B. Guy, and Martin O. Heisler. 1983. "Thinking about Public Sector Growth: Conceptual, Operational, Theoretical, and Policy Considerations." In *Why Governments Grow: Measuring Public Sector Size,* edited by Charles L. Taylor, pp. 177–197. Beverly Hills, Calif.: Sage Publishers.

PETROPERU. *Memorias.* Various issues.

Philip, George. 1978. *The Rise and Fall of the Peruvian Military Radicals 1968–1976.* London: University of London, Athalone Press.

———. 1982. *Oil and Politics in Latin America: Nationalist Movements and State Companies.* New York: Cambridge University Press.

Piazza, Walter. 1971. "La industria y el plan nacional de desarrollo." Speech given at the annual executives' conference. In *Anales de la X Conferencia Anual de Ejecutivos CADE '71.* Lima: Instituto Peruano de Administración de Empresas. pp. 209–221.

Pinelo, Adalberto. 1973. *The Multinational Corporation as a Force in Latin American Politics: A Case Study of the International Petroleum Company in Peru.* New York: Praeger Publishers.

Pinzas, Teobaldo. 1981. *La economía peruana 1950–1978, un ensayo bibliográfico.* Lima: Instituto de Estudios Peruanos.

Ponce, Luis. 1985a. *Gestión pública de los programas de inversión: El caso de SIDERPERU.* Lima: Escuela de Administración de Negocios para Graduados, Proyecto de Gestión Pública, no. 4.

———. 1985b. "Gestión pública de los proyectos de inversión: El caso de SIDERPERU." Licentiate Thesis. Pontificia Universidad Católica del Perú.

Pontoni, Alberto. 1981. *Transnacionales y petróleo en el Perú.* Lima: Centro de Estudios para el Desarrollo y la Participación.

———. 1983. *Politica petrolera y precios de los combustibles 1973–1983.* Lima: Fundación Friedrich Ebert, Diagnostico y Debate, no. 11.

Potash, Robert. 1959. *El Banco de Avío de México: El fomento de la indústria, 1821–46.* Mexico City: Fondo de Cultura Económica.

Portocarrero, Felipe. 1982. "The Peruvian Public Investment Programme, 1968–1978." *Journal of Latin American Studies.* 14(20):433–454.

Portugal Vizcarra, José A. 1983. *Parcelación de las empresas asociativas — nueva estructura agraria en el Perú.* Lima: Consultoría

de proyectos agro-industriales.
Prakash, Om. 1971. *The Theory and Working of State Corporations with Special Reference to India.* 2d ed. London: George Allen & Unwin.
Premchand, A. 1983. "Government and Public Enterprise: the Budget Link." In *Government and Public Enterprises: Essays in Honor of Professor V.V. Ramanadham,* edited by G. Ram Reddy, pp. 24–47. New Delhi: N.M. Tripathi Private.
Presidencia de la República. 1971. Instituto Nacional de Planificación. *Plan Nacional de Desarrollo para 1971–1975.* vol. 1, *Plan Global.* Lima.
———. 1975. *Plan Nacional de Desarrollo 1975–1978.* Lima.
———. 1977. *Plan Nacional de Gobierno "Tupac Amaru" 1977–1980.* Lima.
———. 1979?. Instituto Nacional de Planificación. *Plan Nacional de Desarrollo para 1979–1982, Plan Global.* Lima.
———. 1982. "Proyecto de Plan Nacional de Desarrollo para 1982–1985, Plan Global." Lima. Unpublished.
Pryke, Richard. 1971. *Public Enterprise in Practice: The British Experience of Nationalization over Two Decades.* London: MacGibbon & Kee.
Pryor, Frederic. 1976. "Public Ownership: Some Quantitative Dimensions." In *Public Enterprise: Economic Analysis of Theory and Practice,* edited by William Shepherd, pp. 3–22. Lexington, Mass: D.C. Heath and Co., Lexington Books.
Quijano, Aníbal. 1971. "Nationalism and Capitalism in Peru: A Study in Neo-Imperialism." *Monthly Review.* 23(3):1–122.
Radetzki, Marian. 1985. *State Mineral Enterprises.* Washington: Resources for the Future.
Raiffa, Howard. 1981. "Decision Making in the State-Owned Enterprise." In *State-Owned Enterprises in the Western Economies,* edited by Raymond Vernon and Yair Aharoni, pp. 54–62. New York: St. Martin's Press.
Ramanadham, V.V. 1972. "Substantive Working Document." Paper presented at the meeting of consultants on Administration of Public Enterprises, Santiago, 27-29 Nov. Economic Commission on Latin America.
———. 1974. *Organization, Management and Supervision of Public Enterprises in Developing Countries.* New York: UN, Department of Economic and Social Affairs.
———. 1984. *The Nature of Public Enterprise.* London: Croom Helm.
Ramanadham, V.V., and Yash Ghai. 1981. *Parliament and Public Enterprise.* Ljubljana, Yugoslavia: International Centre for Public, Enterprises in Developing Countries, ICPE Monograph Series, no. 1.
Ray, Anandarup. 1975. *Cost Recovery Policies for Public Sector Projects.* World Bank Staff Working Paper, no. 206.
Reforma de la administración pública. 1969. Lima: Ediciones "ESEDAL."

Remy, Felix. 1985. "Hacia una gestión eficaz de la empresa estatal."
Paper presented at the Instituto Peruano de Administración de Em-
presa's first National Management Conference, Lima, 3–6 July.
Revesz, Bruno. 1982. *Estado, algodon y productores agrarios*. Lima:
Centro de Investigación y Promoción del Campesinado.
Revilla, Julio E. 1987. "The Peruvian State and Its Economic Policies:
From the Guano Age to the Beginning of the Twentieth Century."
Master's Thesis. University of Texas at Austin.
Robles Chávez, Marcos. 1985. "El empleo estatal en el Perú." In
Alberto Giesecke S.L. *Reporte de investigación: La organización del
sector público peruano*. Lima: Escuela de Administración para
Graduados. pp. 75–112.
Roel, Virgilio. 1968. *La planificación económica en el Perú*. Lima:
Editorial Gráfica.
Roemer, Michael. 1970. *Fishing for Growth: Export-led Development in
Peru, 1950–1967*. Cambridge, Mass.: Harvard University Press.
Rose, Richard. 1983. "Disaggregating the Concept of Government." In
Why Governments Grow: Measuring Public Sector Size, edited by
Charles L. Taylor, pp. 157–176. Beverly Hills, Calif.: Sage Publishers.
Rose, Stanley. 1981. *The Peruvian Revolution's Approach: Investment
Policy and Climate, 1968–1980*. Buffalo, N.Y.: Wm. S. Hein & Co.
Rossi, Claudio. 1983. "Aspectos do controle das empresas públicas no
exercío da política econômica." Paper presented at the ECLA
seminar on State Control and Planning of Public Enterprises,
Brasília, 15–17 June.
Rothrock, Van Edwin. 1969. "The Autonomous Entities of the
Peruvian Government in Perspective." D.B.A. dissertation. Indiana
University.
Samuels, John, et al. 1981. *Advanced Financial Accounting*. London:
McGraw Hill.
Sánchez, Fernando. 1981. *Mineria, capital transnacional y poder en el
Perú*. Lima: Centro de Estudios y Promoción del Desarrollo.
———. 1983. "Perú: Política de desarrollo y empresas públicas." Paper
presented at the ECLA seminar on State Control and Planning of
Public Enterprises, Brasília, 15–17 June.
Sánchez, Fernando, and Jesús Esteves. 1978. "Cooperation between
State Trading Organizations in Latin America." Geneva: United
Nations Conference on Trade and Development.
Saulniers, Alfred. 1979a. "The Case of SUPEREPSA." Austin: Institute
of Latin American Studies Case Study Materials.
———. 1979b. "The Case of ENCI." Austin: Institute of Latin American
Studies Case Study Materials.
———. 1980. "ENCI: Peru's Bandied Monopolist." *Journal of
Inter-American Studies and World Affairs*. 22(4):441–462.
———. 1981a. "State Trading Organizations: A Bias Decision Model
and Applications." *World Development*. 9(7):679–694.
———. 1981b. "Public Enterprise." *Discovery*. 5(4):20–24.

———. 1983. "Public Enterprises in Latin America: The New Look?." Paper presented at the ECLA seminar on State Control and Planning of Public Enterprises, Brasília, 15–17 June.

———. 1985a. "The State Companies: A Public Policy Perspective." In *The Politics of Energy: Essays on the Oil Companies in Latin America*, edited by John Wirth, pp. 226–261. Lincoln, Neb.: University of Nebraska Press.

———. 1985b. *Public Enterprises in Latin America: The New Look?*. Austin: University of Texas, Institute of Latin American Studies, Office for Public Sector Studies, Technical Papers Series, no. 44.

———. 1985c. "Public Enterprises in Latin America: Their Origins and Importance." *International Review of Administrative Sciences* 51(4):329–348.

———. 1985d. *Public Enterprise: An International Bibliography*. Austin: Institute of Latin American Studies Special Publications Series.

———. 1985e. "Quatro mitos acerca de las empresas públicas en América Latina: Imagen, teoría y realidad." In *Quatro mitos sobre las empresas públicas en América Latina*, edited by Alfred H. Saulniers et al., pp. 9–34. Lima: Fundación Friedrich Ebert, Taller de Investigación.

———. 1985f. *A Systems Approach to Public Enterprises*. Arusha, Tanzania: Eastern and Southern African Management Institute, ESAMI Monograph Series, no. 1.

———. 1985g. "Mas allá del control gerencial: Un enfoque sistémico a las empresas públicas." In *Las empresas públicas en el Perú*, edited by Alfred H. Saulniers et al., pp. 11–61. Lima: Centro Peruano de Investigación Aplicada.

———. 1985h. *Beyond Management Control: Neglected Dimensions of Public Enterprise Analysis*. Austin: University of Texas, Institute of Latin American Studies, Office for Public Sector Studies, Technical Papers Series, no. 48.

———. 1986. *Public Sector Archive: Peru*. Austin: Institute of Latin American Studies, Office for Public Sector Studies.

Saulniers, Alfred, and Julio Revilla. 1983. "The Economic Role of the Peruvian State, 1821–1919." Paper presented at the XI International Congress of the Latin American Studies Association, Mexico City, 29 Sep.–1 Oct.

Saulniers, Alfred, et al. 1985. *Las empresas públicas en el Perú*. Lima: Centro Peruano de Investigación Aplicada.

Scharpf, Fritz. 1978. "Interorganizational Policy Studies: Issues, Concepts, and Perspectives." In *Interorganizational Policy Making: Limits to Coordination and Central Control*, edited by Kenneth Hanf and Fritz Scharpf, pp. 345–370. Beverly Hills, Calif.: Sage Publishers.

Schydlowsky, Daniel, and Juan Wicht. 1979. *Anatomía de un fracaso económico: Perú, 1968–1979*. Lima: Universidad del Pacífico.

———. 1983. "Anatomy of Economic Failure." In *The Peruvian Experiment Reconsidered*, edited by Cynthia McClintock and Abraham

Lowenthal, pp. 94–143. Princeton: Princeton University Press.
Senado. n.d. "Proyecto de ley de constitución y transferencia de las empresas del Estado." Lima. Unpublished.
Sharp, Daniel. 1972. "The Context for U.S. Policy for Peru." In *U.S. Foreign Policy and Peru*, edited by Daniel Sharp, pp. 3–14. Austin: University of Texas Press.
Sheahan, John. 1976. "Public Enterprise in Developing Countries." In *Public Enterprise: Economic Analysis of Theory and Practice*, edited by William Shepherd, pp. 205–233. Lexington, Mass: D.C. Heath and Co., Lexington Books.
Shepherd, William. 1976a. "Objectives, Types and Accountability." In *Public Enterprise: Economic Analysis of Theory and Practice*, edited by William Shepherd, pp. 33–48. Lexington, Mass: D.C. Heath and Co., Lexington Books.
———. 1976b. "British and United States Experience." In *Public Enterprise: Economic Analysis of Theory and Practice*, edited by William Shepherd, pp. 103–122. Lexington, Mass: D.C. Heath and Co., Lexington Books.
Sherif, Fouad. 1973. *Measures for Improving Performance of Public Enterprises in Developing Countries*. New York: UN, Department of Economic and Social Affairs.
Shirley, Mary. 1983. *Managing State-Owned Enterprises*. Washington: World Bank Staff Working Paper, no. 577.
Short, R.P. 1984. "The Role of Public Enterprises: An International Statistical Comparison." In Robert H. Floyd, Clive S. Gray, and R.P. Short. *Public Enterprise in Mixed Economies: Some Macroeconomic Aspects*. Washington: IMF. pp. 110–196.
Sicherl, Pavle, and Praxy Fernandes. 1980. "The Identity and Character of Public Enterprises: A Building Blocks Approach." Paper presented at the expert group meeting on Concept, Definition, and Classification of Public Enterprises, Tangier, Morocco, 15–19 Dec.
Sigmund, Paul. 1980. *Multinationals in Latin America: The Politics of Nationalization*. Madison: University of Wisconsin Press.
Silva, Javier. 1978. "Plan económico." In *Anales de la IX Conferencia Anual de Ejecutivos CADE '78*. Lima: Instituto Peruano de Administración de Empresas. pp. 241–257.
———. 1981. *Yo asumí el activo y el pasivo de la Revolución*. Lima: Centro de Documentación e Información Andina.
Sishtla, V.S.P. 1982. *Working Capital Management in Public Enterprises*. Ljubljana, Yugoslavia: International Centre for Public Enterprises in Developing Countries, ICPE Monograph Series, no. 5.
Sobhan, R., and Muzaffer Ahmad. 1980. *Public Enterprise in an Intermediate Regime: A Study in the Political Economy of Bangladesh*. Dacca, Bangladesh: Bangladesh Institute of Development Studies.
Sociedad Nacional de Industrias. 1969. "Análisis de la economía industrial del Perú y política para el desarrollo." Paper presented at the Second National Congress of Manufacturing Industries. Lima.

Mimeo.

Solberg, Carl. 1979. *Oil and Nationalism in Argentina: A History.* Stanford, Calif.: Stanford University Press.

Sorensen, Georg. 1985. "Public Enterprise Interlinkages: A Structural Approach." In *The Management of Interlinkages*, edited by Ricardo Acosta, pp. 232–265. Ljubljana, Yugoslavia: International Center for Public Enterprises in Developing Countries.

Sorj, Bernardo. 1976. "The State in Peripheral Capitalism with a Case Study of Peru after 1968." Ph.D. dissertation. University of Manchester.

———. 1977?. "The Socio-Economic Structure of the Peruvian Public Enterprise Sector." Lima?. Mimeo.

———. 1983. "Public Enterprise and the Question of the State Bourgeoisie, 1968–1976." In *Military Reformism and Social Classes: The Peruvian Experience, 1968–1980*, edited by David Booth and Bernardo Sorj, pp. 72–93. New York: St. Martin's Press.

Stefani, Giorgio. 1980. "Machinery for the Control of Public Enterprises by the Public Authorities." Paper presented at the 13th International Congress of Public and Cooperative Economy, Lisbon, 2–4 June. Mimeo.

Stepan, Alfred C. III. 1978. *The State and Society: Peru in Comparative Perspective.* Princeton: Princeton University Press.

Stevens, Evelyne. 1980. *The Politics of Workers' Participation: The Peruvian Approach in Comparative Perspective.* New York: Academic Press.

Strasma, John. 1972. "Agrarian Reform in Peru." In *U.S. Foreign Policy and Peru*, edited by Daniel Sharp, pp. 156–205. Austin: University of Texas Press.

Talavera, Óscar, and Victor Villar. 1978. "Modelo de sistema integrado aplicado a las empresas públicas en el Perú." Undergraduate thesis. Lima: Universidad Nacional de Ingeneria.

Tantalean, Javier. 1970. Speech given at the annual executives' conference. In *Anales de la IX Conferencia Anual de Ejecutivos CADE '70*. Lima: Instituto Peruano de Administración de Empresas. pp. 204–210.

———. 1971. Speech given at the annual executives' conference. In *Anales de la X Conferencia Anual de Ejecutivos CADE '71*. Lima: Instituto Peruano de Administración de Empresas. pp. 71–84.

———. 1978. *Yo respondo*. Lima: Talleres de Maturano.

Taylor, Charles L. ed. 1983. *Why Governments Grow: Measuring Public Sector Size.* Beverly Hills, Calif.: Sage Publishers.

Tello, María del Pilar. 1983. *Golpe o revolución? hablan los militares del 68*. Lima: Ediciones SAGSA.

Thorndike, Guillermo. 1976. *No, mi general*. Lima: Mosca Azul Editora.

Thornhill, C. 1983. "The Malfunctioning of Traditional Control Methods and Bodies." Paper presented at the 19th International

Congress of the International Institute of Administrative Sciences, Berlin, 19–23 Sept.

Thorp, Rosemary. 1983. "The Evolution of Peru's Economy." In *The Peruvian Experiment Reconsidered*, edited by Cynthia McClintock and Abraham Lowenthal, pp. 39–61. Princeton: Princeton University Press.

Thorp, Rosemary, and Geoffrey Bertram. 1978. *Peru 1890–1977: Growth and Policy in an Open Economy*. New York: Colombia University Press.

Topik, Stephen. 1979. *The Evolution of the Economic Role of the Brazilian State, 1889–1930*. Austin: University of Texas, Institute of Latin American Studies, Office for Public Sector Studies, Technical Papers Series, no. 15.

Trebat, Thomas. 1981. "Public Enterprises in Brazil and Mexico: A Comparison of Origins and Performance." In *Authoritarian Capitalism: Brazil's Contemporary Economic and Political Development*, edited by Thomas Bruneau and Phillipe Faucher, pp. 41–58. Boulder, Co.: Westview Press.

————. 1983. *Brazil's State-Owned Enterprises: A Case Study of the State as Entrepreneur*. New York: Cambridge University Press.

Turk, Ivan. 1984. *Accounting Analyses of the Efficacy of Public Enterprises*. Ljubljana, Yugoslavia: ICPE Monograph Series, no. 19.

Ulloa, Manuel. 1980. "Mensaje al congreso del presidente del consejo de ministros, Doctor Manuel Ulloa." *El Peruano*, 29 Aug.

UN, DESA, Department of Economic and Social Affairs. 1976. "Capital Structure of Public Enterprises in Developing Countries." In *Financing of Public Enterprises in Developing Countries: Co-ordination, Forms and Sources*, pp. 33–73. New York.

UN, ECLA, Economic Commission for Latin America. 1969a. "Some Administrative Problems of Public Enterprises." Paper presented at a meeting of experts on Administration of Public Enterprises in Latin America and the Caribbean, Santiago, 17–22 Nov. Mimeo.

————. 1969b. "Report on the meeting of experts on Administration of Public Enterprises in Latin America and the Caribbean." Santiago, 17–22 Nov. Mimeo.

————. 1971. "Public Enterprises: Their Present Significance and their Potential in Development." *Economic Bulletin for Latin America*. 16(1):1–70.

UNIDO, United Nations Industrial Development Organization. 1969. "Profitability and Efficiency Measures of Public Enterprises." Paper presented at a meeting of experts on Administration of Public Enterprises in Latin America and the Caribbean, Santiago, 17–22 Nov. Mimeo.

————. 1970. *Financial Aspects of Manufacturing Enterprises in the Public Sector*. Report and Proceedings of Interregional Seminar held in Rome, Italy, 1–2 Dec. 1969. New York.

UN, ILPES, Instituto Latinoamericano de Planificación Económica y

Social. 1981. "Notas sobre los estilos de planificación y el sector de empresas públicas." Paper presented at the seminar in Public Enterprises in Planning for Development in Central America and the Caribbean, 1–5 July.

UN, Statistical Commission. 1976. "Reconciliation of the United Nations 'Draft manual in public sector statistics' and the International al Monetary Fund draft 'Manual on government finance statistics,' Report of the Secretary General." Paper prepared for the Nineteenth Session of the Statistical Commission, New Delhi, 8–19 Nov. Mimeo.

Velasco, Juan. 1970. "Queremos una industrialización que contribuya a liberar nuestra economía de tradicional sujeción." *El Peruano*. 7 Apr. 1970.

Vernon, Raymond. 1981. "Introduction." In *State-Owned Enterprises in the Western Economies*, edited by Raymond Vernon and Yair Aharoni, pp. 7–22. New York: St. Martin's Press.

Villanueva, Victor. 1982. "Peru's 'New' Military Professionals: The Failure of the Technocratic Approach." In *PostRevolutionary Peru: The Politics of Transformation*, edited by Stephen Gorman, pp. 157–178. Boulder Co.: Westview Press.

Villegas del Solar, Gustavo, and Gonzalo Ansola Cabada. 1982. "El control gubernamental." Law Thesis. Pontificía Universidad Católica del Perú.

Webb, Richard. 1977. *Government Policy and the Distribution of Income in Peru, 1963–1973*. Cambridge, Mass.: Harvard University Press.

Whitaker, Arthur. 1941. *The Huancavelica Mercury Mine*. Cambridge, Mass.: Harvard University Press.

Winn, Peter. 1986. *Weavers of Revolution*. New York: Oxford University Press.

Wils, Frits. 1979. *Industrialization, Industrialists, and the Nation-State in Peru: A Comparative Sociological Analysis*. Berkeley: University of California, Institute of International Studies, Research Series, no. 41.

Wittich, Bernhard. 1983. "La situación operativa y productiva de las empresas de CORDE." Santo Domingo: Corporación Dominicana de Empresas Estatales.

Wolfenson, Azi. 1981. *El gran desafío*. Lima: Intergráfica de Servicios.

Zimmerman, Augusto. 1975. *El Plan Inca — objetivo: Revolución peruana*. Lima: *El Peruano*.

Index

EMATINSA (Empresa Estatal
Minera Asociada Tintaya,
S.A.), 8
Employment, 26, 97–98
Empresa Editora, 31
ENAFER (Empresa Nacional de
Ferrocarriles del Perú), 27,
47(n67), 109(n5), 129
ENAPU (Empresa Nacional de
Puertos)
creation of, 19
and customs, 163
externalities, 170
finances, 116
subsidies, hidden, 167
ENATA (Empresa Nacional del
Tabaco), 8, 37, 48(n86),
143, 144(table)
ENATRU (Empresa Nacional de
Transporte Urbano del
Perú)
billing, 126
creation of, 31
inventory, 129
profits, 132
ENCI (Empresa Nacional de Comercialización de Insumos),
8
board of directors, 153
creation of, 25
debt, 102–104, 110(n8)
development of, 30, 33–34, 39,
48(n89)
externalities, 170–172
and fertilizers, 163–164, 170
financing, 33
insolvency, 119
management turnover, 145
monopsony, 166
objectives, 145
reform of, 38
subsidies: arrears, 164;
hidden, 167
value added, 106
Energy and Mines, Ministry of.
See MEM
ENI (Ente Nazionale

Idrocarburi), 152
ENRAD (Empresa Nacional de
Radiodifusión del Perú), 31
ENTEL (Empresa Nacional de
Telecomunicaciones del
Perú), 21, 26–27, 102, 143
Environment, physical, 170
EPADESA (Empresa Peruana de
Apuestas Deportivas),
144(table)
EPAPRODE (Empresa Pública de
Administración de Prognósticos Deportivos), 31,
144(table)
EPCHAP (Empresa Peruana de
Comercialización de Harina
y Aceite del Pescado)
board of directors, 154
creation of, 23
development of, 33, 48(n89),
54, 75(n10)
finances, 117
inventory, 129
profits, 133
ships for, 165
EPF (Empresa Petrolera Fiscal),
8
creation of, 16
development of, 19–21
management of, 57
reform, 19
See also Loret de Mola,
Carlos
EPSA (Empresa Pública de
Servicios Agropecuarios)
creation of, 21, 27, 43(n31)
debt, 102, 104
development of, 27, 33
epsitis, 74
finances, 33, 169
income, 83
insolvency, 119
inventory, 129
monopoly, 166
objectives, 145
profits, 85, 132
scandal, 175(n18)